THE HAND REVE[...]

Dylan Warren-Davis has been involved in the study a[...] of handreading for the past 15 years, as well as being a practising Medical Herbalist for 11 years. He originally became interested in the subject through its diagnostic potential while a student of herbal medicine. Dylan teaches Cheiromancy by private tuition as well as giving handreadings. He also gives seminars and lectures on the subject in the UK and overseas.

THE HAND REVEALS

=

A Complete Guide to Cheiromancy
The Western Tradition of Handreading

=

DYLAN WARREN-DAVIS

Edited by
STEVE EDDY

ELEMENT

Shaftesbury, Dorset ● Rockport, Massachusetts
Brisbane, Queensland

Published in Great Britain in 1993 by
Element Books Limited
Longmead, Shaftesbury, Dorset

Published in the USA in 1993 by
Element Inc
42 Broadway, Rockport, MA 01966

Published in Australia in 1993 by
Element Books Limited for
Jacaranda Wiley Limited
33 Park Road, Milton, Brisbane 4064

Cover design by Max Fairbrother

Illustrations by Kris Warren-Davis

Text design and DTP by Pete Russell, Faringdon, Oxon

Printed and bound in Great Britain by
Loader Jackson Ltd

British Library Cataloguing in Publication
data available

Library of Congress Cataloging in Publication
data available

ISBN 1-85230-353-0

To all my teachers who have made this work possible

Foreword

By Olivia Barclay

IT is my conclusion that the physical body is an outward expression of the soul, whether it is the body of a human being, or of a creature, or of a plant, or the earth itself. It therefore stands to reason that if you can read the tangible body which you can see, you gain insight into the intangible nature that produces it.

The human body is unique in that it can be read not only from its whole, but from many of its separate parts, and most particularly, and very exactly, from the hand, as this book explains to us. Some have tried to read it from the shape of the head, as did Lavater and Fuseli, others from the lines of the forehead, which is called metoposcopy, and others from the position of the moles on the body. Astrologers read it from the heavens, good traditional astrologers could give clear descriptions of physical appearance as well as character, circumstances and events from an astrological chart.

The reason our predecessors devoted such energy to the study of appearances was because they believed in the Oneness of life, and the interaction of one part of the whole on the other parts of the whole, and the great intangible reality leaving imprint on solid matter. Beauty was of greater value. Nowadays in our materialistic society a body is simply a body, there is no need to study its appearance. Few distinguish between beauty and ugliness, an observation apparent in most of our arts.

The art of cheiromancy is extremely old, as astrology is. It can well be expressed in astrological symbolism. Many famous men, Paracelsus for one, have studied both subjects. Great men of the past have spent a lifetime in the pursuit of such knowledge, and there is much that the two subjects have in common. Both have been besieged by charlatans, whose dishonesty has led, in part, to their present discredited position. They are further misunderstood because the premise upon which they are based is not materialistic, and so they have become subjects of ridicule or entertainment.

Yet despite these similarities, the astrologers and cheiromancers work from different points of view. Astrologers look at the vast heavens and from them deduce the lesser details in life and events on earth. An astrologer sees the wood and later the trees, and even the twigs. A cheiromancer on the contrary, looks at the small detail on the hand, and from it builds greater information. He sees the trees first and then the wood. The cheiromancer works for the human race, while the astrologer is dealing with everything God created.

In this book our author has sought to bring these two arts closer together, not only by his use of astrological symbolism, but by introducing us to the work of Rothmann, an astrologer-cheiromancer who lived in the sixteenth century. Rothmann drew the subject's hands within the natal chart, with some intriguing ideas from that era for us to absorb. It was Wharton, astrologer to Charles I, who translated the work of Rothmann from Latin into English.

Now the time has come for those of us who study these subjects seriously to re-examine the achievements of our predecessors, to find and translate books that have remained inaccessible, to re-graft our arts onto their ancient root stock. This trend is strongest in America. I hope therefore our author will produce more from Rothmann.

Dylan Warren-Davis is a practising herbalist who uses astrology in its traditional context. Of his herbalism I can only tell you that his Ascendant conjoins Culpeper's Sun and his Sun conjoins Culpeper's Ascendant! Need I say more!

And so, although I may not agree with every single word our author writes on astrology, especially regarding the outer planets, I greatly enjoyed this thought-provoking book. The painstaking care with which the subject has been treated is a welcome contrast to the plethora of whimsical astro-psychological books which have recently flooded the market. I recommend it to you as a scholarly achievement worthy of your careful study and attention.

December 1992   O.B

Acknowledgements

The Hand Reveals has evolved from much personal research which has spanned a decade. In making this research possible I should like principally to acknowledge and thank a number of my teachers. Firstly Barbara Lewis who by spontaneously grabbing my hand and giving me an impromptu reading (while waiting for the second course of an Indian meal), unwittingly sowed the seeds for my interest in handreading. I should like to thank Priscilla Osband and Terry Dukes – Priscilla for sympathetically showing me the rudiments of handreading and Terry for revealing the intricacies of Elemental symbolism and its application to the hand.

I should also like thank my astrological teachers, Maggie Hyde, Geoffrey Cornelius and Derek Appleby, who collectively taught me the symbolic language of astrology and inspired me with its potential.

A particularly warm thank you to Stéphanie Spindler whose friendship and encouragement so critically nurtured the early stages of the research for this book.

I would like to thank my editor Steve Eddy who, at precisely the moment I felt it was time to write, offered me the opportunity of a book contract. I would also like to thank Julia McCutchen and all at Element Books who have helped in the production of this book.

An enormous thank you must go to my wife Kris who, in addition to drawing the large number of illustrations for the book, has made many valuable criticisms and suggestions that have significantly enhanced the book.

I would like to give a special thanks to Olivia Barclay, whose expertise in the field of classical astrology has been invaluable in spotting astrological anachronisms in the text and in the definition of astrological terms used in the Glossary. Her contribution to the Foreword is deeply appreciated. Thanks also to Gary Price for researching astrological calculations in Chapter 18.

I would like to acknowledge the Warburg Institute, University of London for their kind permission to use the illustrations in Figure 2.1, 2.2, and 2.3. I would also like to acknowledge Regulus Publishing Co. Ltd for their kind permission to use the illustration in Figure 20.1.

I also must thank those who have given me permission to use their handprints to illustrate the text. Last but not least, I would like to thank the many students and clients, too numerous to mention individually, who in one way or another have led to the furthering of the knowledge found in this book.

D. W. D

Contents

PART 3

SYNTHESIS AND
APPLICATION OF
CHEIROMANCY

Illustrations

Introduction

CHEIROMANCY (pronounced KIRO-mancy) is the art of handreading in which all aspects of a person's hand are considered in order to gain an accurate picture of their inner nature. Cheiromancy is distinct from the fortune telling of palmistry. What has come down to us as palmistry today is a rather degenerate and effete form of this ancient discipline. The word cheiromancy comes from the Greek *chir* meaning 'hand' and *manteia* meaning 'divination', literally meaning 'divination through the hand'.

In classical times cheiromancy, as its name suggests, was considered a valuable skill and held in high esteem. Cheiromancy today, however, tends to be regarded as an obscure topic. This is understandable for in the last 300 years it has been suppressed by the Church and spurned by reductionist science. Despite this, handreading still attracts much popular interest as a gentle pastime, though one which is unfortunately not taken very seriously.

What is the value of cheiromancy today? Despite biological science demonstrating the predominant neurological connection between brain and hand and acknowledging the importance of the hand for translating ideas into action as a part of man's evolution, it cannot see any significance in handreading. This is more than a case of one hand not knowing what the other is doing: it seems that modern man does not know what either hand is up to!

It is time to re-evaluate the topic. Contemporary physics no longer believes in matter as an absolute objective reality, as it did in the eighteenth and nineteenth centuries. Instead it sees the consciousness of the observer as being integrally linked with the observed material world. The study of just how consciousness interacts with matter is the very basis of cheiromancy; for the premise of handreading is that the hand, and indeed the whole body, is symbolic of the psyche within it. In our technological age where medical science prides itself on being able to print out heart and brain rhythms, it is curious that the continuous print-out of the psyche on the palm is ignored!

It is understandable that after 300 years of negation, the scepticism that surrounds cheiromancy is very deep. It has so closed people's minds that it is very hard for them to accept that handreading has any validity at all.

Consider a historian who knows nothing whatsoever about music, finding an untitled music score in some archive. With no knowledge of musical notation he completely fails to recognize it as a musical score. 'Perhaps it is some sort of secret message in code,' he muses to himself. A passing musician just glances at the score and mentally hears the music written on it. On recognizing the melody he exclaims, 'That's one of Bach's sonatas.' The sceptical historian remains unconvinced, 'He's just making it up,' he argues. In order to demonstrate his point the musician gets his violin and plays it to him. Alas to no avail, the historian still remains unconvinced and accuses the musician of playing Bach's sonata from memory just to prove his claim. 'The score is definitely a hidden message,' he maintains. The only possible way left for the musician to convince the sceptic is to teach him the violin so that he can play the musical notation directly. Finally, after many months the historian might be able to hear Bach's sonata coming from his own violin.

Just like musical notation, the hand has its own language that needs to be learnt first before 'reading' the hand is possible. Unless one learns the basic principles of cheiromancy, the hand is as meaningless as a musical score is to a non-musician. The validity of cheiromancy lies in being able use this knowledge to interpret a person's hand successfully. It is in the actual experience of reading a hand that the knowledge is verified. In the same way that a musician on reading musical notation and hearing the sounds emitted from their instrument gradually learns to 'hear' the music in the score, so, too, it is possible for the skilled cheiromancer to 'see' intricate psychological patterns in the hand.

This book sets out to explain the principles of cheiromancy whereby diligent students should be able to read hands for themselves. It will first explain the cultural context of this knowledge and then elucidate the cosmology and symbolism used in reading the hand. As the book unfolds, this symbolism will be applied to the various aspects of the hand, thus enabling their interpretation. Finally all the strands of symbolism will be woven together so that successful handreadings may be done.

It is hoped that those who gain proficiency in reading hands will be able to see the immense potential and cultural importance of cheiromancy in many human spheres. In education it can help recognize the innate abilities that need to be drawn forth if an individual is to flourish. In medicine its diagnostic potential can enable patients to see how their psychological and emotional nature influences their physical health, so assisting the healing process. In the vocational sphere it would help people to find work that accords with their temperament and thus enhance their fulfilment in life. In psychology it offers a very practical way of gaining insight into people's minds and behaviour. Whereas spiritually cheiromancy can help people to find inner meaning in their lives.

This book will introduce people to many ideas that have long been buried in our cultural heritage. Readers at first glance can be forgiven for thinking that these ideas are out of date. The Three Worlds presented in the following chapter – Elemental, Celestial and Intellectual – may seem somewhat medieval in conception. However, when seen in terms of physical, emotional and mental experience respectively, the material is just as valid today as it has been in former centuries. *The Hand Reveals* is written as a practical guide to reading hands; it is not merely theoretical. As various points are described, throughout the book, try to apply this knowledge at every opportunity to find confirmation of the ideas. There is a considerable amount of knowledge and information compressed into these pages, and even the most diligent student would have difficulty in digesting it in one reading. It is recommended that you refer back as often as necessary to the material you have read, to allow your understanding of cheiromancy to grow gradually.

In writing a book of this nature one needs to sustain interest without getting bogged down by instructions. For this reason some of the instructional detail is intentionally cryptic, requiring the student to work out their own information using the given symbolic principles. A workbook demonstrating more of the techniques of cheiromancy 'in action' will follow this book.

PART ONE

—

THE PHILOSOPHY AND SYMBOLISM OF CHEIROMANCY

—

CHAPTER 1

A Cultural Perspective of Cheiromancy

THOUGH handreading is found in many cultures, *The Hand Reveals* largely focuses on the practice of handreading as it existed in Europe from classical times to the seventeenth century. The practice of cheiromancy is intimately linked to the spread of Hermetic thought within European culture. This is vividly illustrated by the works of Cornelius Agrippa (1483–1533), Paracelsus (1493–1541) and Robert Fludd (1574–1637), who were all exponents of the art, while deeply immersed in Hermetic philosophy and its related disciplines. In order to understand the principles of cheiromancy it is necessary to contemplate a number of Hermetic ideas. Various aspects of Hermetic philosophy will be explained throughout the book as the chapters unfold.

The history of Hermeticism is obscure, mainly because its teachings are esoteric in nature, seldom written down and only communicated when students were inwardly ripe to receive it. Despite this, through the centuries many of the most illuminated minds have been inspired by Hermeticism. Throughout their works and writings on science, alchemy, art, literature, architecture, theology, astrology and medicine, the Hermetic spirit can be detected.[1]

Prior to the seventeenth century many of the ideas and principles behind these disciplines overlapped and learned minds often embraced several subjects. Within academic circles cheiromancy never became a major discipline in its own right, but it was often included in the study of physiognomy – the divination based upon the form and structure of the body; or as Paracelsus defined it, *'the art of discovering what is within and hidden in man'*.[2]

The great classical physicians Hippocrates and Galen were serious exponents of cheiromancy. Within medieval medicine cheiromancy was a very important part of diagnosis. In the fifteenth and sixteenth centuries physicians were not considered properly trained unless they had an understanding of cheiromancy or physiognomy. For, as Paracelsus additionally explains, when the principles of cheiromancy are transposed to the herbal world they enable the physician to understand how to use plants medicinally:

. . . the physician should also study the lines of the herbs and the leaves, and by application of cheiromancy, he should discover their efficacy and virtues.[3]

In earlier centuries, artists such as Hieronymous Bosch and Albrecht Dürer used cheiromancy and physiognomy in their work. Considerable attention was placed upon the detailed structure of the hand, so that a portrait would reflect the subject's inner temperament. Gesture, too, was a common device to conceal hidden meaning in a painting. For example, the frontispiece of William Lilly's *Christian Astrology* (1647), Figure 20.1, page 197 shows the author with his left index finger pointing to the 3rd house cusp of an astrological chart. The full significance of this detail is explained in Chapter 20.

In a religious context, symbolic positions of the hand, such as the Christian sign of the cross made during the blessing or the clasping of hands in prayer, are all highly significant when seen in terms of cheiromancy. The placing of rings on particular fingers such as the Papal seal – 'The Ring of Fishes' – on the index finger or the wedding ring on the ring finger are symbolically profound. These symbolic ideas will be explained in the sections on each individual finger in Chapter 13.

Paracelsus, the maverick physician of the early sixteenth century, held cheiromancy in high regard:

Many arts have come to the light of day through genuine cheiromancy; and the cheiromancers of the hand, of herbs, or of wood have introduced cheiromancers to the art. Not without good reason was cheiromancy so highly favoured by the ancients. We use it only for soothsaying, but the ancients used it as a means for learning the arts.[4]

Some readers may be puzzled by this link that Paracelsus makes between cheiromancy and herbs or wood. However, the principles used to interpret the palmar lines in terms of a person's character, are not so dissimilar to those formerly used to deduce the medical actions of herbs from the vein patterns of the leaves, or to understand the nature of wood from the quality of its grain.

Despite the obvious cultural importance of cheiromancy and the reverence in which the art was held, written material on the topic is notably sparse. Even Paracelsus, a prominent proponent of cheiromancy, devotes comparatively little space within his prolific output to the subject. Moreover, the available material contains very little explanation of how meaning is attributed to features on the hand.

One reason for this absence of written information is that the art was largely communicated from master to student by oral means. One advantage to oral transmission is that it ensures the perpetuation of a high standard of knowledge. A second advantage is that it protects the knowledge from abuse and exploitation. Thirdly it protected the student and teacher, since there have been times when cheiromantical knowledge was suppressed by the Church.

There was a flowering of astrology and its related disciplines, including cheiromancy, in seventeenth century Britain, thanks largely to the political changes brought about by the Civil War (1642–9). One consequence of the war was the ending of official censorship by the Company of Stationers in 1641. The Company of Stationers had a monopoly over all publications, granted to it by James I in 1603. The Company was initially under the ecclesiastical control of Cambridge University. From 1632 control was additionally shared by Oxford University. All publications were brought under their scrutiny and naturally anything that contravened the authority of the Church was banned.

Under this censorship astrologers and cheiromancers were severely restricted as to what they could publish. Printing or selling astrological books which had not been seen and revised by the ecclesiastical authorities could incur corporeal punishment. The collapse of official censorship during the Civil War allowed a rapid proliferation of all astrological works.[5] In particular, a number of works on cheiromancy appeared through the work of two astrologers.

In 1652 Sir George Wharton (1617–81) translated Johannes Rothmann's principal text *Cheiromantia* (1595) from German into English under the title *The Art of Divining, by the Lines and Signature Ingraven on the Hand of Man*. The contemporary astrologer Richard Saunders (1613–75) also brought together as much information on handreading as was possible at the time. His writings include *Physiognomie and Cheiromancy* in (1653), and *Palmistry (the Secrets thereof Disclosed)* in (1676).

This freedom to print lasted about twenty years till Charles II was restored to the throne in 1660. By 1662 the Company of Stationers had been reinvoked and it sought particular revenge against astrological writings and almanacs. It is significant that the latter of Saunders' works was entitled *Palmistry* and not *Cheiromancy*, since it was published after the Restoration. This suggests that it was the divinatory aspect or *manteia* of cheiromancy that was seen to clash with the authority of the Church so leading to its suppression.

It is hardly surprising, given the nature of the knowledge and the extent to which it has been suppressed, that over three centuries later what has come down to us as palmistry today is a rather degenerate form of this ancient discipline. To inject new life into cheiromancy we must explore the Hermetic principles behind its practice, which elevates it from mere 'fortune-telling' to the noble art of 'divination through the hand'.

The Greek philosopher Aristotle is cited as having written several works on cheiromancy. According to tradition his interest in the subject was first aroused by finding an ancient Arabic text lying on an altar to Hermes – an allusion to the Hermetic source of his knowledge. The nature of Hermetic philosophy and its cosmology is presented in the following chapter.

CHAPTER 2

Hermetic Philosophy

HERMETIC philosophy is the source of the principles used in the practice of cheiromancy. Hermeticism is a school of esoteric knowledge emanating from the mythical figure Hermes Trismegistus, whose wisdom is derived from Thoth – the Egyptian scribe of the gods. Hermeticism is an eternal fountain of wisdom from which anyone may drink, provided they develop their intuition so that they can receive it. Though Hermetic teachings have given rise to a body of scriptures called the *Corpus Hermeticum*, dated between the first and third centuries, the teachings are timeless in nature. They have flourished many times in many different forms through the centuries and so will continue to do in years to come. Hermeticism is a perennial wisdom that flowers when times are favourable and disappears without trace in adversity. Many have been deeply inspired by it, including such people as Agrippa, Paracelsus and Fludd.

The Jacobean philosopher and Hermeticist Robert Fludd (1574–1637) was profoundly interested in cheiromancy. He included a chapter on it in the second volume of his major opus *Utriusque cosmi maioris scilicet et minoris, metaphysica, physica atque technica historia* (1619). Figure 2.1 prefaces the section within the second volume of Fludd's work, which deals with the microcosmic arts, including cheiromancy, physiognomy, astrology, art of memory, geomancy, prophecy and the science of the

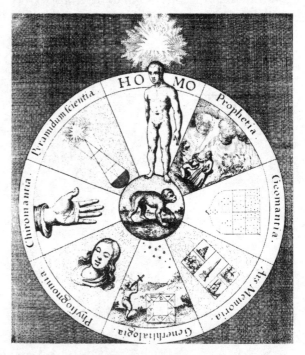

Figure 2.1 Preface in Second Volume of Robert Fludd's work *Utriusque cosmi maioris scilicet et minoris, metaphysica, physica atque technica historia* on the Microcosmic Arts (Oppenheim, 1619), reproduced by kind permission of the Warburg Institute, University of London.

pyramids. Each of these topics are included as separate chapters of Fludd's work.

Close inspection of Figure 2.1 reveals the spiritual teachings of Hermeticism. An image of Man (*Homo*) is found standing above an ape with the Divine Triangle representing the Light of Creation above his head. Mankind is so depicted standing between animal existence and spiritual illumination.

Within the circle, cheiromancy is located along with other divinatory arts. All of these practices Fludd saw as having the potential of pointing towards the soul and revealing Man's inner nature. This idea is subtly concealed in the illustration by use of the Solar glyph (☉) hidden in its basic format. The central Dot contains the ape while the outer Circle contains the names of all the disciplines. The Solar glyph alludes to the opening and purifying of the heart, which Hermetic teaching sees as being the seat of the soul.

Subtle shading to the segments composing the circle of the Solar glyph reveals the Greek form of the Christian cross. Fludd perceived a link between Hermetic teachings and Christianity, pointing out that the objectives of these divinatory arts were consistent with finding the Light of Christ within the heart.

In relation to cheiromancy or 'divination through the hand' this recalls the following biblical quotation that was often used in defence of cheiromancy when challenged by the ecclesiastical authorities: '*God has placed signs in the hands of all the sons of men, that all the sons of men may know His work.*'[6]

THE CREATION OF THE THREE WORLDS

Another of Robert Fludd's illustrations, The Three World View (Figure 2.2), shows the pro-

cess of Creation as perceived within Hermetic philosophy. The material world which is represented by the Elements in the centre of the circle – *Ignis* (Fire), *Aer* (Air), *Aqua* (Water) and *Terra* (Earth) – is shown created out of the realm of Light. The spiral pattern describes the descent of Light from God (Deus) into matter. In this descent, three distinct Worlds are formed. Commencing with *Mens*, the universal mind, the spiral leads down through the names of the various Angels and Archangels: *Seraphin, Cherubin, Dominationes, Throni, Potestates, Principatus, Virtutes, Archangeli, Angeli,* to the *Caelum Stellatum* – the 'stars in the heavens'. This first segment is called the **Intellectual World** and is linked to the Divine Air Element.

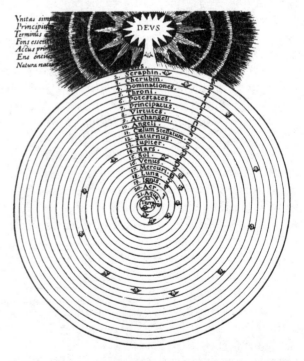

Figure 2.2 The Three World View: Robert Fludd, *Utriusque cosmi maioris scilicet et minoris, metaphysica, physica atque technica historia* (Oppenheim, 1619), reproduced by kind permission of the Warburg Institute, University of London.

Figure 2.3 Title page of John Dee's *Monas Hieroglyphica* (Antwerp, 1564), reproduced by kind permission of the Warburg Institute, University of London.

Next the spiral leads down through the names of the Planets: *Saturnus, Jupiter, Mars, Sol, Venus, Mercuri* and *Luna*. This second segment is called the **Celestial World** and is linked to the Divine Water Element.

Finally the spiral leads down through the names of the Elements: *Ignis, Aer, Aqua* and *Terra*. This third segment is called the **Elemental World** and is linked to the Divine Earth Element.

THE RULERSHIP OF THE THREE WORLDS

Each World has rulers which have dominion over each of the three realms. The Intellectual World is ruled by the Angels and Archangels. The Celestial World is ruled by the Planets. The Elemental World is ruled by the Elements. In Figure 2.2, Fludd also connects the twenty-two letters of the Hebrew alphabet with each of the rulers of the Three Worlds as the spiral of Light descends to earth.

In summary, Hermetic cosmology visualizes the universe as having four distinct realms in accordance with the Four Elements; Fire, Air, Water and Earth respectively. Existence consists primarily of a realm of Light (Fire) or God, from which three worlds are created. Out of the Light the Intellectual World (Air) is generated. Next the Celestial World (Water) descends from the Intellectual World. Finally the Elemental World (Earth) precipitates from the Celestial World. All matter is thus seen to incorporate the energy that created it. The symbolism of the Elements and the Planets will be explained in the following chapters.

John Dee (1527–1608), astrologer to Elizabeth I, is a particularly good example of someone whose life was inspired by Hermetic teachings. For Dee the Hermetic teachings came to him inwardly as a composite symbol, his *Monas Hieroglyphica* (Figure 2.3). Dee was particularly excited by this revelation, for within its intricate structure a dazzling array of astrological, alchemical, and mathematical ideas can be found.

This symbol deserves close attention, for it encapsulates both the cosmology of Hermeticism and the symbolic principles necessary for understanding cheiromancy. It shows how symbolism is used within Hermetic philosophy.

Furthermore it demonstrates the interrelationship of the Three Worlds with Elemental, Planetary, Zodiacal and alchemical symbolism.

The genesis of the hieroglyph is reflected in its central motif, which is the Planetary glyph for Mercury ($\mercury$), located above a flattened form of the Zodiacal glyph for Aries ($\aries$) = ($\aries$). When Mercury is equated with the god Hermes, and Aries is equated to the head (the part of the body traditionally ruled by Aries), one can visualize an image of the wisdom and knowledge of Hermes coming down and entering Dee's head. This very image is descriptive of the nature of Hermetic revelation. Since Aries is a Fire sign it indicates that energy needs to be focused onto the symbol in order to derive knowledge from it.

As has been explained above, Hermetic philosophy visualizes the universe as having three distinct Worlds manifested out of a realm of Light. When transposed into Man the Intellectual World corresponds to the spirit, the Celestial World to the soul and the Elemental World to the body. This tripartite cosmology is reflected within the glyph of Mercury ($\mercury$), as the three component shapes respectively; the Crescent of the spirit, the Circle of the soul and the Cross of matter. The Crescent corresponds to the Intellectual World. The Circle corresponds to the Celestial World. The Cross corresponds to the Elemental World.

The location of the central glyph within an egg is important, for this is an ancient Egyptian symbol that alludes to the source of Hermetic knowledge. The egg has as its sequel the hatching out of a bird, which is ultimately able to fly. The flying of the bird through the Air, or the Intellectual World of spirit, is symbolic of Man's spiritual unfoldment. Thus the reception of Hermetic knowledge leads to spiritual development.

The archway symbolizes Creation as perceived within Hermetic philosophy. Despite the substantial appearance of the pillars that compose the arch, the stars located in its dome suggest that Creation should be interpreted on a universal cosmic scale. The crescent-shaped dome is separated from a much larger circle. If this circle was completely present its circumference would encompass the two bottom corners of the pillars. When the complete circle is seen to symbolize the unity or oneness of life, then the splitting away of the crescent dome from the circle forming the two pillars shows symbolically the generation of duality out of the unity. Embodied in the shape of the pillared archway can be found the Roman numeral II, which is the glyph for the Zodiacal sign Gemini. Since Gemini is an Air sign, relating to the mind and ruled by Mercury the Planet of communication, linked with the god Hermes, this alludes to the Hermetic teachings. The Latin inscription at the top the pillars – *Qui non intelligit, aut taceat, aut discat* – means, 'He who does not understand should be silent or learn.'

If one imagines standing underneath the archway looking forwards, on the right-hand pillar there is an image of the Sun, and on the left-hand pillar an image of the Moon. Thus between these two pillars the whole range of duality is symbolized, including day and night, light and darkness, masculine and feminine, positive and negative, Sulphur and Salt, manifest and hidden, hot and cold, and dry and moist.

While still standing beneath the archway, at each of the four corners, at the top and bottom of the pillars, are found representations of the Four Elements: top right, *Ignis* (Fire); top left, *Aer* (Air); bottom right, a rural vista (Earth); and bottom left, the Lunar goddess Diana swimming in the waves (Water).

The Four Elements have a quintessential relationship to the fifth Element, Ether, whereby the Four evolve out of the fifth. Ether was known to the alchemists as the *Aqua Vitae*,

meaning 'the Water of Life'. On the pillars of the hieroglyph the *Aqua Vitae* is seen in the 'droplets' present between the Luminaries (Sun and Moon) and the basins seen below. A subtle circulation of the *Aqua Vitae* is also symbolically described, for on the right pillar the Sun (hot and dry) evaporates it from the Earth, while on the left pillar the Moon (cold and moist) condenses it back to the Water.

The Hermetic Three Worlds are also reflected vertically in the pillars. At the top, above the Luminaries (Sun and Moon), is located the Intellectual World. In the middle; between the Luminaries and the basins, is located the Celestial World. At the bottom, below the basins where the pillars are substantially larger, is located the Elemental World. Subtle details on the pillars highlight these three realms. The Elements present in the Intellectual World (the realm of ideas) are shown as words – 'ideas' – whereas the Elements present in the Elemental World (the realm of matter) are expressions of their physical forms. The 'droplets' of the *Aqua Vitae* are only found in the Celestial World, since Ether forms the medium of this realm.

An idea central to Hermetic philosophy is that Man is made in the image of the heavens, summed up by the oft-quoted phrase, 'As above, so below'. The *Monas Hieroglyphica* reflects this correspondence in a variety of ways. In the macrocosm, the Four Elements located at the corners of the pillars correspond to the Four Elements reflected by the four angles of the Cross within the microcosm of the central Mercury glyph. Ether is readily seen in the macrocosm as the 'droplets', but its microcosmic counterpart is more abstruse. The *Aqua Vitae* is also alluded to by alchemists as the Philosophical Mercury. Hence the glyph of Mercury represents Ether in the microcosm within the egg.

The Sun and Moon located on the pillars too, have their counterpart in the central glyph, since their symbols (☉) and (☽) = (◡) are found composing the upper two sections of the glyph. Again, the Three Worlds reflected vertically in the pillars correspond to the three sections of the Mercury glyph.

The three Alchemical Principles, Sulphur, Salt and Mercury are covertly reflected in the *Monas Hieroglyphica*. The Sun connects with the masculine, dynamic, fiery, Sulphur Principle and the Moon connects with the feminine, passive, watery Salt Principle. Their synthesis, the Mercury Principle, is once again reflected by the central glyph.

The Dot, forming the Solar glyph inside the Mercury glyph, intentionally coincides with the centre of the pillars and the radius of the dome. In Hermetic philosophy the 'opening of the heart' is central to understanding the nature of the universe. When the Sun is seen to symbolize the heart – the seat of the soul – and the pillars to symbolize the Hermetic vision of the Creation of the Three Worlds, then the concordance between the Dot within the Solar glyph and the centre of the pillars symbolically reveals how the opening of the heart leads to the understanding of Creation. This is a particularly powerful confirmation of Man being made in the image of the heavens.

This idea concords with Christian teachings in which Jesus says, '*The kingdom of heaven lies within.*'[7] The Sun is a symbol of a kingship, as well as of the soul's residence in the heart: '*Blessed are the pure in heart for they shall see God.*'[8] A Christian cross is visible within the shaft of the central glyph. A further Christian connection is made by the Latin inscription found at the base the pillars. This extract from Genesis 27 means '*May God give thee the dew of heaven and of the fatness of the earth.*'[9] Hermetic knowledge, despite the views of the Church, was seen to be in harmony with true Christian teachings.

At the top of the Mercury glyph the Crescent of the Moon lies over the Sun with its concave aspect receptive to the impressions from above. Since the Moon symbolizes the visual imagination, this illustrates the importance of the imagination in the development of intuition. Once a person's intuition is developed they can receive the necessary inspiration for their own spiritual development.

By purifying the heart (☉) and developing the imagination (☽), the inspiration of Hermes (☿) can flow. This point is highlighted by certain Zodiacal signs located around the egg. At the top are the claws of Cancer; at the bottom is the head of Leo; on the right is the head of Aries; on the left is the head of Taurus. The two twins of Gemini are found one on either side of Cancer, each bearing a caduceus (a further Hermetic symbol).

To see the significance of this we must refer again to the three main Planetary glyphs found within the central glyph. Traditionally the Sun is dignified in the sign of Leo and exalted in the sign of Aries. The Moon is dignified in Cancer and exalted in Taurus. Mercury is dignified in Gemini. Thus symbolically these are the conditions that enhance the 'hatching out of the egg' – in other words, a person's 'spiritual unfoldment'.

Do not be discouraged if you have found it difficult to follow all the symbolism in this explanation of the *Monas Hieroglyphica*. Much of it will be developed further in the following chapters. Symbolic understanding grows through repetition of ideas, in the same way that repetition of a piece of music leads to its greater appreciation.

It would be worthwhile to read this section again after going through the following chapters on symbolism. Not only will the exercise show you how much your symbolic understanding has grown, but it will also help you to participate further in the complex subtlety of Dee's symbol. To the experienced symbolist the *Monas Hieroglyphica* is a wellspring of inspiration, for each contemplation will give rise to new ideas.

This exposition of Dee's *Monas Hiero-glyphica* is by no means exhaustive. The above ideas have been extracted from the symbol purely to illustrate Hermeticism as a spiritual teaching and source of the symbolic ideas used in cheiromancy. It should be pointed out that Dee, though a powerful exponent of Hermetic ideas, was not known to be a cheiromancer.

THE THREE WORLDS IN THE HAND

The Hermetic cosmology of the Three Worlds can be seen projected onto the hand in Figure 2.4. The illustration shows the Intellectual World – the fingers and phalanges, the Celestial World – the lines and thumb, and the Elemental World – the palm of the hand and the four Elemental quadrants.

Symbols

Corresponding to the Three Worlds, three orders of symbols are also used to classify the various features of the hand. The glyphs used to represent these symbols are shown in Figure 2.4, the glyphs of the Zodiac are shown on the phalanges: Zodiacal symbolism is used to interpret the mental or Intellectual World of the fingers. The glyphs of the Planets are shown connected with the lines: Planetary symbolism is used to interpret the emotional or Celestial

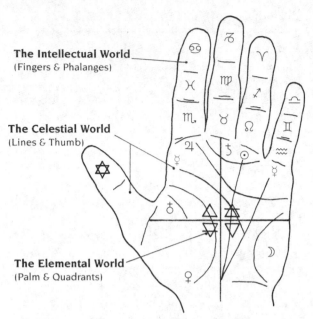

Figure 2.4 The Three Worlds in the Hand

World of the lines. The triangular glyphs of the Elements are shown at the centre of the palm: Elemental symbolism is used to interpret the physical or Elemental World of the palm.

The names of these symbols have been intentionally given initial capitals. This is to draw your attention to what is symbolized by the word, in contrast to its more literal meaning.

Each category of symbolism will be explained in the following chapters. Elemental symbolism will be covered next, in Chapter 3. Planetary symbolism will be covered in Chapters 4 and 5, and Zodiacal symbolism will be left until Chapter 13, which deals with the fingers.

Elemental Symbolism

SYMBOLISM is an essential part of cheiromancy, for it provides the tools for extracting information from the hand. This enables inner connections to be made and the features to be interpreted. Cultivation of this symbolic perspective is at the heart of successful handreading. The more time spent developing these symbolic ideas, the richer and deeper the understanding of handreading will be. Therefore this chapter attempts to promote this perspective.

The basic premise of cheiromancy is founded on the body symbolizing the psyche that resides in it, the two being visualized in tandem. A simple analogy of a slide projector illustrates this relationship. Light from the bulb inside shines through the image on the slide and carries it to the screen. The image formed on the screen corresponds to the body, while the image on the slide corresponds to the inner psyche. Just as one may define the image on the slide by describing the image on the screen, so one may may define a person's character and inner psyche by a symbolic description of the hand.

Imagination plays a vital role in the understanding of symbols, for it is in their visualization that they come alive and their numerous meanings are comprehended.

THE ELEMENTS

The first category of symbols used in cheiromancy comprises the Elements which are seen to rule the material or Elemental world. Primarily the Elements are readily perceptible to the senses and exist all around us as the forces upon which life depends.

The Element of Earth corresponds to the *terra firma* of the planet, providing the structure, substance and foundation of the material world. It is the soil from which plants grow, in turn providing food for other forms of life. Earth nutritionally provides the substance from which our physical bodies are composed. Earth provides the material out of which houses are built, contributing to our sense of material security.

The Element of Water corresponds to the rivers, lakes and oceans which irrigate the soil, fertilizing it and enabling plants to grow. It is the universal solvent in which biochemical processes take place. Through drinking water it becomes the medium of the blood, which connects all the cells in the body together providing essential nutrition and eliminating wastes.

The Element of Air corresponds to the atmosphere, winds and clouds which surround us. With each breath life-giving oxygen enters the blood via the lungs. When carried to the tissues, respiration occurs releasing energy.

The Element of Fire corresponds to the Sun in the sky, which provides heat and light. By photosynthesis energy from the sunlight is harnessed by plants. Ultimately this energy is released again from food by tissue respiration. In the body Fire connects to the muscles where this energy is transformed into action, generating heat once more.

The Hermetic mind perceives a fifth Element, Ether, that animates the material or Elemental World. It is immaterial and indiscernible to the sense organs. The alchemists referred to it by various names, including *Aqua Vitae*, meaning 'the Water of Life', or the Philosophical Mercury. They also called it the *Prima Materia* meaning the 'First Matter', since it is the matrix from which the Elemental World was born.

Ether is identified as the vital force within the body. The order and structure of the physical body is seen to be differentiated and maintained by the Etheric vital force. The flow of the vital force through the body is the basis of emotional experience. Each emotion has its own pattern of energy flow. For example in love the flow of vital force is smooth and peaceful, whereas in anger the flow of the vital force is intense and frenetic. Ether is seen as the basis of mental experience, for all ideas and images within the mind are formed from its substance. Etheric energy flows through the nervous system, relaying sensory information and translating ideas into action.

By using your imagination to visualize the Elements, their cosmology comes alive. Their images are formed out of the 'Ether' of your imagination. To illustrate this, contemplate the word *fire*.

Instantly images of dancing flames, radiating light and heat are created in the mind. Consider these images; the dynamism of the flames

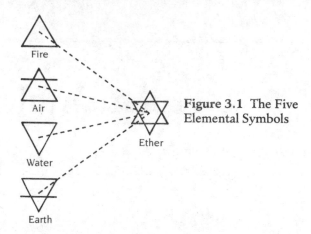

Figure 3.1 The Five Elemental Symbols

symbolizes the energy that propels us into action; the light is the understanding that comes through performing actions; and the heat connects with the heat generated in the body through physical expression.

This exercise shows that the understanding of the Elements can be seen to arise from the Ether. For this reason Ether is described as embodying all Four Elements.

The relationship of the Elements (Earth, Water, Air, Fire) is demonstrated by their alchemical symbols in Figure 3.1, which combine to form the symbol of Ether. When the fifth Element Ether is seen as the Essence from whence the other four arise, the meaning of another of its names, *Quintaessentia* – the 'fifth essence' – becomes apparent.

It is not possible to give an exhaustive description of Elemental symbolism; that would be a sisyphean task! However, contemplation of the following word-lists will facilitate an understanding of Elemental symbolism. It is important to note and value the images and associations that come to mind in performing this exercise, for this is an essential part of developing an understanding of the symbols.

There are five lists, one for each Element, and each is divided into two parts. The first part is abstract, capturing the essence or quality of the Element. The second part is personified, demonstrating how the Element can symbolize different aspects of human experience.

Earth (▽̶)

Abstract

Massive, solid, concrete, material, dense, fundamental, basic, supportive, nurturing, substantial, repetitive, stable, permanent, rigid, enduring, durable, steadfast, compact, inert, immobile, stagnant, resilient, natural, mundane, rocky, rugged, rough, dusty, muddy, ashen, fossilized, barren, deserted, abandoned, desolate, mountainous.

Personified

Bodily manifestation, constitution, skeleton, bones, robustness, sustenance, nourishment, concentration, reliance, persistence, endurance, dependence, security, acquisition, selfishness, rhythm, equilibrium, momentum, magnitude, tradition, dogma, institution, inertia, repression, inhibition, apprehension, fear, melancholia, lethargy, apathy, dullness.

Water (▽)

Abstract

Liquid, fluid, solvent, deep, profound, salty, stagnant, wavy, flowing, fluent, tidal, meandering, cascading, glacial, icy, wet, rainy, foggy, misty, humid, damp, swollen, sodden, drenched, saturated, soaked, dewy, swampy, boiling, scalding, steamy, vaporous, formless, unstructured, mutable, untenable, impressionable, effervescent, sparkling, passive, translucent, reflective, interpenetrative.

Personified

Emotion, feeling, reception, affection, attraction, seduction, passion, relationship, attachment, impulse, response, frigidity, love, devotion, compassion, grace, charity, mercy, sympathy, tenderness, fidelity, intuition, humility, modesty, meditation, reflection, perception, imagination, vision, dream, art, fantasy, myth, secrecy, clairvoyance, prophecy, delusion, lunacy, aura, mood, humour, blood, fertility, anaemia, drowsiness.

Fire (△)

Abstract

Direct, active, energizing, stimulating, forcible, invigorating, climatic, potent, intense, sunny, bright, radiant, luminous, vivid, volcanic, hot, burning, blazing, boiling, simmering, baking, scorching, scalding, molten, inflammatory, aflame, virulent, aglow, incensed, sublime, sharp, ferocious, vigorous, rash, rapid, spontaneous, explosive, changeable, volatile, ephemeral, consuming, exhaust, destroy, warm, tepid.

Personified

Personal energy, stimulation, initiation, action, movement, achievement, satisfaction, pleasure, prestige, fame, ambition, motivation, drive, enterprise, creativity, acceleration, promotion, execution, enthusiasm, excitement, exercise, muscle, potency, power, strength, zeal, impatience, passion, lust, form, structure, friction, tension, anger, animosity, hostility, rage, violence, wrath, conflict, reaction, destruction, effect, frustration, anxiety, stress.

Air (△̶)

Abstract

Invisible, intangible, transparent, light, rarefy, delicate, frail, faint, subtle, tenuous, diffuse, gaseous, spacious, pervasive, dispersive, expansive, metaphysical, spiritual, cavernous, reverberant, acoustic, hollow, bubbly, fair, balmy, pleasant, serene, calm, tranquil, cloudy, humid, foggy, dank, frosty, chilly, windy, breezy, gusty, stormy, tempestuous, changeable, swayed.

Personified

Mind, intelligence, intellect, reason, rationality, thought, conception, idea, comprehension, understanding, brain, breath, wit, fiction, pretence, inspiration, invention, fashion, deceit, trickery, illusion, falsehood, exaggeration, confusion, appreciation, communication, information, knowledge, skill, talent, science, speech, language, voice, music, deafness, wisdom, culture, education, judgement, logic, laws, commentary, criticism, tact, diplomacy, joy, elation, joviality, perception, detection, discovery, analysis, inquiry, attention, inspection, awareness, consideration, observation, discrimination, cleverness, attitude, opinion, religion, creed, doctrine, study, abstract, conceit, arrogance.

Ether (✡)

Abstract

Light, lucid, radiant, shining, magnificent, tenuous, delicate, subtle, discreet, volatile, mercurial, ethereal, metaphysical, sublime, buoyant, ecstatic, pervasive, rarefied, immaterial, incorporeal, imponderable, insensible, invisible.

Personified

Life, consciousness, vital force, vitality, sexual energy, healing, aura, *quintaessentia, aqua vitae, prima materia.*

You can enhance your Elemental knowledge by directly observing and experiencing nature. Simply walking in the countryside or digging the garden, or engaging more specialized outdoor pursuits like hang-gliding, scuba-diving, rock-climbing or marathon-running, can all generate a wealth of ideas. Listen to the variety of sounds associated with each Element. Whether it be the crunching of gravel underfoot or the heavy silence of a deep cave; the gentle chuckle of a small stream or the cascade of a waterfall; the crackle and hiss of a bonfire or the roar of a powerful inferno; the delicate echo reverberating through a valley or the crashing drama of a thunder-storm. After observing these qualities try to think what human experience could be described by them.

The ancient philosophers defined each of the Four Elements in terms of the primary qualities: hot or cold and dry or moist. These qualities are perceived from direct sensory experience and are attributed to the Elements as follows:

- Earth = cold and dry.
- Water = cold and moist.
- Air = hot and moist.
- Fire = hot and dry.

The association of hot and moist for Air may well seem unclear till it is seen that air mediates the heat of the Sun and the moisture of the rain.

ELEMENTAL COMPATIBILITY

You may further enhance your understanding by visualizing the interactions between the Elements. Of the six possible Elemental combinations only two are compatible: The spontaneous combustion of Fire and Air and the sustained fertility of Earth and Water. All the other combinations are incompatible:

- Fire and Water are explosive or depletive.
- Fire and Earth are intense or barren.

• Air and Water are foggy or diffusive.

• Air and Earth are static or sterile.

As a valuable exercise consider each of the above Elemental combinations in turn. What associations come to mind? Write down the images as they form in your mind. Now look back at the previous lists of Elemental correspondences and select the most appropriate words to describe the images in your mind. For example if you contemplate the interaction between Air and Water, the following words would be most appropriate from the Air, Abstract list: *bubbly, cloudy, foggy, stormy*. The following words would be most appropriate from the Water, Abstract list: *wavy, rainy, misty, damp, dewy, steamy*. From the Personified list for Air; *deceit, illusion, confusion*. From the Personified list for Water; *imagination, vision, dream, art, fantasy, myth, clairvoyance, prophecy, delusion, lunacy*.

The above lists are by no means exhaustive of all the possible Elemental patterns. If other words come to mind then add them to the list. As you select and list these words, they will evolve into a very useful set of correspondences for use whenever you need to consider Elemental combinations in the hand.

Through developing knowledge of this rich spectrum of Elemental qualities it is possible to develop powerful insights into the material world. Philosophers have derived these insights since the time of Plato, who is credited with coining the name 'Element'. As these Elemental ideas grow within your imagination, so you will be able to grasp the validity of the Three World view central to Hermetic philosophy. So, too, you will be able to perceive just how intimately the material world is connected to our psyche.

This Elemental symbolism will be applied to various aspects of the hand, including hand shape, skin texture, quadrants, lines, thumb and fingers. These will be explained further in Part 2 of the book.

CHAPTER 4

Planetary Symbolism

THE second category of symbols are the seven traditional Planets – Saturn, Jupiter, Mars, Sun, Venus, Mercury and the Moon – which rule the Celestial World. The Planets have an integral relationship with the Elements, whereby they are able to influence the material world. This influence is mediated through the fifth Element, Ether.

The exposition which follows intentionally breaks with the traditional order of the Planets given above, in order to draw out some subtleties in Planetary symbolism lost to current astrological understanding. The Trans-Saturnian Planets, Uranus, Neptune and Pluto have only been comparatively recently discovered and are not therefore included in this relationship. The symbolism of the Trans-Saturnian Planets will be explained in Chapter 5.

MERCURY (☿)
==

The Planet Mercury is synonymous with Ether. Ether, as mentioned in the last chapter, is the matrix of the Elemental World.

The glyph for Mercury shown in Figure 4.1 is unique amongst the other Planetary glyphs, since it encapsulates all three primary shapes used in Planetary glyphs; the Crescent of the spirit, the Circle of the soul and the Cross of matter. As the illustration shows, the Crescent corresponds to the Intellectual World, the Circle to the Celestial World and the Cross to the Elemental World. The triangular star at the top corresponds to the Realm of Light. The Mercury glyph embraces all Three Worlds; Intellectual, Celestial and Elemental respectively, created from the Realm of Light. The fifth Element of Ether, symbolized by Mercury, is shown to pervade all Three Worlds.

As the illustration shows, the Intellectual World embraces the mind, where ideas are formed out of spirit. The Celestial World of the soul is the source of will. It is also connected with the flow of emotions through the heart. The Elemental World of matter corresponds to the physical body and its sensations.

The Cross of matter situated below the Circle in the glyph for Mercury describes the manifestation of the Four Elements from the Ether. The Crescent of spirit, with its concave surface uppermost, shows the receptiveness of the Ether to the inspiration descending from the Intellectual World. This symbolically describes how ideas are formed within consciousness.

The alchemists saw the shining liquid

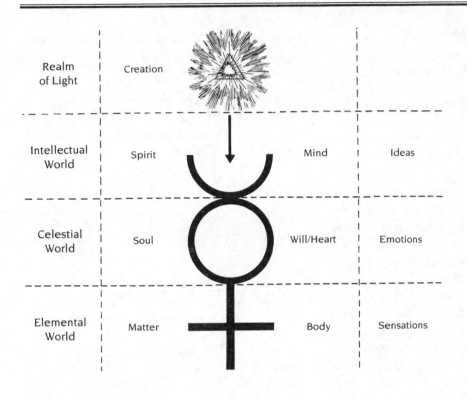

Realm of Light	Creation		
Intellectual World	Spirit	Mind	Ideas
Celestial World	Soul	Will/Heart	Emotions
Elemental World	Matter	Body	Sensations

Figure 4.1 The Cosmology of the Three Worlds in the Mercury Glyph

mercury or quicksilver as symbolizing the fifth Element, Ether. They called the metal *Hydrargyre*, which literally means 'the water that joins together', coming from the Greek *hydor*, meaning 'water' and *ageiro*, meaning 'to gather, bind or join'. The name *Hydrargyre* alludes to their perception of Ether as permeating all Three Worlds, joining everything together.

The contemporary explanation of the name is that it is derived from *hydor*, meaning 'water', and *argyros*, meaning 'silver' – which gives rise to the idea of 'silver water'. Since silver was used by the alchemists to symbolize the reflective nature of the Moon, this reflects another property of Ether – its susceptibility to the Moon. This will be explained further in the section on the Moon in this chapter. So strong are these symbolic connections that the name mercury for the metal is derived from the Roman deity Mercurius, the 'Messenger of the Gods'. In modern chemical textbooks Hg, short for *Hydrargyre*, is still found as shorthand for the metal.

Within the human body Mercury correlates with the Etheric vital force. Specifically this energy flows through the nervous system. Modern physiology divides the nervous system into two principal functions; the sensory function and the motor function. The sensory function receives the impulses from the senses and conveys them to the brain. The motor function conveys impulses from the brain to the muscles that move and co-ordinate the body.

These two functions can be symbolically perceived within the Mercury glyph ($\cdot$). The sensory function involves stimulation of the sensory organs (+), generates feelings in the heart (○), that give rise to understanding in the mind (∪). By contrast the motor function involves ideas arising from the mind (∪), being energized from the realm of will (○), and executed in the physical world (+). In Figure 4.2 the Circle of the soul in the Mercury glyph shows the generation of the vital force in the heart, the Cross of matter shows the vital force activating the body, and the Crescent of spirit shows the receptivity of the vital force to impressions from the spiritual world.

Surrounding the egg and the Zodiacal symbols in Dee's *Monas Hieroglyphica* (Figure 2.3 page 10), is a scroll that twists around the central motif. Its Latin inscription means '*Mercury* [Stilbon] *becomes the parent and the King of all planets when made perfect by a stable pointed hook.*'[10] This enigmatic phrase alludes to the alchemical perception of Mercury as symbol-ically embodying all the other Planets. Just as Ether is seen as the *Quintaessentia* of the Four Elements, so too, Mercury embodies all the other six traditional Planets. The '*stable pointed hook*' refers to the Dot in the central glyph forming the Solar glyph. Once this Dot is in place all other Planetary glyphs can be found within the glyph for Mercury, hence the idea of it becoming a parent. The Sun is symbolically connected with kings, so the presence of a Solar glyph at the centre of the Mercury glyph makes it '*King of all planets*'. The name Stilbon is Greek meaning 'Glistener', another allusion to the fifth Element, Ether.

The position of each Planet within the Mercury glyph will be explored in the appropriate sections to follow. Since Mercury is synonymous with Ether, this relationship of the Planets to Mercury in the heavens symbolically shows how the Planets influence the Elements below: 'As above so below'. This will become more apparent as the other Planets are described.

Each Planetary section will conclude with a list of symbolic associations to aid understanding of the symbol.

Symbolic Associations for Mercury

Mind, thought, idea, intellect, reason, common sense, conception, understanding, perception, detection, knowledge, interest, belief, learning, study, writing, books, news, subtlety, inquisitiveness, communication, language, speech, eloquence, wit, gossip, commerce, administration, siblings, brain, nerves, hands, medicine, vitality, vital force, healing, hermetic knowledge, magic, skill, invention, imitation, tricks, dishonesty, perjury, boasts, idiocy, superficiality, restlessness, fickleness, forgetfulness.

THE SUN (☉)

The glyph of the Sun is composed of a Circle enclosing a Dot. In order to draw out the full symbolic significance of each of the remaining Planets, each Planetary glyph will be projected against the glyph for Mercury. Since the Mercury glyph embodies the Three Worlds, the effects of each Planet can then be considered in relation to these Three Worlds.

Figure 4.2 shows the Sun in relation to the Three Worlds. The Circle shape of the Solar glyph aligns it within the Mercury glyph to the soul, located in the Celestial World of the heart. In Hermetic teachings, the Dot represents the source of Light or God (Fire) which in each incarnation descends through the Intellectual World of the Air Element and acquires an emotional body (celestial vehicle) whereby it resides within the heart as the soul. Here the soul remains with the potential for mankind's inner illumination.

The following two sections from Agrippa's *De Occulta Philosophica* illustrate the Hermetic perception of the soul and its descent into the body. Regrettably this 1651 translation from

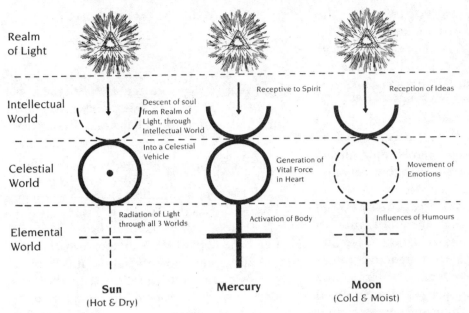

Realm of Light

Intellectual World

Receptive to Spirit

Reception of Ideas

Figure 4.2 Mercury, Sun, Moon and the Three Worlds

Descent of soul from Realm of Light, through Intellectual World

Into a Celestial Vehicle

Celestial World

Generation of Vital Force in Heart

Movement of Emotions

Radiation of Light through all 3 Worlds

Activation of Body

Influences of Humours

Elemental World

Sun
(Hot & Dry)

Mercury

Moon
(Cold & Moist)

Latin is awkward.

The soul of man is a certain divine Light, created after the image of the word,[YHVH] the cause of causes and first example, and the substance of God, . . .also the soul of man is a certain divine substance, individual and wholly present in every part of the body,

Therefore mans soul being such, according to the opinion of the Platonists, immediately proceeding from God, is joyned by competent means to this grosser body; whence first of all in its descent, it is involved in a Celestiall and aeriall body, which they call the celestial vehicle of the soul, others the chariot of the soul: Through this middle thing, by the command of God who is the centre of the World, it is first infused into the middle point of the heart, which is the centre of mans body, and from there it is diffused through all parts and members of his body,[11]

In the Mercury glyph shown in Figure 4.2 the Circle is the vacant Celestial vehicle of the soul,

while the presence of the Dot in the Solar glyph shows the descent of the soul from the realm of Divine Light into the heart. From the interaction of the Dot within the Circle, as seen as part of the Mercury glyph, there arises the idea of the Light from the soul generating the vital force of the body. This idea is succinctly captured by Nicholas Culpeper:

The Vital spirit hath its residence in the heart, and is dispersed from it by the Arteries; and is governed by the influence of the Sun. And it is to the body, as the Sun is to Creation; as the heart is in the Microcosm, so is the Sun in the Megacosm. For as the Sun gives life, light and motion to the Creation, so doth the heart to the body. Therefore it is called Sol Corporis [The Sun of the body], as the Sun is called Cor Coeli [The heart of the heaven], because their operations are similar.[12]

The Sun in the heavens is the source of light and heat which, once captured by the photosynthesis of plants, ultimately provides the energy for all life. During the summer the Sun reaches the zenith of its cycle, which is also when life is at its most abundant. Just as the Sun is the principal light in the heavens with all life on earth dependent upon it, so, too, the Sun symbolizes monarchs and rulers on earth.

The Sun symbolizes the Light from the soul which illuminates the ideas arising in the conscious mind (∪), provides energy to the will in emotional expression (○) and, as mentioned above, is the source of vital force that pervades the body (+).

The Sun symbolizes true creative expression. Here inspiration from the source of Light very rapidly propels the will to action. The Sun provides immense physical strength to accomplish tasks, often quite effortlessly despite the long duration. The resultant work is permeated by a light making it outshine and endure similar works. In time it is regarded as a masterpiece. The recognition leads to fame and celebration for the creator.

The hot and dry nature of the Sun connects it to the Fire Element. In humoral physiology the Sun is linked to the choleric humour. Humoral physiology will be explained later in the section on the Moon. Intense sunshine can cause drought and devastation; under certain circumstances the Sun is considered a minor malefic Planet.

Symbolic Associations for the Sun

Soul, heart, will, light, illumination, clarification, power, charisma, strength, courage, king, monarch, majesty, potentate, ruler, government, authority, domination, command, gold, dignity, loyalty, creativity, originality, mastery, honour, fame, glory, fortune, extravagance, pride, haughtiness, arrogance, vanity, fire, heat, energy, choler, circulation, masculinity, father, laziness, restlessness.

THE MOON (☽)

Figure 4.2 shows the Moon in relation to the Three Worlds. The Crescent shape of the Lunar glyph aligns it within the Mercury glyph to the spirit permeating the Intellectual World. Once the Sun has created the vital spirit, symbolized by Mercury, the Moon moves the spirit, causing it to wax and wane. In the same way that the Moon moves the waters of the oceans, so, too, it moves the 'Waters of Life'.

The Moon lacks its own light: instead it reflects the light of the Sun. Similarly the spirit by itself does not possess light, but reflects the Light of Creation. Seen as part of the Three World view, the Crescent located at the top of the Mercury glyph with its concave surface upwards, shows the Moon receiving Light and inspiration descending through the Intellectual World. Imagination is connected to the Moon, for as the Waters of the spirit are moved, so images are formed out of the Ether in response to impressions from the Intellectual World.

This subtle visual world is the realm of dreams. At night, once the Sun has set, the light of the Moon reveals softer gentler images of the world around us. Similarly while asleep, when conscious awareness (+) of the body is absent, the inner darkness of sleep is illuminated by images from the dream world (∪).

Emotional responses are powerfully influenced by the Moon. When the Moon appears at night, the air is cool and moisture condenses. Thus it is described as having a cold and moist nature. The Moon has particular affinity with the cold and moist Water Element. Water symbolically describes emotional experience; since the Moon causes the rising and falling of the tides, the Moon reflects the range of emotional expression and withdrawal.

The Moon symbolically describes the flow of

vital force through the body within the blood and body fluids. This is the basis of humoral physiology. The Moon has a powerful influence over humoral circulation generally, while specifically co-ruling the phlegmatic humour along with Venus.

Humoral Physiology

Having now touched upon the ideas of the humours, it is necessary to explain briefly what they are since humoral physiology is no longer understood by modern medicine. Up until the seventeenth century, medicine was based upon the humoral ideas first attributed to Hippocrates. The word humour derives from the Latin *humor*, meaning 'fluid' or 'liquid'. This term encompassed not only the body fluids but also the Etheric vital force that was perceived as flowing through the blood.

The four humours are all contained in the blood. They were symbolically perceived and differentiated using the Four Elements: the sanguine humour (L. *sanguineous* = bloody) corresponds to Air, the choleric humour (Gk *chole* = bile) corresponds to Fire, the melancholic humour (Gk *melanchole* = black bile) corresponds to Earth and the phlegmatic humour (Gk *phlegma* = phlegm) corresponds to Water.

Each humour has its own temperament in terms of hot and cold, wet and dry;

• Choleric – hot and dry.

• Sanguine – hot and moist.

• Phlegmatic – cold and moist.

• Melancholic – cold and dry.

Each humour is sympathetically ruled by a Planet. For example the Sun co-rules the hot and dry choleric humour.

In health the harmonious combination of humours is held in balance or temper, which allows the *Aqua Vitae* or vital force to flow freely through the body, whereas in disease the temper of the humours is lost. A particular humour predominating over the others causes a characteristic distemper. The humour can be identified by the symptoms it produces, whether they are hot or cold, dry or moist. The 'common cold' is classically a phlegmatic condition which should more accurately be diagnosed as a cold and moist!

The therapeutic objective of humoral physiology is to counteract the dominant humour and so restore the temper to the blood. For example a fever is a hot and dry condition which is helped by medicines that are cooling and moistening. One herb with the reputation for dealing with fever is the willow, perceived by the ancient herbalists as having a cold and moist Lunar nature.

The Moon, with its influence upon the Ether, from which the Four Elements are born, has been described as the Universal Mother, the counterpart of the Sun – the Universal Father.

A further development of these ideas is found within Dee's *Monas Hieroglyphica* (Figure 2.3, page 10). Instead of the usual Crescent elevated over the Circle as found in the Mercury glyph, the Crescent is allowed to overlap the Circle of the soul, while a Dot is placed at the centre of it. The additional Dot forms the Solar glyph (☉), while the two symbols overlapping form the shape of a *vesica piscis*. The elliptic shape of the *vesica piscis* (◗) alludes to a vulva and it is a potent symbol of the Universal Mother through which all matter is born.

The Dot – symbolic of the Light of the soul – can now be seen to have passed through this cosmic vulva in its descent into the material (L. *Mater* – mother) world. Thus following the union of the Universal Parents (☉) and (☽) a soul can symbolically be seen to incarnate. Dee also mentions that the Dot can also represent the Earth, with the Sun, Moon and Planets revolving around it – seen from a geocentric perspective.

Symbolic Associations for the Moon

Receptivity, intuition, premonition, visualization, reflection, spirit, imagination, images, dreams, vision, psychic, fantasy, myth, hallucination, illusion, lunacy, emotions, impulses, feeling, moods, ambience, sensitivity, devotion, sanctity, sadness, mother, femininity, fertility, nurse, affection, protection, softness, water, humour, phlegm, fluids, milk, rhythm, waves, pulse, cycles, vacillation, silver, passivity, nocturnal, subconscious.

SATURN (♄)

The glyph of Saturn, shown in Figure 4.3, is composed of the Cross of matter located above the Crescent of spirit, showing that matter is exalted over spirit in this glyph. When the glyph

is projected against an inverted Mercury glyph (defined by the dotted line in the illustration), then its deeper significance is revealed.

The Crescent recalls the Lunar glyph with its connection to the Water Element (as mentioned in the last section on the Moon) in which case the Cross of matter (+) comes between the Light of Creation and the Waters of the spirit (∪). Without heat and Light from the realm of Creation, the Waters of the spirit freeze. The quality of Saturn is cold and dry and has an affinity with the Earth Element.

Winter is the time when Saturn prevails. Without the heat and light from the Sun, water freezes and leafy vegetation withers. Throughout the night, when the first frosts strike, the 'scythe of the reaper' cuts down the vegetation leaving the Earth barren. The vitality of nature withdraws into the soil and is concentrated into the roots. Ephemeral forms of life that lack the strength of Earth to buffer and protect them perish.

Within the body, Saturn connects to the

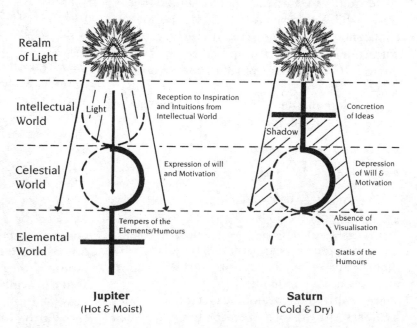

Figure 4.3 Saturn, Jupiter and the Three Worlds

skeletal system which provides structure and foundation for the tissues. In the living body, bones are highly dynamic tissues continually being formed and broken down at the same time. When bedridden, without the pressure exerted by gravity (also ruled by Saturn) upon the skeletal system, the bones become more frail and prone to fractures. After death, when the vitality is lost from the body, the tissues decay but the bones endure (Earth).

From its placing within the inverted Mercury glyph, the Cross of matter is projected into the Intellectual World or mental realm. Hence the Planet is associated with the building of ideas into solid structure, theories, laws and sciences – which may in time come to be accepted blindly as dogmas.

The density of ideas that the Cross of matter creates in the Intellectual World blocks out the Light from reaching the Celestial and Elemental Worlds. The heart is often gripped by fears and the soul plummeted into darkness. The Crescent leaves the Circle of the soul incomplete (as indicated by the dotted line in the illustration). The vitality of the body becomes severely depressed, leading to chronic ailments (*Khronos* is the Greek equivalent of Saturn) becoming entrenched in the body, leading ultimately to death.

The cold and dry nature of Saturn aligns it with the melancholic humour, which was formerly described as the 'sediment of the blood'. In the context of modern physiology this can be equated with the blood clotting mechanism. Though normally vital to seal against the loss of blood from the body, the inappropriate formation of clots in the blood vessels deprives vital organs of blood. This can rapidly cause loss of function of an organ, even death, in a matter of minutes. Mythologically Saturn is the Lord of Death.

The absence of Light reaching the lunar-shaped Crescent symbolizes the receptive visual part of the mind being blocked. Saturn denies receptiveness to the spiritual world.

Symbolic Associations for Saturn

Concentration, condensation, matter, darkness, discipline, resolution, course, plan, responsibility, restriction, control, method, procedure, indoctrination, conditioning, repression, prohibition, science, law, logic, regulation, institution, patience, endurance, solitude, secrecy, deficiency, severity, fear, caution, hesitation, selfishness, ostracism, time, building, structure, prison, pessimism, depression, melancholia, sorrow, ice, skeleton, skin, teeth, spleen, apathy, coldness, dullness, decay, death.

JUPITER (♃)

The glyph for Jupiter shown in Figure 4.3 is the inverse of Saturn, here the Crescent of spirit is located over the Cross of matter, showing the exaltation of spirit over matter. The elevated Crescent acts as a receptacle to the Intellectual World, drawing down its inspiration into the material or Elementary World. The Lunar Crescent above the Cross of matter enables the Light of Creation to warm the Waters of the spirit. The quality of Jupiter is hot and moist and has an affinity with the Air Element. Water when heated expands and evaporates. The influence of Jupiter causes growth and expansion.

Within the human body Jupiter traditionally rules the lungs. With each inspiration the chest expands, air flows into the lungs and diffuses into the blood. (Saturn rules expiration.) Condensation of hot, moist air onto a mirror or plate of glass held in front of the nose is a sign of life. No condensation occurs when the body is dead.

Jupiter rules the sanguine humour, the

principal humour of the blood which embodies the other three. The seat of this humour is the liver – the largest organ in the body – which is responsible for maintaining the balance of the humours in the blood. Modern physiology recognizes that the function of the liver is precisely reflected in the biochemical composition of the blood. Jupiter ensures that the sanguine humour is properly composed of its three constituent humours – choleric, phlegmatic and melancholic – thus facilitating the flow of the vital force through the body and maintaining health.

Mythologically Jupiter is a sky god and is ruler of all the other gods in the pantheon. When angry he exerts his authority by throwing down thunderbolts. The hot, moist and muggy weather before a thunderstorm is the anger of Jupiter. The lightning bolts clear the air, release tension and restore temper to the atmosphere.

In Roman times the sites where thunderbolts fell were immediately considered sacred, and temples dedicated to Jupiter were built there. This reflects how Jupiter draws the spiritual world down to earth.

When compared to the Mercury glyph, the Cross of matter is located firmly in the Elemental World with the Lunar Crescent drawing down the Waters of the spirit. When the vital force of nature is in harmony with the material world it brings about growth, expansion, healing and regeneration.

The soul's openness to intuitions from the Intellectual World leads to an expansion of ideals and aspirations. The broadened horizons create enthusiasm and optimism as the will is inspired towards new goals.

Symbolic Associations for Jupiter

Temperance, justice, judgement, equity, ambition, expression, enterprise, initiative, goal, aspiration, hope, wish, expansion, religion, priesthood, faith, confidence, fidelity, spirituality, prophecy, philosophy, liberation, optimism, joy, pleasure, altruism, generosity, charity, largess, privilege, compassion, grace, mercy, clemency, tolerance, modesty, humility, vanity, ostentation, gluttony, dissipation, evaporation, lungs, liver, sanguine, thunder.

VENUS (♀)

The glyph of Venus in relation to the Three Worlds (seen in Figure 4.4) is composed of the Circle of the soul joined to the Cross of matter. The Circle embodies the vital force generated by the Sun so the glyph describes the drawing down of the vital force into the material or Elemental World. Venus symbolizes the mother and is identified with the creative energy of nature which arises every spring.

Mythologically Venus is a goddess of love. Fertilization of an ovum following an act of love results in a soul incarnating into material form. After nine months gestation in the womb, also ruled by Venus, the soul emerges from its Watery world clothed in a new physical body.

This Venusian action, the drawing down of the vital force into the material world, is captured by the phrase 'falling in love'. From the glyph the vital force is seen to be drawn away from the realm of Light. Hence Venus is cold and moist and has an affinity with the Water Element.

Venus in the body traditionally co-rules, with the Moon, the phlegmatic humour – the plasma portion of the blood. Phlegm has its seat in the lungs. Various secretions which are essentially exudations from the blood plasma, like tears, sweat and urine are all ruled by Venus. The kidneys, which filter the blood, forming urine, and the flow of blood around the body – the

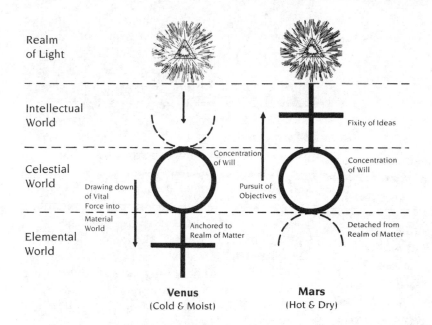

Realm
of Light

Intellectual
World

Celestial
World

Elemental
World

Figure 4.4 Venus, Mars and the Three Worlds

Fixity of Ideas

Concentration of Will

Concentration of Will

Drawing down of Vital Force into Material World

Pursuit of Objectives

Anchored to Realm of Matter

Detached from Realm of Matter

Venus
(Cold & Moist)

Mars
(Hot & Dry)

'venous' circulation – are traditionally ascribed to Venus.

When compared to Mercury, the glyph of Venus lacks the crescent at the top, indicating that the love of Venus lacks knowledge received from the Intellectual World. Human love is often described as 'blind'; hence Cupid depicted shooting his arrows of love blindfold.

Through love comes a sense of value, so Venus relates especially to material items that are loved and cherished for their beauty. The bond of love draws people together in harmony and co-operation. Love within a family provides the security which nurtures the children and enhances the unfolding of their individuality. Love also facilitates the material security of a home base.

Venus rules food, from which energy is drawn into the body. The substance of the food forms new tissues in growth and regeneration.

Philosophy was originally a Venusian pursuit, being derived from the Greek words *phileo* meaning 'love' and *Sophia* the goddess of

wisdom, thus literally meaning 'love of Sophia'. This understanding is apparent in the way that Culpeper referred to philosophy.

For caution, consider that the ancient Philosophers followed, and regarded Nature herself in all her ways, and nothing else. They knew the steps of Nature were clearly seen in the procreation and generation of man, where she observes her own law and rules, and they being contented with the plain way of Nature alone, attained to the utmost period of all their studies and hopes also, and found out those things which the wits of modern Alchemists would not.[13]

Symbolic Associations for Venus

Love, amorousness, passion, glamour, attachment, affection, union, marriage, emotion, feeling, joy, pleasure, amusement, flirtation, pleasantness, tranquillity, sweetness, serenity, grace, kindness, fortune, prosperity, money, gifts, sensuality, lasciviousness, incest, adultery, sloth, philosophy, music, harmony, art, beauty, material, Water, phlegm, veins, kidneys, nocturne, food, semen, femininity, mother.

MARS (♂)

The glyph of Mars (♂) has in modern times become distorted from its earlier form, in which the Cross of matter is elevated over the Circle of the soul (♂). It should now be easily recognized that this glyph is the symbolic opposite of Venus (♀).

Figure 4.4 shows Mars in relation to the Three Worlds. The Cross of matter is now elevated, showing the projection of the Four Elements into the Intellectual World. The vital force from the soul is directed into the realm of ideas. This rising of the vital force brings it closer to the realm of Light. Hence the quality of Mars is hot and dry and has an affinity with the Fire Element.

The presence of the Cross in the Intellectual World generates fixed goals and ideas. The focusing of vital force towards the Intellectual World provokes the will-power to pursue these objectives. Mythologically Mars is a god of war; under the influence of martial rule, ideas are forcibly imposed upon others. The contemporary use of a barb instead of a Cross symbolically captures the sharpness of weapons, knives, spears, bullets and so on, while the link with Fire symbolizes the energy that propels their use and the destruction they cause. Mars symbolizes anger and in accordance with the motion of the glyph, people are said to 'rise up in anger'.

The Cross of matter is not firmly anchored in the Elemental World, as it is in the Venusian glyph; instead its projection into the Intellectual World describes a radical upheaval of the Elemental World. Consider the aftermath

of war. Mars is a powerful agent of change. Martian knowledge lacks inspiration; instead its ideas are based upon practical experience and empirical observation. Knowledge of a mystical or intuitive nature is generally vehemently eschewed or dogmatically asserted.

Within the body the hot and dry influence of Mars connects it to the choleric humour or yellow bile – the Fire portion of the blood. In contemporary physiology this is linked to the red blood cells. The red blood cells transport oxygen from the lungs to the tissues, enabling the cells to 'burn up' the sugar from the blood and generate energy. Mars is traditionally connected to the metal iron (used in instruments of war). The principal molecule inside the red blood cells responsible for carrying oxygen is called haemoglobin. It contains iron as part of its molecular structure. When the haemoglobin combines with oxygen forming oxyhaemoglobin, the blood turns bright scarlet. Mars is the 'red planet' in the heavens. By contrast when the haemoglobin releases its oxygen it returns to a dark red colour, which when seen through the skin appears pale blue. It is this blue colour that has linked Venus with the flow of blood through the veins, hence 'venous' circulation. Venus is the 'blue planet' in the heavens.

The symbolic link between Mars and energy is dramatically shown in anaemia. Anaemia is a condition where there is a lack of red blood cells in the blood, often due to a shortage of iron. Its main symptoms are tiredness and lethargy, with diminished resistance and vitality.

The choleric humour or yellow bile in humoral physiology has its seat in the gall-bladder. The yellow colour of the bile is formed from the breakdown products of haemoglobin when the red blood cells are destroyed.

The muscles are ruled by Mars. When they contract energy is translated into actions that move and propel the body. In the process heat is generated that contributes to the body's warmth.

Mars rules the male sexual organs. Once again the upward thrust of the Martian energy is found in the ejaculation of seminal fluid. In illness Mars is linked to fevers, in which excessive heat is generated in the body, and particularly to acute (L. *acutus* = sharp) illness which has a short duration.

Symbolic Associations for Mars

Power, energy, force, dynamism, change, drive, *esprit de corps*, thrust, vigour, fortitude, virility, violence, brutality, rape, murder, aggression, attack, belligerence, resistance, soldiers, action, battle, execution, gallantry, valour, cowardice, desire, hunger, lust, obscenity, stubbornness, anger, animosity, quarrel, annoyance, assertion, argument, sport, muscles, penis, masculinity, bile, choler, fever, rashes, surgery.

As already described, each Planet has a particular affinity with one of the Four Elements. However, every Planet by its nature does have an effect on all the other Elements as well. This is summarized in Figure 4.5.

The Planetary symbolism shown in Figure 4.5 will be applied to the rulership of the palmar lines and used in the understanding of phalanges. This will be explained in Part 2 of the book.

Figure 4.5 Table of Elemental Compatibility

Planet	Element			
	Earth	Air	Water	Fire
Saturn	Strengthens	Limits	Freezes	Suppresses
Jupiter	Weakens	Expands	Thaws	Expresses
Sun	Dries	Activates	Evaporates	Intensifies
Moon	Moistens	Clouds	Moves	Dampens
Mars	Burns	Heats	Boils	Strengthens
Venus	Softens	Moistens	Cools	Extinguishes

CHAPTER 5

The Trans-Saturnian or Outer Planets

CHEIROMANCY has largely been in decline since the seventeenth century; since then three more Planets – Uranus, Neptune and Pluto – have been discovered by astronomers. Their symbolic significance has been rapidly taken up by astrologers, but not by cheiromancers – which perhaps reflects just how stagnant cheiromantical knowledge has become in the last three centuries. In Chapter 12 the symbolism of the three outer Planets will be used to interpret some of the less well understood lines of the hand.

A substantial body of ideas connected to these symbols has been worked out by astrologers. This has largely been done by noting what was happening in the world, in all spheres of life, at the time when these Planets were born into consciousness and what subsequently developed directly after their discovery. For cheiromantical purposes this section is intentionally limited to the scientific discoveries and developments of the time, since the ascendancy of 'scientific thought' has contributed to the decline of symbolic understanding, and to that of cheiromancy. When, however, scientific ideas are seen symbolically, it reveals just how valid symbolic knowledge is. Rather than showing the 'triumph of reason over superstition' described in the history of science, it shows

how this symbolic knowledge can be used in tandem with scientific ideas.

URANUS (♅)

Uranus was discovered by William Herschel (1738–1822), on 13 March 1781, while looking up at the heavens through his telescope. This discovery had an enormous impact upon the body of symbolic knowledge surrounding the traditional seven-Planet system (the Sun is included as a Planet). The neatness of this system of correspondences involving the Planets 'above' influencing the Elements 'below', as expounded in Chapter 4 on Planetary symbolism, was apparently shattered by the discovery of a new Planet.

Up until this time Saturn was the furthermost Planet visible to the eye, which thus defined the boundaries to this symbolic knowledge. The discovery of Uranus radically undermined all the ideas that had been built up through the centuries from classical times. Uranus is symbolically connected to the flashes of intuition that spark off new discoveries, inventions and innovations that lead to far reaching economic, social and political effects.

The abrupt, iconoclastic ideas of Uranus cause radical change. Uranus embodies a powerful search for truth and a seeking out of the principles underlying blind conventions. It was this mode of analysis that underlay the development of modern scientific thinking which, at the time of Uranus' discovery, started increasingly to probe into the nature of matter.

The scientific changes at the time of Uranus' discovery illustrate its energy and symbolic nature. The state of scientific thought during the hundred years prior to this is powerfully symbolized by Robert Boyle's work, *The Skeptical Chemist* (1661). Boyle (1627–91), who is considered one of the patriarchs of modern chemistry, in this work destructively criticizes the Four Elements – Earth, Water, Air and Fire – and the three Philosophical Principles – Salt, Sulphur and Mercury. He explains his doubts from being unable to equate findings in the laboratory with the Philosophy of the Elements. Throughout the work he interprets the Elements solely from a literal rather than a symbolic point of view. This is shown where he doubts

. . . that from the mixture of the Peripatetick [Aristotelian] four Elements there could arise but an inconsiderable variety of compound Bodies.[14]

Boyle particularly commends the use of Fire to analyse different substances. He then cites many examples of the changes brought about by heating different substances that cannot be explained by the substances containing the Elements or the Philosophical Principles. Boyle compares the number of substances formed by Fire with the number of Elements and Principles to disprove their validity. His work concludes that his experimentation

. . . sufficiently prov'd that these distinct Substances which Chymists are won't to obtain from Mixt Bodies, by their Vulgar Distillation , are not pure and simple enough to deserve, in Rigor of speaking, the Name of Elements, or Principles.[15]

In dismissing the validity of the Elements Boyle dogmatically denies the metaphysical and philosophical ideas that he acknowledged were based upon them. Since Boyle was a deeply religious man also known to be interested in astrology,[16] this critique of the Elements and Philosophical Principles was a distinct about-face. It is perhaps significant that *The Skeptical Chemist* was written just after the Restoration in 1661, reflecting the same political pressures of censorship that led to the decline of astrology and cheiromancy.

In place of the Four Elements Boyle defined a chemical element in terms of a substance incapable of being decomposed into simpler constituents:

I now mean by Elements, as those Chymists that speak plainest by their Principles, certain Primitive and Simple, or perfectly unmingled bodies; which not being made of any other bodies, or of one another, are the Ingredients of which all the perfectly mixt Bodies are immediately compounded, and into to which they are intimately resolved.[17]

Seen symbolically, this definition is a very Saturnine materialistic view of what can be expressed and understood by the Elements. Using this definition Boyle was still unable to draw up a list of chemical elements in his lifetime.

This was an era when chemists put a lot of energy into experimenting with the combustion of metals and the nature of gases. Despite the activity in the laboratory, scientific thinking was in a 'vacuum'. The suppression of metaphysical knowledge had led to a stagnation of Elemental understanding. Philosophers sought to explain the physical world solely through a literal interpretation of the Elements, that predictively proved to be deficient.

This situation persisted until 1787 when the French chemist Antoine Lavoisier (1743–94) grasped the ideas necessary to understand combustion and set about pragmatically to prove the truth of his discoveries.

Lavoisier's most famous experiment consisted of heating liquid mercury in a retort enclosing a sealed volume of air. The heated metal combined with the oxygen in the air to form the red oxide of mercury. In a separate experiment Lavoisier then found that when the oxide was reheated gently it returned to the liquid metal, releasing the same volume of gas as it had taken up from the air.

From various experiments Lavoisier concluded that there were two principal gases in the air. Firstly there was the active portion that supported combustion and combined with heated metals. This portion additionally supported life through respiration. Secondly the passive portion, that took no part in the changes of combustion and did not support life. The outcome of this analysis and experimentation was that Air was no longer seen as an element in Boyle's definition of the term, since it could be reduced into two separate portions.

Symbolically it is very interesting that Lavoisier made his breakthrough using mercury, the metal traditionally ruled by Mercury – the god of Hermetic knowledge; while the phenomenon of combustion (the burning of Fire in Air) should lead to new ideas being sparked off in the quest to understand the nature of matter.

The English philosopher Henry Cavendish (1731–1810) had discovered a gas in 1766 which he called 'inflammable air', given off when dilute sulphuric acid was dripped onto zinc. In 1781 (the year of Uranus' discovery) he burnt the gas in air, forming water. Lavoisier repeated the experiment in 1783 and called the gas hydrogen after the Greek meaning 'water producer'. As a result it was realized that Water could no longer be considered an element.

Thus within the space of ten years from the time of Uranus' discovery, Water and Air were no longer seen as Elements. Water was found to be composed of hydrogen plus oxygen, while air was found to contain oxygen and nitrogen. In accordance with Boyle's definition, since they could be reduced to simpler constituents, they were no longer considered as Elements. With the discovery of chemical elements supporting Boyle's definition, Elemental knowledge was seen to have no physical basis and so fell into marked decline.

This decline led to the collapse of the Three World view and all the metaphysical ideas associated with it. The combination of these discoveries with the effects of renewed censorship by the Company of Stationers at the time of the Restoration had a tremendous cultural impact. This radical destruction of traditional knowledge powerfully illustrates the energy of Uranus.

Under the influence of Uranus matter was seen to exist in its own right. Any metaphysical explanations of the material world were intensely denied. Scientists sought to explain matter solely in terms of its own composition.

Parallel to these developments in chemistry, advances in the understanding of electricity were being made. In 1746 the American Benjamin Franklin (1706–90), famous for flying his kite in a thunderstorm, described positive and negative charges in the flow of electricity. At the time of Uranus' discovery, the Italian physiologist Luigi Galvani(1739–98) demonstrated an electrical component to nervous conduction when he induced the violent twitching of a frog's leg using metal wires.

The English chemist Sir Humphrey Davy (1778–1829) used the newly developed battery (invented by A. Volta in 1796) for electrolysis (the splitting of substances by electrical current). In 1807 Davy isolated sodium and potassium from soda and potash respectively. In conclusion to his work Davy postulated that the chemical affinity between atoms was an electrical phenomenon. Thus under the influence of Uranus electricity was used to investigate the material world.

Recently physiologists have found that sodium and potassium ions are vital in the conduction of nervous impulses. Thus the functioning of the nervous system can be linked to Uranus.

Electricity and all the technologies that have evolved from it are all ruled by Uranus. The somewhat unconventional glyph for Uranus incorporates an 'H' – the initial of its founder William Herschel (see Figure 5.1). It has been thought, appropriately, to look like a TV aerial! The role that electronics now plays in traditional Mercurial domains such as communication, commerce and medicine is enormous. As a consequence the rulerships of Uranus and Mercury distinctly overlap. Take a fax machine – is it ruled by Mercury the traditional ruler of documents or Uranus, ruler of electronic inventions?

On a global scale the way the media now functions through satellite technology has linked up the civilized world like a giant electronic nervous system, relaying news, information and entertainment while providing a conscience for humanity.

The Uranus glyph in Figure 5.1 shows the Cross of matter elevated over the Circle of the soul, projected into the Intellectual world. Thus intense energy is focused into investigating and questioning the nature of matter. The Cross of matter being uprooted from the Elemental World symbolically reflects the radical upheaval of Elemental knowledge. The Cross in the Uranus' glyph is further differentiated by the H shape, showing the redefinition of the chemical elements. In science, matter is no longer rooted in nature but abstracted into a realm of theory. Like Mars, Uranus' glyph shows the will being directed upwards into the realm of ideas. The Cross of matter elevated towards the realm of Light makes its temperament hot and dry,

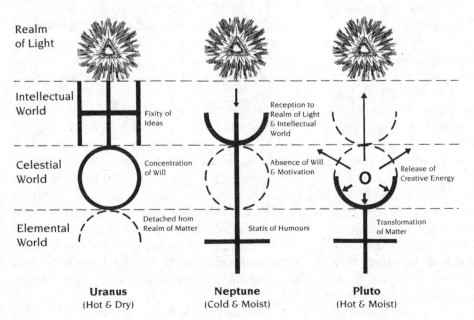

Figure 5.1 Uranus, Neptune, Pluto and the Three Worlds

giving the Planet an affinity with the Fire Element. Fire describes the zeal with which science has analysed the material world and reduced it to its component particles, like flames consuming a piece of wood and reducing it to ash.

Symbolic Associations for Uranus

Intuition, insight, discovery, revelation, perception, detection, inquiry, investigation, experimentation, observation, explanation, hypothesis, analysis, breakthrough, invention, innovation, revolution, iconoclast, heretic, science, electricity, technology, computing, media.

NEPTUNE (Ψ)

In contrast to the stark discovery of Uranus, Neptune's arrival into awareness was surrounded by controversy concerning whether it existed or not. Slight perturbations noted in the orbit of Uranus had been attributed to the gravitational pull of another planet. The position of the planet was predicted by the astronomers Adams and Leverrier, both men working quite independently. (The synchronicity of scientific discoveries is a common theme of the Neptunian era.) The English astronomer John Couch Adams (1819–92) had been working on the irregularities of Uranus' motion and by October 1845 had completed his investigations determining the position of the planet. Although he sent his results to the Astronomer Royal, George Biddell Airy (1801–92), they were not published.

The French astronomer Urbain Jean Joseph Leverrier (1811–77), also working on the Uranian motion problem, published the results of his calculations in June 1846. His unknown planet was assigned to within a degree of Adams' calculations. Finally Neptune was found on 23rd September 1846, by Johann Galle in Berlin, near the point in the sky predicted by Leverrier. Since Adams' calculations were not published, it was only later that he was accredited as a co-discoverer of Neptune. Neptune has come to be associated with confusion and deception.

The glyph for Neptune in Figure 5.1 is composed of the Cross of matter projected upwards through the Crescent of spirit and forming a trident. Thus the symbol focuses upon the relationship between spirit and matter. It is where dream and imagination interface with the material world.

In the scientific world the discovery of Neptune coincided with the development of anaesthesia. A cluster of substances were found to be very useful as anaesthetics within four years surrounding its discovery; nitrous oxide in 1844, ether in 1846, chloroform in 1847 and ethyl chloride in 1848. Anaesthesia was a very important development for surgery, as the control of pain enabled more advanced procedures to be undertaken. Under the influence of the anaesthetic the patient's consciousness is induced into the spirit world (∪) and dissociated from the body (+), allowing the surgeon to probe ever more deeply into the tissues and organs of the body without the patient feeling pain.

In 1853 the French physiologist François Magendie (1783–1855) injected an extract from opium into the blood of patients. This caused depression of brain activity, and induced deep sleep and a pronounced insensitivity to pain. This action of opium was found to be related to the concentration of morphine present (L. *morphina*, from *Morpheus* – the god of sleep). In this connection opium is the resinous exudation from the opium poppy *Papaver somniferum*, a plant symbolically connected to the Moon.

It was also in 1853 that another Neptunian invention made the injection of opium possible:

Alexander Wood developed the hypodermic syringe. The skin, which is traditionally ruled by Saturn, provides a protective barrier around the body dividing that which is visible from that which is invisible. It is symbolically appropriate that a trans-Saturnian invention should penetrate through the skin into the humours or body fluids. When it is recalled that the Moon rules the humours or body fluids generally, the central prong of the Neptune glyph (⊥) can be seen as a needle penetrating the Crescent of the Moon (∪). The Cross of matter forms the handle on each side of the syringe barrel and the tip of the plunger (♆). This creates an image of the syringe injecting the drug into the blood.

Anaesthesia illustrates an important Neptunian quality – that is, the dissociation of the mind from the body. This characterizes a whole pattern of scientific investigation whereby in the pursuit of objectivity the subjective is excluded from the situation. This is particularly shown by the birth of psychology as a science separate from medicine in the Neptunian era.

Photography has been linked to Neptune through the connection between images in the imagination and the images on the film. The phenomenon subtly evolved through about 120 years of gradual observation and experimentation prior to the discovery of Neptune. It began with the observation that silver salts reacted to light. Through the years different mediums were used to carry the silver compounds, from paper to glass and finally celluloid. The medium enabled the image to be captured and preserved. Since both silver and the imagination are traditionally linked with the Moon, it is most appropriate that silver salts were so instrumental in the birth of photography.

The development of the camera, which controls the amount of light reaching the film, coincided with Neptune's discovery. By the year 1889 amateur photography was possible. In contrast to the slow speed of painting, images in the mind of the photographer could now be captured instantaneously. The same development facilitated the birth of cinematography. A rapid succession of fixed images were found to simulate the illusion of movement, as in a dream.

In Figure 5.1, page 35, the Neptunian glyph is projected against the Hermetic Three World view. It symbolically shows how Light emanating from the realm of Creation is captured by the Lunar shaped Crescent and the resultant image fixed by the Cross of matter. Photography illustrates another Neptunian association of fixing images from the realm of the imagination.

Since Uranus' discovery matter had been seen to exist in its own right, being composed of tiny atoms. Each atom was perceived as a tiny solid lump, as exemplified by Dalton's atomic theory of 1808. With Neptune's discovery chemists started increasingly to visualize how atoms joined together as molecules.

This was the time when organic chemistry (based upon the carbon chain) was born in the laboratory. Chemists started to see that there was no end to the way that carbon atoms could be joined together. This was when organic chemicals like acetic acid, found in vinegar, were first synthesized.

The role of the imagination in visualizing how atoms joined together in molecules is shown by an anecdote about how the German chemist Friedrick Kekulé (1825–99) discovered the structure of benzene. Kekulé spent many hours contemplating the structure of benzene. In 1866 the solution came to him while asleep. He dreamt about an ouroboros, an alchemical symbol of a serpent or dragon devouring its own tail. The circle defined by the body of the creature, amongst other things, describes the Unity of life. On waking Kekulé realized that the structure of benzene consisted of a ring of carbon atoms.

The success of the organic chemists in the laboratory in this era led them to believe that they could explain all living processes solely by organic chemistry. The idea that living matter was animated by a vital force and was fundamentally different from inanimate matter, a view maintained by the 'vitalists' of the day, was vigorously eschewed by the organic chemists.

Closer inspection of the Neptunian glyph is particularly interesting in this respect. Apart from the central shaft that unites the Cross of matter with the Crescent of spirit, the middle section of the glyph lacks the Circle of the soul, when compared with the glyph for Mercury. When it is recalled that the Sun generates the vital force symbolized by Mercury and that the Solar glyph is linked to the missing Circle of the soul, then the denial of that vitalism at this time is especially appropriate. The science from this Neptunian era, in dissociating mind from the body, evolved a soulless mechanical perception of Man.

Symbolic Associations for Neptune

Imagination, dreams, vision, deception, illusion, mirage, controversy, confusion, perplexity, sensitivity, subtlety, anaesthesia, dissociation, hallucination, synthesis, pharmaceutical, narcotic, mind-body split, materialism, photography.

PLUTO (♀)

The discovery of Pluto was quite enigmatic. Once again perturbations had been noted in the orbit of Uranus (the Planet of new discoveries and innovations) which could not be explained by the gravitational pull of Neptune. In 1915 the American astronomer Percival Lowell (1855–1916) had been working on the problem and, after doing his calculations, set about looking for a trans-Neptunian planet. The technique he used was time lapse photography, a recent Neptunian development, which involved taking a photographic plate of the segment of the heavens under consideration through a telescope. Two plates were exposed two or three nights apart, allowing time for a planet to move. Once developed their images were superimposed. In this short period of time any moving planet would appear to have a 'split' image while the bulk of the stars would have remained stationary. Lowell was unsuccessful in his attempt and died the following year.

His calculations were published in 1918 in a pamphlet on the perturbations of Uranus by a planet beyond Neptune, but despite this the discovery lay dormant for another fifteen years until January 1930, when Pluto was finally found by fellow American astronomer Clyde Tombaugh. Its position was very close to where Lowell had predicted it to be, and the same time-lapse photographic technique was used. It is noteworthy that a Neptunian medium had to be used in order to discover what lay beyond it.

Fifteen years later the original plates made by Lowell were re-examined in the light of his calculations being so accurate. If Pluto had been where he said it was, why had he not found it in 1915? On closer examination of one of the original plates a slight fissure was found in the photographic emulsion precisely at the point where Pluto was located. The fissure had obscured the split image which should have highlighted Pluto's position.

Between 1890 and 1930, as Pluto gradually emerged into consciousness, the scientific understanding of matter became radically transformed. These developments powerfully reflect the symbolism associated with Pluto. As will be explained, Pluto is symbolically linked to the relationship of energy to matter.

Dalton's concept of atoms existing as solid 'billiard ball' like particles was shattered by the discoveries and developments of this period. Various atomic phenomena were found that did not fit in to such a neat conception of atoms, in particular the discovery of radioactivity by Henri Becquerel (1852–1908) in 1896.

In 1889 the New Zealander Sir Ernest Rutherford (1871–1937) investigated radioactivity and found that there were two kinds of radiation from uranium, which he called alpha and beta particles. In 1903 Curie and Laborde found that radioactive substances emitted heat. Physicists concluded from all these phenomena that vast amounts of energy must be stored inside atoms.

In 1911 Rutherford performed a highly significant experiment which showed that atoms were not solid particles. He directed a fine beam of positively charged alpha particles through very thin gold leaf. To his astonishment he found that the bulk of particles passed straight through the gold leaf undeflected. A few were slightly deflected in their path, while only occasionally some were directly repelled and bounced back from the leaf. If the atoms had been solid, as Dalton had conceived them to be, then all these alpha particles would have been repelled.

In conclusion Rutherford went on to describe how each atom had a positively charged nucleus that was tiny in relation to the rest of the atom. Therefore the bulk of the alpha particles passed through the 'empty space' of the atom undeflected. Those alpha particles that passed close to the nucleus were slightly repelled (like charges repel) and so deflected in their path. A small number of particles actually hit the nucleus causing them to be powerfully repelled and rebound back again. So the classical model of a solid atom was dispelled, revealing a more composite nature: comparatively 'hollow' and storing vast amounts of energy.

Parallel to all these developments, Albert Einstein (1878–1955) produced his theories of relativity; his special theory of relativity in 1905 and his general theory in 1915. His most famous equation '$E = mc^2$' essentially means that matter is nothing but a form of energy. Any physical object at rest contains vast amounts of energy stored in its mass, as shown by the decay of radioactive elements. From the equation; when matter (m) is accelerated beyond the speed of light (c), it becomes energy (E). The reverse is also true. Matter (m) is energy (E) that has decelerated from the speed of light (c).

Modern nuclear physics basically demonstrates the same process as the Hermetic Philosophers who, 300 years before, visualized the material or Elemental World precipitating out of a realm of Light, as shown by Robert Fludd's illustration (Figure 2.2 page 9). The Hermetic Philosophers perceived all matter as incorporating the energy that created it.

Another realization of modern physics is that matter, rather than consisting of 'component building blocks', appears to consist of a series of relationships between the various parts of the whole. This includes the observer watching over the phenomena; the behaviour of any atomic structure can only be understood in terms of the structure's interaction with the observer. Matter cannot be considered separately from the person observing it.

This relationship between energy, matter and the observer has always been obvious and apparent to the alchemist through the centuries within the cosmology of the Five Elements; Ether is the all-pervasive universal energy that provides the matrix of the psyche and from which the material world of Earth, Water, Air and Fire is generated.

Boyle's Saturnine interpretation of an element as a substance incapable of being decomposed into smaller constituents can now be seen as totally erroneous according to the modern understanding of atoms. It is also symbolically significant that gold (the metal of the Sun) should have shed light on the nature of matter (Saturn).

Since the modern conceptions of matter can now be seen to be compatible with the cosmology of the Five Elements, the Four Elements that rule the material world can be symbolically linked to the infrastructure of an atom.

Earth corresponds to the atomic nucleus, composed of the protons and neutrons, which constitutes 99 per cent of the atom's mass. Despite the protons and neutrons travelling at speeds of 40,000 miles per second inside the nucleus, it is remarkably stable.

Water corresponds to the electrons that spin around the nucleus, in a series of 'shells', at 600 miles per second. In the light of quantum theory, electrons are seen to behave sometimes as particles and sometimes as waves; both properties are easily grasped using the symbolism of Water, since it can exist as a particle, as in a raindrop, or waves, as in a large body of water. Water is the Element used to describe joining together; the exchange of electrons between atoms is the basis of the chemical bonding of molecules.

Air describes the space inside an atom. If an atom is visualized inflated to the size of a large football stadium, then the nucleus would be present in the middle, the size of a football. On this scale electrons would be like grains of salt travelling at vast speeds throughout this space.

Fire links to the energy contained in an atom, in the motion of the electrons, protons and neutrons. When electrons absorb energy from an electric arc, discharge, spark or heat, they move into higher 'orbit' within the 'shells', as they spin round the nucleus. On spontaneously returning to their lower 'orbits', they release this absorbed energy as light.

Since the cosmology of the Five Elements dynamically describes the relationship of the mind and the emotions to the matter of the body, it can be used to describe the relationship between the observer and the observed. Specifically this knowledge shows how consciousness and matter are interconnected.   The potential of this knowledge is vast. For example, it could enable physiologists to see how mental decisions are translated into physical movements of the body, or how emotional states directly influence the physical health and performance of the body. The study of cheiromancy demonstrates the potential of this knowledge.

The glyph for Pluto in Figure 5.1 is composed of the Cross of matter anchored in the Elemental World with the Crescent of spirit lying immediately above it, within the Celestial World. Inside the Crescent lies a small Circle, which cannot be taken to be the Circle of the soul since it would need to have the same diameter as both the Cross and the Crescent. The Circle is reminiscent of the Dot found in the centre of the Solar glyph – which is symbolic of the Light from the realm of Creation descending into matter. The expansion of the Circle in contrast to the Solar Dot suggests a release of this energy which is partially captured by the Crescent of spirit. Thus the Pluto glyph embodies the release of the Creative Energy that is locked in matter. Energy 'radiates' from above the horizon of the Crescent, while that energy captured by the Crescent leads to transformation of the material or Elemental World. This reflects the phenomenon of the transmutation of elements, whereby as an atom undergoes radioactive decay releasing vast amounts of energy, it is transformed into another chemical element of less mass.

The invention of the electron microscope in 1932 illustrates another aspect of Pluto – namely, the ability to penetrate into the heart of the matter, in great detail. The electron microscope made an important contribution to the understanding of the intracellular chromosomes. The chromosomes bear the genetic material along the length of their nucleic acids. Their discovery provided a molecular basis to heredity. The nucleic acid DNA was defined and prepared by Altman in 1889. Since then a fascinating jigsaw puzzle has developed, fitting together the means by which the nucleic acids store the genes – the characteristics of inheritance – along their length and how, through protein synthesis, the physical characteristics of the body are generated.

Physiology gained enormously from the endocrine discoveries made during this period. Endocrinology stems from 1855 when the French physiologist Claude Bernard described the liver cells directly secreting into the blood. The word endocrine is Greek in origin, meaning to 'secrete within'. Historically endocrinology is Neptunian in its discovery. However, the developments that took place at the turn of the century are particularly interesting when projected against the emergence of Pluto.

Professor Starling coined the term 'hormone' in 1905, when describing the action of these chemical messengers in the body. The word hormone also comes from the Greek meaning 'to excite or arouse' – a very Plutonian metaphor. Of the steroidal sex hormones, various oestrogens were isolated from 1920 to 1938, progesterone in 1934, and testosterone in 1935. This is particularly significant since the counterpart of the energy contained in the atom is the sexual energy of the body.

Tying all these discoveries together it is noteworthy that the genetic information present in the chromosomes is particularly vulnerable to damage by radiation from radioactive substances. Damage to the molecular structure of DNA carries the risk of distorted physical characteristics being perpetuated through procreation to the future generations.

Symbolic Associations for Pluto

Hidden knowledge, intelligence, penetration, power, radiation, energy, destruction, devastation, transformation, relativity, connection between mind and body, subjectivity and objectivity, sexuality, procreation, heredity, genetics, hormones.

PART TWO

—

READING THE HAND

CHAPTER 6

The Taking of Handprints

MATERIALS NEEDED

You should be able to obtain most of the following items at a good art supplier:

- 1 lino printing roller, 2.5" – 3.0" wide;
- 1 tube of water-soluble block printing colour – blue, purple or black are the most suitable colours;
- 1 pad of plain white A4 paper; 70 gms – recommended thickness;
- 1 bathroom tile or plastic square, approx. 3" × 3";
- pair of scissors;
- ballpoint pen.

PRELIMINARY CONSIDERATIONS

Make sure that the person having their handprints taken has clean hands, free from creams, detergents and grease removers, as these will effect the quality of the print. They should also remove all rings if possible as this will make the technique easier.

The taking of handprints is best done with the subject sitting comfortably at a table. It is recommended that novices cover the area of table to be used with newspaper or plastic to prevent ink from marking the surface. For ease of taking handprints you will need to stand on the subject's right or left side, depending on whether you are right- or left-handed respectively. Have all your materials ready, placing the pad of paper on the table in front of the subject.

THE PROCEDURE FOR TAKING HANDPRINTS
(see Figure 6.1)

Main Print

1. Carefully squeeze a small amount of ink onto the tile in a series of little dabs. Taking handprints requires far less ink than you might imagine. (6.1 A)

2. Use the roller to flatten ink out over the surface of the tile. Apply pressure to ensure that the ink is thinly and evenly spread over its surface.

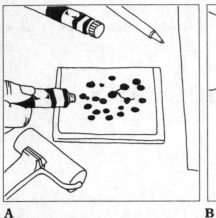

A

B

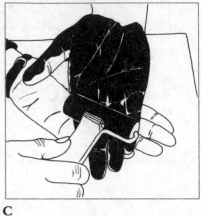

C

Figure 6.1 The Procedure for Taking Handprints

(A) Dab ink onto the tile

(B) Spread ink over tile, evenly coating roller with ink

(C) Using roller, cover hand with ink

(D) Direct subject to place inked hand onto paper, and apply gentle pressure on subjects hand

(E) Draw around hand with ball point pen

(F) Ask subject to lift up their hand with the paper still attached

(G) Ink subject's thumb, taking print on bottom edge of the paper

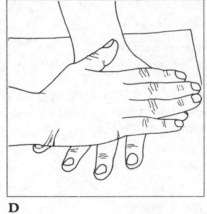

D

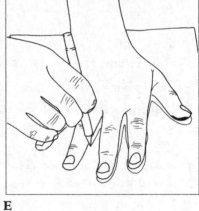

E

F

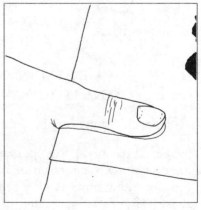

G

3. Draw the roller back and forth across the tile, ensuring that the ink spreads uniformly around the roller and along its width. (6.1 B)

4. Taking only one of your subject's hands at a time, apply the ink to the hand using bold strokes of the roller. Make sure that the ink covers the hand fully, taking the ink around the edges of the palm and the sides and tips of the fingers. Be careful not to apply too much ink to the hand; otherwise the lines will become smudged and obliterated. Too little ink will produce a very faint print. (6.1C)

5. Once the hand is fully covered with ink, direct the subject to place their hand in a natural, relaxed but definite way onto the paper. Ensure the hand and wrist are placed level on the surface of the table with the hand and lower arm in a straight line. Make sure the pad of paper is positioned so that there is no bending of the wrist when placing the hand upon it. Also prevent the subject from additionally pressing their hand down onto the paper, as this can lead to distortion of the handprint.

6. Use your hands to press down gently but firmly onto the back of your subject's hand and fingers. (6.1 D)

7. While their hand is still on the paper draw around it with a slender ballpoint pen. Ensure that the pen is held vertically and does not slant, as this would distort the outline of the hand. Do not be concerned if you cannot get the pen between the fingers. If certain fingers are held close together, this is significant, as will be explained later in Chapter 13. It is important not to move the fingers from their natural placing. (6.1 E)

8. Next, ask the subject to lift their hand, gently and with the paper still attached, and turn it over so that the palm is facing upwards with the paper still covering it (6.1 F). Place your passive hand underneath the subject's hand to act as a support. With your other hand, use the base of your palm to press the paper down into the central hollow of their palm. Take care to prevent the paper from slipping as this will cause the print to become smudged. Additionally, extra pressure at the base of their fingers and in the angle of their thumb may be needed to get good, clear details printed on the paper.

9. Peel the paper smartly off the hand and then set it aside for a few moments for the ink to dry. Repeat the whole process until you get at least three or four satisfactory handprints of the same hand and then repeat the procedure for the other hand.

The Thumb

Due to the oblique angle of the thumb on the side of the hand, the impression that the thumb makes on the paper while taking a handprint only includes one side of its length. In a handreading it is important to assess the development of the thumb. For this purpose it is best to make separate imprints of the thumbs, that can be placed at the base of their respective handprint.

1. Place the paper bearing the handprint so that its base is level with the edge of the table. Ink the thumb with the roller once more, as described in point 4 above.

2. With the thumb now covered with ink, direct the subject to clench their hand as in the 'thumbs up' gesture. Demonstrate how to place the thumb at the bottom edge of the handprint, so that the edge of the table is firmly located in the angle of the thumb and the fingers are still tightly clenched. It is best to get the person to place their thumb directly at the bottom right or left corners of

the paper. In this manoeuvre it is very important to make sure that the person places the lower phalanx onto the paper as well as the upper phalanx – which they will normally only do if specifically instructed.

3. Press down gently on to the thumb. Again discourage your subject from additionally pressing down onto the paper. Then draw around the thumb, as in point 7, above. (6.1 G)

4. Finally ask the subject to lift their thumb gently off the paper. Make sure that the imprint of the right thumb is placed at the base of the right handprint and vice versa. It is easy to get the wrong thumb printed at the base of a handprint. To help avoid this error it is perhaps best to take the thumbprint immediately after making each handprint.

ADDITIONAL TIPS

A satisfactory handprint is one that captures the definition of the lines with clarity, without smudges or faint areas. The skin ridge patterns, especially of the fingertips, should be clearly visible.

The whole procedure should be executed as quickly as possible without being careless; otherwise the ink may dry on the subject's hand before a satisfactory print can be taken. If this happens blend a little more ink on the tile and apply it to the hand.

Should the ink become caked up on the palm, obliterating detail of the lines, then simply take a series of prints without any further inking of the hand until the detail reappears. Sometimes it may be necessary to wash the hand and start again.

Sometimes the lines do not form a clear imprint, particularly in elderly hands. After having taken a set of handprints as best you can, missing areas of the hand can be more easily imprinted onto small cut-out pieces of paper, pressed directly on to the problem area.

CUT-OUTS

Refer to Figure 6.2. Cut out a paper square of about 3" × 3". Ink over the desired part of the palm and place the cut-out square directly over the area. Press the paper square lightly onto the palm and then peel it off. This technique does consistently obtain clear impressions of the lines in the central hollow of the palm. The serious handreader might like to include this technique as a regular part of their procedure for taking handprints, as this will obtain the optimum amount of detail for performing a reading.

After the handprints have been taken, shampoo or washing up liquid and warm water should easily remove ink from the hands, roller and tile. Once the prints have been taken write the name,

Figure 6.2 Taking a Cut-Out Palmprint
Press cut-out square onto palm, then peel it off.

date of birth, date of taking the handprint and whether the person is left- or right-handed on to the print, preferably on the reverse side. Additional details may also be useful to have for research purposes, such as time and place of birth for astrological correlations, or the placing of rings on particular digits emphasizing psychological traits. Additional details are best kept separately on a card system, this avoids further writing on the actual print and obscuring or damaging its detail.

It takes time to master the skills involved in taking handprints. The more prints you take the more skilful you will become.

BUILDING A HANDPRINT LIBRARY

A handprint library is enormously valuable to the serious cheiromancer. The collection of handprints that accumulates with time and experience can become the source of valuable research material. It is common for themes to emerge spontaneously amongst the collection, such as familial patterns, similarity of profession, nationality, education, religion or disease. Sometimes it is a specific feature within the palm, fingers or lines that recurs with astonishing synchronicity. These themes provide considerable opportunity for exploring underlying Elemental and Planetary patterns and amplifying upon your knowledge directly from experience. Choosing a particular theme to concentrate on can provide further focus for your study of cheiromancy.

Depending upon your particular cultural background, education, and profession, it is possible to explore much more specific themes within your immediate circumstances. Therapists can obtain handprints from their patients, astrologers or counsellors can obtain hand-

prints from their clients, tutors can obtain handprints from their students, just to mention a few of the many possibilities. Even if you are not directly involved with such vocations that provide a comparatively easy opportunity of obtaining handprints, perhaps you know a friend who does. Is it possible to get their assistance? Most people will readily let you take their handprints.

A second important reason for building a handprint library is that it records the patterns on the hand at a particular time in a person's life. After a year or more the same person may want to have another handreading. Alternatively you may be interested in discovering what effects certain experiences or courses of therapy have had on a person as reflected in their hands. In both cases a second set of handprints enables their comparison to be made with their previous set and change to be identified. Handprints taken regularly at yearly intervals in people's lives can provide fascinating studies of change. Obtaining children's handprints as they grow up particularly reflects their psychological development and the unfolding of their talents.

On a practical note to assist observation of change it is useful to use different colour inks for each new set of handprints. This visual aid helps eliminate anachronisms when interpreting the changes.

For storage and display purposes the most convenient way to keep your handprints is in plastic wallets in a lever arch file. The water-soluble ink used for making handprints is prone to smudging and the plastic wallets protect the prints from damp and, worst of all, cups of tea!

If you are serious about building up a substantial library an index system needs to be thought about at an early stage of collecting handprints so that a lot of hassle, time and energy is saved. There are two main ways that this can be done, firstly by alphabetical order of surnames or secondly by date order of taking the print. If you are going to explore specific themes such as illness, vocation and so on amongst your handprint collection, you will need to record certain key details that arise from doing the reading. A simple card system is a very inexpensive way of recording personal details and the salient features of the person's life. If you have chosen the date order system of filing your handprints, then the date of the first and subsequent handreadings can be included on the card.

Addresses and telephone numbers are useful if you want to pursue follow-up handprints and capture changes in the hand.

A computer with a database facility, with its ability to cross-reference material, can be an enormously valuable tool for accessing information from the handprint collection. However, unless one already has a computer for other purposes this would be an expensive undertaking in comparison to the card system.

CHAPTER 7

Hand Shape
Part 1

HAVING covered the necessary information on symbolism and obtained a number of hand prints, it is now possible to apply this information to the hand. First, Elemental symbolism will be applied to the physical structure of the hand. Since the Elements rule the material or Elemental World they are the most appropriate symbols with which to interpret the nuances of the hand's structure. The next three chapters examine hand shape, skin texture, and the quadrants – the parts of the hand that reflect a person's experience of the Elemental World. Further use of Elemental symbols will be made when explaining the lines and fingers in later chapters.

As the symbolism unfolds through hand shape, skin texture, quadrants, lines and fingers, it is important to superimpose all the symbolic patterns, layer by layer, to create the picture of a person and their specific experience of life.

The assessment of hand shape incorporates the overall structure of the palm and fingers. The overall hand shape reflects of the type of vehicle a person is born into. It describes their physical body and their basic temperament. The Four Elements – Earth, Water, Air and Fire – are directly used in the classification of shape. In identifying hands it is possible to find hands that have a mixture of two or even three of these Elemental shapes. The most important thing to grasp here is how each Elemental shape is composed, so that each one, and that of the composite hand shapes, can clearly be recognized. Figure 7.1 displays the four main Elemental hand shapes. These shapes are exaggerated to display the proportions of palm to fingers. Compare them to the actual prints of Elemental hand shapes in Figures 7.2–7.5, pages 53–58. It is important to note that only the shape of the hand is being assessed at this point, and not such details as lines and skin texture, which come later.

HAND SHAPE AND THE THREE WORLDS

The allocation of the Elements to hand shape stems from the relationship between the palm and fingers. When the Hermetic Three Worlds are superimposed onto the hand, the palm connects with the Elemental World or physical experience and the fingers with the Intellectual World or mental experience. Since the fingers grow out of the palm from embryo to adulthood, in allocating each Elemental shape, the palm is considered first and then the fingers in relation to it.

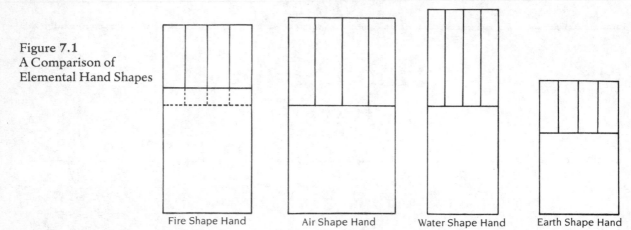

Figure 7.1
A Comparison of
Elemental Hand Shapes

Fire Shape Hand   Air Shape Hand   Water Shape Hand   Earth Shape Hand

Of the four main hand shapes, two have square palms and two have oblong palms. As can be seen in Figure 7.1, both the Earth and Air hands have square palms. These are differentiated by general size of palm and length of fingers. In the Earth hand the square palm is small and compact, while the fingers are short and squat. In addition there is a chubby, heavy appearance that gives the impression of Earth. The Air hand has a much larger square palm, with long, well formed fingers and an expansive appearance that gives a much lighter impression than the Earth hand.

As shown in Figure 7.1, both the Fire and Water hands have oblong palms. These are differentiated by the width of the palm in relation to the length and shape of the fingers. In the Fire hand the broad oblong palm has wide fingers that are shorter than the palmar length. By contrast, the Water hand has a long, thin oblong palm with long, thin fingers that may well reach the same length as the palm.

ELEMENTAL PERSONALITIES

Each of the Elemental hand shapes, corresponds to a distinct personality type. These personality pictures can also be applied when a person has other features within their hand (covered later in the book) that indicate a strong presence of a particular Element, such as quadranture, skin texture and line widths. So you may wish to refer back to this section later on to enhance your Elemental understanding of these features.

Additionally you might also like to refer back to the Elemental correspondences lists in Chapter 3 to build on your Elemental understanding for each personality.

The Earth Personality

The shape of the Earth hand reveals someone whose life is centred upon physical experience. The well developed palm in relation to short fingers shows that physical experience predominates over intellectual or mental experience. Figure 7.2 shows an Earth shape hand.

The qualities of the true Earth type are perhaps best exhibited in tribal communities that live in close harmony with the earth; where their whole existence and culture depends upon an instinctive understanding of nature. A strong Earth Element naturally creates an affinity with earth in all its forms, so these

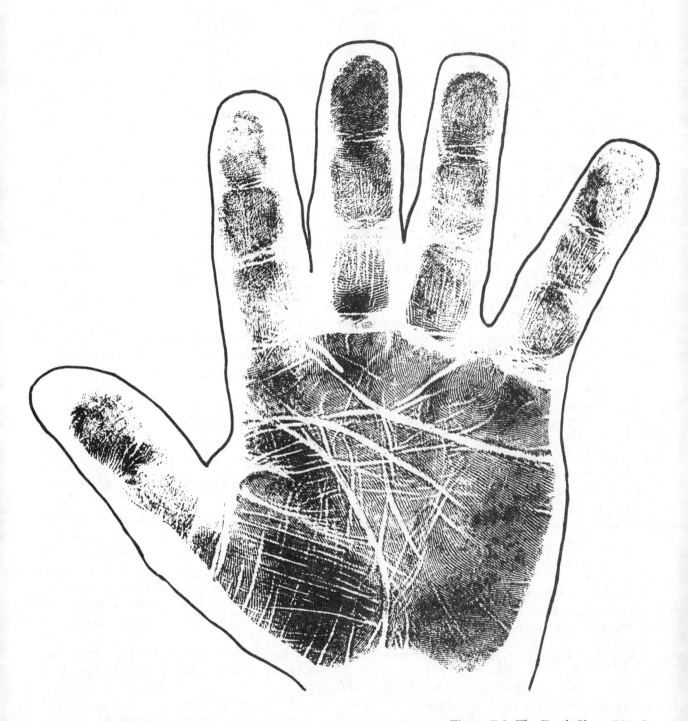

Figure 7.2 The Earth Shape Hand

people have an innate knowledge of working with natural materials such as mud, stone, wood and clay, and of the cultivation of plants. They have a strong practical sense and are keen builders.

The number of pure Earth types in Western culture today is few. Professions like mining or farming, where these types would have been found, have now been taken over by the Fiery influence of technology. Occasionally in rural communities you will find people still in touch with the Earth Element.

On a physical level Earth connects with the bones, the densest part of the body that provides structure and foundation for the rest of the bodily tissues. The physical build of an Earth type is generally short, squat and compact, with strongly formed bones. They generally have robust health, though digestion tends to be a weak spot due to overindulgence in food which Earth types are generally fond of. They are generally free from stress as they like to lead their life in close harmony with nature.

In terms of work they tend to do what their parents did, being very conservative in their outlook and disliking change. They exhibit an intense suspicion of anything new, preferring to stay with what they know and feel secure with rather than risk experiencing anything unfamiliar. They enjoy the simple things in life, having a rhythmic, persevering and enduring quality. You will find them involved with such activities as gardening, cooking, crafts, pottery, masonry and carving.

In relationships they are rather unadventurous, tending to choose those they have grown up with in the community.

The Air Personality

The Air hand shape has long fingers, so experience for the Air type is centred in the mind. Figure 7.3 is an example of an Air-shaped hand.

The Air personality will dwell and delight in the whole realm of ideas, spending much of their time absorbed in the numerous studies and mental activities that spark their interest. Air types are naturally found in universities or other places of higher education, in writing, journalism, the media, teaching – indeed anywhere that chiefly involves the communication of ideas.

Due to their strong intellectual nature, emotional relationships are usually very difficult for them because they intellectualize their feelings.

Air types have strongly charged nervous systems and are subject to worry and stress. They often have weak digestions due to their nervous nature and irregular eating habits. Their bodies tend to be rather lean and lanky. They are often impractical and dwell within their mind all day long. They tend to spend a lot of their time making plans, but often fail to act them out. Air types like variety and diversion though their energies often become overly dispersed.

The Fire Personality

The Fire hand shape has an elongated broad palm which reflects a strong practical sense. Figure 7.4 is an example of a Fire-shaped hand. By nature the Fire type is characterized by an abundance of energy which surges forth, propelling them into actions of all sorts. The shortness of the fingers in relation to the palm suggests that as soon as they get an idea, rather than think it through or develop it, they will immediately put it into action. Thus they are more pragmatic in their thinking than the Air type.

Fire types are generally highly motivated and need to be active in order to feel fulfilled. They cannot endure routine or humdrum situations where they are unable to express their energies to the full. They easily fall prey to boredom and

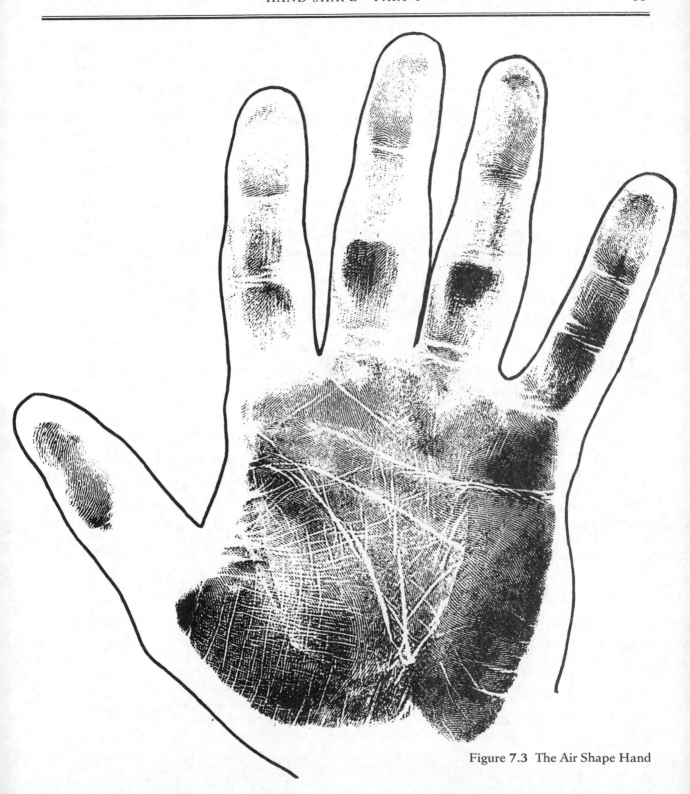

Figure 7.3 The Air Shape Hand

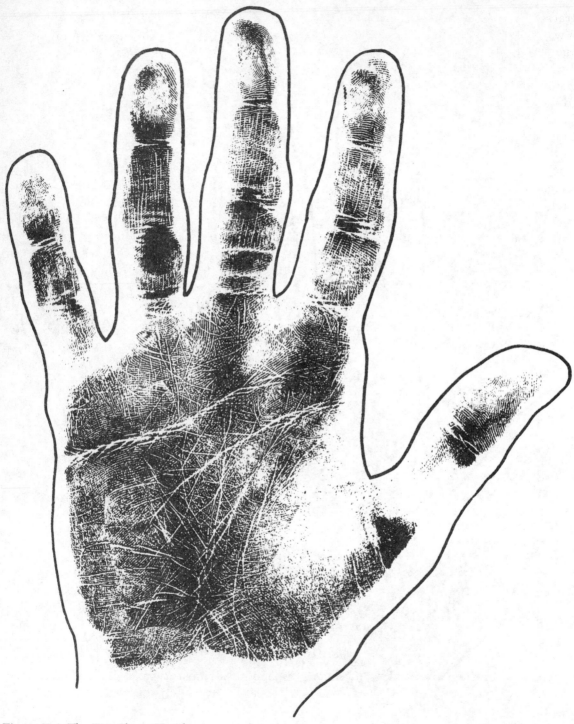

Figure 7.4 The Fire Shape Hand

frustration. They enjoy initiating change, but do not always see the project through to its end as they generally dislike attention to small detail.

Fire types like challenge, excitement, adventure and pioneering. Consequently they are found in such areas as the armed services, sport, engineering, industry and technology. Naturally they prefer to lead and give orders rather than take them.

In relationships the Fire type tends to be intensely drawn to a partner and gets passionately involved with them for a while until they get bored and want to change for someone else. In their lifetime they tend to notch up a number of relationships rather than find one that is really fulfilling.

Their bodies are physically very strong with powerful muscles and have a good resistance to infections. Inner tension makes them prone to stress illness like heart attacks and ulcers while they are susceptible to arthritis and liver disorders through a passion for rich, spicy foods and alcohol.

The Water Personality

In the Water hand shape there is a strong emphasis on the slenderness of the palm and fingers, indicating a lack of foundation in both mental and physical realms. Figure 7.5 is an example of a Water-shaped hand. Water symbolically connects with the Celestial World or emotional experience, which can be seen in the Three World view as being halfway between the mind and body. The Water type experiences life through their feelings, making the whole realm of emotional expression and relationships of immense importance to them. They have an innate need to share their feelings with others. A Water type needs caring, affectionate, intimate relationships where they can feel secure and nurtured by someone sensitive.

Their deeply feeling nature makes them highly receptive to all forms of artistic experience. A Water type usually enjoys theatre, ballet, concerts and art galleries, where the influence of colour and music has an emotive effect on them. They like to express their feelings through fashion, clothes and perfumes, while they are drawn to the sea and love all kinds of water sports.

Water types are often found in caring environments involving children, the elderly, the sick, animals or charity work. They are drawn to healing through their concern for the suffering of others. They like to feel part of a team and seldom like to work in isolation. Typical jobs for Water types include nursery school teaching, research, social work, nursing, child care, therapy, counselling, art teaching or painting – especially using watercolours.

Their bodies tend to be slim, effeminate and graceful in appearance. They are not strong and lack a powerful vitality. Their joints are usually very flexible and susceptible to strains through poor muscular tone. Their physical health is powerfully influenced by their mood. The female Water type is particularly prone to premenstrual symptoms, water retention, poor circulation, bladder and kidney disorders.

COMPOSITE HAND SHAPES

Where hands have a combination of different Elemental patterns in their shape, then it is important to ascertain which is the primary one. Once this is clear then the secondary and tertiary Elements can be considered in relation to it. The primary Element is found by looking at the palm and considering what Element shape it is most typical of. The secondary Element is shown by looking at the fingers and considering what Element shape they are most typical of. A tertiary Element can in certain

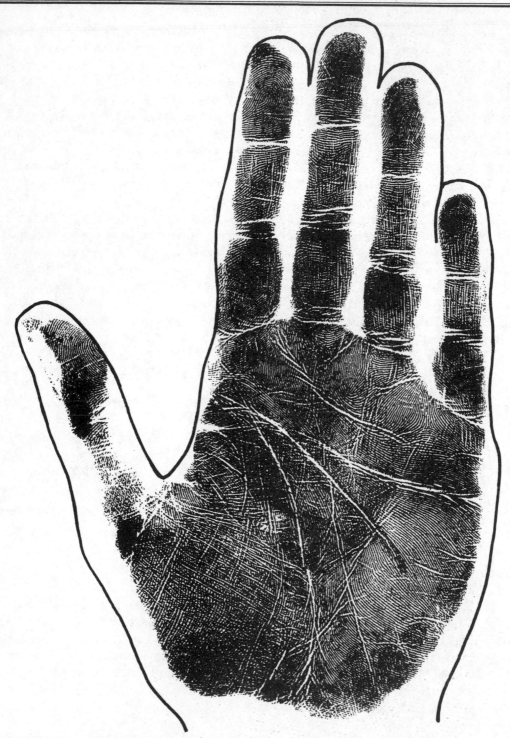

Figure 7.5 The Water Shape Hand

hands be identified from the part of the hand most developed within its overall shape. The recognition of a tertiary Element requires an understanding of all the features in the hand and develops with experience of looking at a wide variety of hands.

For example, a hand with a wide oblong palm would be primarily classified as Fire-shaped. If it had long, broad fingers the secondary Element would be Air. With experience it might be possible to see that the base of the palm is strongly developed, indicating a strong Earth influence. In summary, the hand can be seen as a Fire hand with Air fingers with a strong Earth develop-ment. In the interpretation of this combination each Element is added together in turn. Thus the typically energetic and dynamic Fire type is tempered by the strong mental development indicated by the Air fingers. This would indicate a much greater ability to plan their ideas before rushing headlong into action. The strong Earth influence would temper the Fiery energy, slowing it down and making the person even more practical. Such a combination of energy, intelligence, execution and practicality would be useful to an engineer or athlete. Figure 19.1, page 180, is an example of a composite Air and Earth hand shape.

CHAPTER 8

Skin Texture

WHILE hand shape indicates the type of vehicle into which a person is born, the skin texture indicates how the person makes contact with the environment around them.

The skin texture is an assessment of the overall consistency of the skin and its underlying tissues. By palpation of the skin, four different consistencies can clearly be recognized corresponding to the qualities of the Four Elements. The Elemental texture of the skin describes how someone receives stimuli and responds to impressions from the environment.

The surface of the skin is composed of a series of undulating ridges, called papillary ridges, as shown in Figure 8.1. Along the tops of these ridges tiny openings of sweat pores are located. When the hand is covered with ink, it is the crests of these ridges that form the main impression of the hand on the paper. Close inspection of a handprint with a magnifying glass reveals the pin-prick openings of the sweat glands running along the crest of these ridges.

There are two ways in which the Elemental quality of the skin is determined: firstly by direct palpation of the skin, and secondly by understanding the various impressions made on the paper by the skin while taking a handprint. The qualities to look for will be described under the different skin types to follow.

Palpation is probably the easiest way of getting to know the skin textures. It involves rubbing your thumb over the percussion area (on the side of the hand below the little finger) to directly feel its surface. The percussion area is a good place to begin to get the feel of the different Elemental textures. Different textures may be present across the palm and fingers within one hand.

The different skin textures, when seen in a handprint, reflect the different degrees of space between the papillary ridges. The relative degrees of space found with various Elemental skin

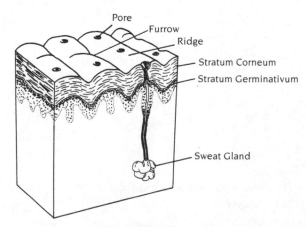

Figure 8.1 Papillary Ridges of the Skin

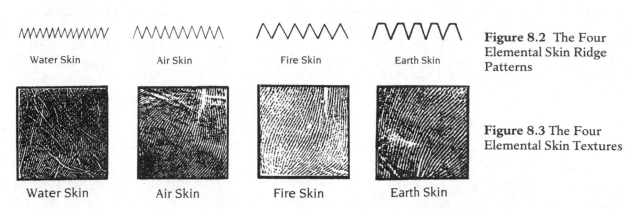

Figure 8.2 The Four Elemental Skin Ridge Patterns

Figure 8.3 The Four Elemental Skin Textures

textures are represented in Figure 8.2. The amount of space between the ridges ranges from the Water-textured skin, which is the narrowest, to the Earth-textured skin, which is the widest. The Air-textured skin is slightly wider than the Water textured, while the Fire-textured skin is wider still than the Air textured but narrower than the Earth textured. Figure 8.3 gives examples of the four Elemental skin textures from actual handprints.

THE WATER SKIN

The Water quality perceived in the skin, on palpation, is soft, spongy and silky. Additionally it may be cool and moist to touch. The velvet-like Water-textured skin tends to produce smudgy handprints. Learning to use less ink is the key to taking clear handprints from a Water skin. Inspection of the skin ridges from the handprint reveals that they are very close together. If the handprint is smudgy it may not be possible to see the individual ridges at all clearly.

People with Water-textured skins are very sensitive to their environment. Their feelings readily pick up the atmospheres of places or sense the presence of other people. A Water skin person needs a calm and tranquil environment free from stress and tension if their qualities are to flourish. Additionally they like companionship at work where they can feel part of a team. Their sensitivity draws them to work that involves nurturing, caring, healing or artistic expression.

THE FIRE SKIN

The Fire quality perceived in the skin is firm, taut and fairly coarse. This texture is like drawing your thumb across the grain of the pages of a closed book. The skin may be hot and dry to the touch. The Fire-textured skin forms clear imprints though, because the skin is unyielding, it is often difficult to take a complete print in one go. The dryness of the skin means it tends to absorb moisture from the ink, which dries quickly on the hand. Inspection of the skin ridges reveals that the spaces between the ridges are broad and distinct.

People with Fire-textured skins react spontaneously to the tension and dynamism all around them. A Fire skin person enjoys challenge, competition and diversity for their excitement and stimulation. Work needs to have a sense of achievement and provide opportunity for promotion. In work, though they respond well under pressure, they typically need sport and exercise to be able to relax and unwind. Their ambition and sense of competition makes them enjoy the cut and thrust of business.

THE AIR SKIN

The Air quality perceived in the skin is smooth and firm. It is not as soft and silky as a Water skin, nor firm and coarse as a Fire skin. This texture, in contrast to the Fire skin, is like drawing your thumb along with the grain of the pages of a closed book – with the grain. The Air skin is generally warm and moist to the touch and usually gives a clear handprint. Inspection of the skin ridges reveals the spaces between the ridges are fine and distinct.

People with Air-textured skins readily tune into the ideas and thought patterns around them. They like an environment of electronic gadgetry, books or conversation to spark off their ideas and interests. They tend to be rather impersonal, being quite happy to live and work in isolation provided they have their thoughts and ideas to occupy them. Nothing engages them quite like a line of thought to pursue. Their skill lies in the thoroughness with which they can research and investigate a particular issue or topic.

THE EARTH SKIN

The Earth quality perceived in the skin is very coarse and rough. This texture may feel like sandpaper to touch. It may well have a cold and dry quality. The uneven surface of the Earth skin produces rough, patchy handprints that lack clarity and definition. The dry skin absorbs a lot of ink. Inspection of the skin ridges reveals that the spaces between the ridges are wide and fuzzy. You might even find splinters or bits of soil embedded in the skin!

People with Earth-textured skins enjoy getting their hands into the earth and working with natural materials. They prefer an environment where they can utilize their instinctive practical sense. Many with Earth-textured skins are naturally 'green-fingered'. Even if they do not work directly on the land, their pastimes will include gardening. In work they are frequently solitary individuals preferring to plod on with what they know best.

SYNTHESIS OF HAND SHAPE AND SKIN TEXTURE

Having arrived at two orders of Elemental patterns, from the hand shape and skin texture respectively, it is possible to compare them. Consider whether the two Elements of each feature are compatible or not. Ideally there should be a degree of concordance between the two Elements, for this enables an ease of expression in the person's temperament. Frequently these two Elements are found to be incompatible, so generating conflict. For example if a Fire hand has a Fire quality skin, then their dynamic and energetic nature is matched by their ability to respond spontaneously to their environment. If by contrast a Fire hand has a Water skin, then the clash between the Elements means their potentially dynamic nature is confused by their sensitivity. The resultant build-up of inner tension makes them hypersensitive to their environment. They react emotionally to situations without clearly being able to see why, frequently becoming quite exhausted in the process – a case of the Fire heating up the Water and the Water putting out the Fire.

CHAPTER 9

The Palmar Quadrants

THE palmar quadrants reveal how a person experiences the Elemental World. The technique involves projecting the Cross of matter onto the palm, dividing it into four sections called quadrants. Each quadrant corresponds to one of the Four Elements. Assessment of the relative size and development of each quadrant shows how a person is utilizing each Element within their temperament. Before going through the procedure for drawing the quadrants upon the palm it is necessary to consider the underlying principles behind this allocation.

THE PRINCIPLES OF QUADRANTURE

See Figure 9.1. First consider the vertical division which runs along the length of the palm from the centre of its base to the base of the middle finger. The thumb side of the palm is Solar in nature, while the little finger side is Lunar in nature. Under the Sun's rays the world is illuminated and activity is promoted. Similarly the Solar half of the palm corresponds to the visible, manifest, outer appearance of a person and the energy they express in worldly activities. When the Moon shines at night only a minimal amount of activity occurs, hidden in

the shadows. Similarly the Lunar half of the palm corresponds to the hidden, non-manifest, inner life of the person, involving their dreams, ideals and deeper motivations. This designation of Solar and Lunar aspects to this vertical division has already been described in relation to the right and left pillars respectively of Dee's *Monas Hieroglyphica* (see Figure 2.3 page 10).

Next consider the horizontal division which runs across the palm, bisecting at right angles the vertical line at its midpoint. The length of the hand can now be considered vertically, as in the prayer position, to reveal the sequential order of the Three Worlds. Below the horizontal line on the palm is the Elemental World, a realm of fixity, passivity, foundation and material order. Above the horizontal line is the Celestial World, a realm of activity, motivation and aspiration. The fingers correspond to the Intellectual World and will be considered in Chapter 13.

ELEMENTAL ALLOCATION

The allocation of each Element to its particular corner of the quadranture is based upon understanding their respective natures. Of the Four Elements, Earth and Fire are more visible

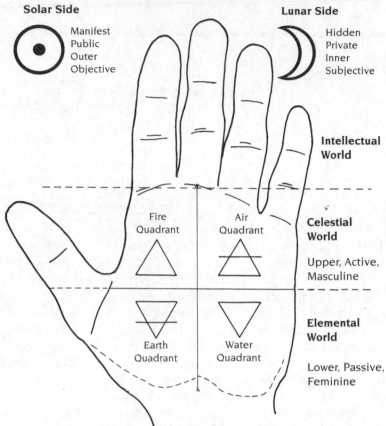

Solar Side

Manifest
Public
Outer
Objective

Lunar Side

Hidden
Private
Inner
Subjective

Intellectual
World

Figure 9.1 The Allocation of the
Elements to the Palm

Fire
Quadrant

Air
Quadrant

Celestial
World

Upper, Active,
Masculine

Earth
Quadrant

Water
Quadrant

Elemental
World

Lower, Passive,
Feminine

and manifest and Water and Air are more hidden. Accordingly Fire and Earth are ascribed to the Solar, manifest side of the palm, and Water and Air to the Lunar, hidden side of the palm. From each coupling of the Elements one naturally gravitates to the bottom, while the other rises to the top. Of Fire and Earth, Earth is the most dense while Fire is the lightest, so Fire is placed above Earth. Of Water and Air, Water is the most dense and Air is the lightest, so Air is placed above Water.

This allocation generates the complementary pairing of Fire and Air – the masculine Elements – in the upper, active half of the palm, and Earth and Water – the feminine Elements – in the lower, passive half of the palm. The Elemental opposites – Fire and Water, Earth and

Air – stand diametrically opposed in the corners, describing the dynamic tension that animates the Elemental World. This point is also exemplified in Dee's *Monas Hieroglyphica* (Figure 2.3 page 10). Here the Fire and Earth Elements are found at the top and bottom corners respectively of the Solar pillar, while the Air and Water Elements are found at the top and bottom corners, respectively, of the Lunar pillar.

THE QUADRANT AREAS

Once the Elements are designated to the particular segments of the palm, their positions remain constant. The Fire and Earth Elements are always found on the Solar, thumb side of the palm and the Air and Water Elements are always found on the Lunar, little finger side of the palm. Each quadrant is linked to particular areas of experience through the symbolic associations of each Element as follows.

The Earth Quadrant

The Earth quadrant connects to the physical structure and constitution of the body, especially the skeletal system and digestion. It indicates an individual's fundamental values, their material wealth, the type of home they like, their family environment and their sense of security. Activities involving the Earth Element are shown here, such as pottery, sculpture, cooking, gardening, rock-climbing, geology, mining, masonry, building and engineering. The Earth Element links the quadrant to the person's understanding of nature and sense of bodily rhythm.

The Water Quadrant

The Water quadrant is associated with sexuality and the expression of emotions and feelings within relationships. This quadrant is linked to the use of imagination and by extension is connected to art, painting, music and poetry. Since Water is linked to intuition, spiritual values are connected with this quadrant. Other activities involving the Water Element include healing, caring, nurturing, drama, swimming and water sports. Within the body the Water quadrant connects with the circulation of blood and body fluids, kidneys and bladder.

The Air Quadrant

The Air quadrant reflects the person's mind, thoughts, ideas and modes of expression. It is symbolically linked to the development of ideas and to communication. By extension, speech and languages are included here. Activities involving the Air Element include education, study, science, electronics, computing, communications, media work, writing, commerce and economics. Within the body the Air quadrant connects with the nervous system and the respiratory system.

The Fire Quadrant

The Fire quadrant is linked to the way a person expresses their energy, whether creatively or stressfully. It reflects their ambition, practical sense and accomplishment. Also their assertiveness and resistance under pressure. Activities involving the Fire Element include business, industry, agriculture, mechanics, sport, athletics, martial arts and armed combat. Within the body the Fire quadrant connects with the muscular system and the heart.

DRAWING UP THE PALMAR QUADRANTS

A practical note before starting; until confidence in drawing up the quadrants is obtained, it may be better to put the handprint inside a clear plastic envelope and draw the lines in a water-soluble marker pen. Alternatively you might choose an inferior quality handprint for drawing quadrants and making notes on, so leaving the best prints free of markings for observation purposes.

Refer to Figure 9.2 for the following steps.

1. The first stage is to mark with a cross the midpoint at the base of the middle finger. The fingers are defined from the palm by the phalangeal lines, which can be taken as the uppermost boundary of the palm. The diagonal crease across the base of the thumb defines the lateral margin of the palm, and the bottom edge of the print defines the lower palmar boundary.

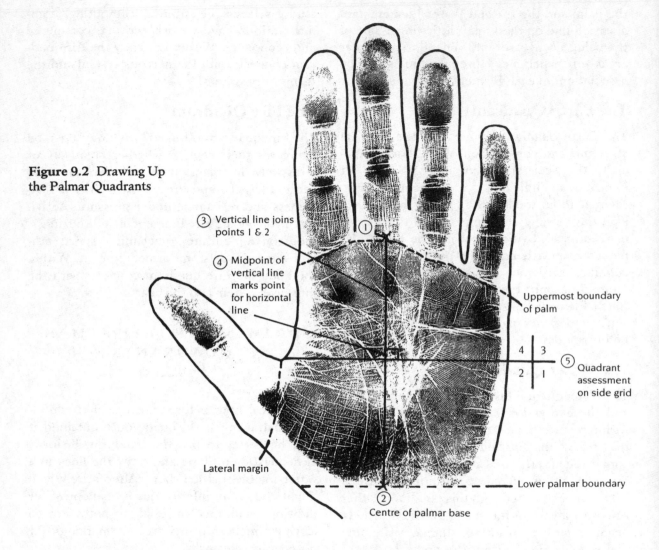

Figure 9.2 Drawing Up
the Palmar Quadrants

③ Vertical line joins
points 1 & 2

④ Midpoint of
vertical line
marks point
for horizontal
line

①

Uppermost boundary
of palm

4 | 3
2 | 1

⑤ Quadrant
assessment
on side grid

Lateral margin

②

Centre of palmar base

Lower palmar boundary

2. The second stage is to find the centre of the palmar base and mark it with a cross. This is best noted by eye as the use of a ruler to measure the width of the palmar base is deceptive. When placing this cross at the base of the handprint, it is important to remember that the hand is a three-dimensional structure that is reduced to a two-dimensional imprint on the paper. The 'white space' between the ink print and the pen line should be visualized as the curva-ture of the palm in a three-dimensional manner.

Figure 9.3 shows how the wider the space between the outline and the print (points A and B), the greater the curvature of the palm. By comparison, a small space (points C and D) indicates a smaller curvature of the palm. This 'white space' needs to be seen as part of the palm in order to define accurately the centre of the palmar base.

Figure 9.4, page 68, shows how the centre of

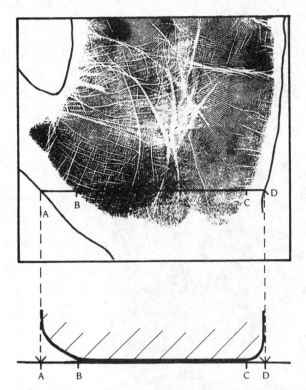

Figure 9.3 The Third Dimension of a Handprint

the palmar base is ascertained by mentally drawing lines down the lateral margins of the hand to the wrist. Then it should be easy to spot by eye where the centre of the palmar base lies.

Until one gets the knack of finding this central point, it is often easier to make your observations from the live hand rather than the print. After noting where on the actual palm this point is located in relation to characteristic lineal patterns, seek its corresponding point on the handprint.

Referring back to Figure 9.2

3. Draw a vertical line joining up the two points you have just marked, bringing the line well down to the wrist, so as to include all the print.

4. The next step is to find the midpoint of the vertical line. Using the ruler measure the length of the vertical line just drawn, from top to bottom. It is important to measure the full length of this line to the exact bottom edge of the print. The imprint may extend a further 1 cm on either side of the palmar base mark, but still be sure to include it all in your measurement. Having measured the length of the palm as a whole, simple division in half will provide the midpoint. At this new point draw a horizontal line across the palm exactly at right angles (90°) to the vertical line. A clear plastic ruler or protractor should provide the necessary accuracy.

5. Allocation of the quadrant order. Now the palm is divided into the four quadrant sections, it should be possible from simple observation to order them by size. Number the quadrants from 1 to 4 in order of the largest, most developed quadrant to the smallest, least developed one. This order gives a particular emphasis to each Element that will be explained fully a little later. Record this order on a side grid, as shown in Figure 9.2, for easy reference.

Once again assessment of each quadrant is more than just looking at its two-dimensional area. It considers the three-dimensional relief. Assuming the handprint in question has had the ink evenly applied over the hand, a raised more developed area of the palm will give a darker imprint. This needs to be taken into account in ordering the quadrants, for if two quadrants appear to be the same size, then the one that is more developed giving the darker imprint is taken to be the larger area. Similarly a wide gap of 'white space' between the imprint and the outline also indicates a particularly developed area of the palm.

If two quadrants still seem very close in relief and development, then take the quadrant that has the most lines in it as being the more developed, larger quadrant. The full significance of this observation will become apparent

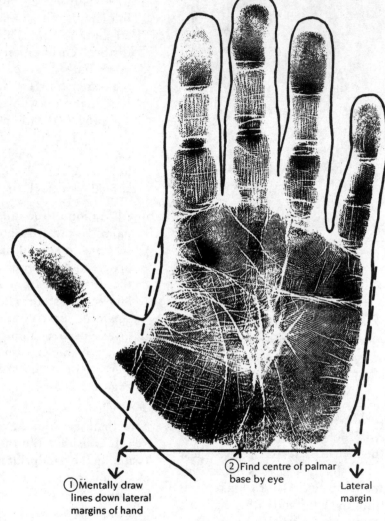

Figure 9.4 Finding
the Centre of the
Palmar Base

① Mentally draw
lines down lateral
margins of hand

② Find centre of palmar
base by eye

Lateral
margin

in Chapter 11. For now this simply indicates that greater energy and awareness is focused in this quadrant, implying its greater use and development.

ELEMENTAL MANIFESTATION

After the order of development within the quadrants from 1 to 4 has been decided they are then interpreted according to a particular pattern. This sequence of manifestation reflects the Hermetic Creation of the Three World view. Seen Elementally, the realm of Light (Divine Fire) generates the Intellectual World of the Divine Air. The Celestial World of Divine Water descends from the Intellectual World. Finally the Elemental World of Divine Earth precipitates from the Celestial World. The sequence of Elemental manifestation used here in the interpretation of the quadrants reflects the Hermetic perception of Creation of the

Three Worlds in reverse. This is because hand-reading deals with what is created, and by using this sequence in reverse it gives insights into what has created the features in the hand.

It is important to note that though the position of the Elements on the palm remains constant for all hands, the particular sequence of development found in the palm is characteristic of the person's temperament.

1. The Largest Quadrant

The Element manifest in the largest quadrant is the Element the person identifies with most strongly. It reveals what they value most and base their life upon. It reflects the constitution and appearance of the body, and the way the person experiences the physical world around them through their senses. This is the Element with which they are most acquainted and it is frequently connected to their work and livelihood. It corresponds to Divine Earth and the Elemental World.

2. The Second Largest Quadrant

Despite the size of the second largest quadrant the second Element manifest in it is weak. The qualities of the Element expressed through this position are conspicuous in a person by their absence. This missing Element is the one that the person has greatest conflict with. Once the conflict is resolved it can become an area of immense inner potential. Despite the weakness and difficulties of expression, this Element often encompasses intense fascination for the person as experience here reminds them of this potential. This Element is frequently sought after by a person within relationships. It corresponds to Divine Water and the Celestial World.

3. The Third Largest Quadrant

The Element manifest in the third largest quadrant in sequence is a resource for the person.

This Element encompasses a realm of knowledge on which they can freely draw. When this Element is well developed it can be easily communicated. Other people recognize this particular Element as strongly developed within them. Since this is an Element of which they are very knowledgeable, it typically combines with their first Element in their vocation and livelihood. It corresponds to Divine Air and the Intellectual World.

4. The Smallest Quadrant

The Element manifest in the smallest quadrant corresponds to the least developed area of a person's life. Qualities linked with the Element are distinctly lacking in the person. However, it is an area of goals and ideals, the vision of what a person aspires to. Since it is the least present it is the most required Element to balance out the other three and thus facilitate change. The healing of crises often comes through the development of this area. It corresponds to Divine Fire – the Realm of Light.

There are twenty-four different possible combinations of Elemental manifestation. To illustrate how a particular sequence of Elements is expressed the following example is included, based upon the sequence shown in Figure 9.2, page 66.

AN EXAMPLE OF ELEMENTAL MANIFESTATION

1. Largest quadrant – Water.
2. Second largest quadrant – Earth.
3. Third largest quadrant – Air.
4. Smallest quadrant – Fire.

1. Largest Quadrant – Water

With Water the largest quadrant, this is the Element with which this person most strongly identifies. As a consequence they are power-fully motivated by their deeply feeling nature and drawn to artistic pursuits in order to express themselves. Physically they have a slender, graceful body which is easily influenced by their emotional state. As a result of this influence the subject is prone to poor circulation, hormonal upsets and water retention. Relationships are immensely important to them as there is a strong need to share their feelings with others.

2. Second Largest Quadrant – Earth

With Earth the second largest quadrant, this is the missing Element. They lack the stability and foundation that a strong Earth Element provides. Their highly fluctuating emotional nature gives rise to insecurity. Consequently they will most likely seek material security and stability in a partner. Issues of self worth and the ability to earn money are likely to be prominent for them. Their digestion is likely to be poor and subject to emotional upsets. There is a tendency to comfort eat to counteract their insecurity.

It is worth noting that when interpreting absent or weak Elements, it is often easier to consider how the Element might manifest were it strongly present. Then mentally take these associations away to perceive what qualities would be missing in the person.

3. Third Largest Quadrant – Air

With Air manifest in the third largest quadrant, this Element describes the person's resources. With a strong Air Element they can commun-icate ideas well. In combination with Water the dominant Element, their ideas will be expressed visually with subtlety and sensitivity. The first and third Elements are described as the mani-fest Elements which combine within the per-son's life and work. They are attracted to music, poetry, literature and the arts generally. This combination of Water and Air makes a good teacher, especially of small children. It is also a good combination of Elements for the caring professions, especially those that involve coun-selling. All forms of research work, particularly hunting down obscure knowledge, are also very appealing to them.

4. Smallest Quadrant – Fire

With Fire the smallest quadrant, this describes the Element that is least developed. They have great difficulty expressing their energy and they often have times when they are completely exhausted. The combination of Earth and Fire being weak Elements in the palm shows they need to have structure and purpose in their life; otherwise they get nothing done. They doubt-less dream about having more energy to fulfil their goals and aspirations.

A contrasting quadrant sequence is described in 'A Cheiromantical Assessment of a Hand' in Chapter 19.

The particular quadrant order found in the hand shows how a person is expressing each of the Elements in their make up. The sequence of Elemental manifestation shows their relative strength and weakness. When the quadrant order is superimposed onto the previous Ele-ments of the hand shape and skin texture, a much fuller picture of how well a person is using their nature and qualities is obtained. Elements that are strong by their placing in the quadrant order (1st and 3rd positions) amplify the power of the same Element found in the hand shape or skin texture. By contrast Elements that are weak by their placing in the quadrant order (2nd and 4th positions) diminish the power of the same Element found in the hand shape or skin texture. For example if a Fire-shaped hand has the Fire Element placed in the third position in the quadrant order, then the abundance of the energy inherent within the person will be very dynamically expressed. Socially they will be very much admired for their abundance of energy, typically becoming the life and soul of a party. In contrast if a Fire-shaped hand has the Fire Element placed in the fourth position in the quadrant order, then the person will have great difficulty in freely expressing this energy and achieving their goals. Frustration will be the inevitable result, leading to a build-up of inner tension. This inner tension usually amplifies conflict between the other Elements in their make-up.

This subtle piecing together of these Elemental patterns and seeing how they interact, complementing or inhibiting one another, provides a true assessment of temperament. The very word temperament is specifically linked to the weighing up of the Elements inside people since it comes from the Latin *temperare* meaning 'to observe proper measure, to mix in the right proportion'.

From the true picture of a person's temperament it is possible to see the hidden concealed Elements – the second and fourth Elements in the quadrant order. These indicate the areas and qualities that the person needs to develop if they are to unfold their full potential in life. The activation of these weak Elements creates a more balanced relationship between them. This enhances the generation of the fifth Element, Ether – the vital force that flows through the psyche. The greater the degree of balance between the Four Elements, the more the flow of Ether is enhanced. The converse is also true; the more disrupted the Elements are, the more the flow of Ether is inhibited.

In Chapter 11, which deals with palmar lines, Ether will be connected with the flow of energy through the lines. The sum total of interaction between the Elements in a person's temperament is reflected in the myriad formations of the palmar lines.

CHAPTER 10

The Mounts

THE mounts are areas of the palm that, with exception of the Lunar and both Mars mounts, are located immediately below one of the fingers or the thumb. Mounts are so called since, when truly present, they stand out above the plain of the palm like little mountains. The traditional placing of the mounts with their Planetary rulers is set out in Figure 10.1. Mountains have long been mythologically associated with deities – Mount Olympus for example. Within the Hermetic Three World view, a mountain peak rising up from the earth is seen symbolically to penetrate up into the Celestial World, ruled by the seven traditional Planets. The mounts are where the influence of the Planets, mediated through the Ether, become manifest in the Elemental World of the palm.

One of the central themes of Hermetic philosophy is the idea that 'Man is made in the image of the heavens'. This idea of the heavens influencing the form and structure of the body is captured by the following quote from the Hermetic philosopher Cornelius Agrippa:

The countenance, gesture, the motion, setting, and figure of the body, being accidental to us, conduce to the receiving of Celestiall gifts, and expose us to the superior bodies, and produce certain effects in us.[18]

The 'superior bodies' are the Planets, while the reception of 'Celestial gifts' refers to their influence from the Celestial World. The Etheric energy, coloured by the influence of the Planets,

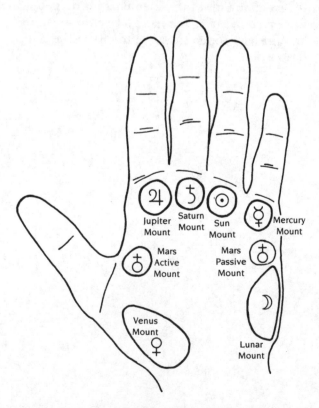

Figure 10.1 The Traditional Palmar Mounts

is received by Man through his hand specifically through the mount areas of the palm. Figure 10.1 shows each traditional mount with its own Planetary ruler. By contemplating the associated Planetary symbolism the student will gain insight into the significance of each mount.

A mount can be visualized as an area of the palm where a particular Planetary energy is contained. When a mount becomes prominent it shows a particular concentration of this energy. The flow of the palmar lines draws from the Planetary energy contained in the mounts. The contact between a line and a mount indicates that the energy from the mount is being used by the person. By contrast the presence of a prominent mount without contact to a line suggests the energies of the mount are latent and unused.

Hyperstriation and grill markings on mounts are linked with negative associations and diseases. These markings indicate that the energy within the mount is confused and discordant. Hyperstriation and grill markings can been seen in Figure 13.9, page 138, and will be explained in Chapter 13 when we look at the phalanges.

We will now consider the symbolic associations of each of the mounts in turn.

THE VENUS MOUNT

Positive

Love, sensuality, passion, pleasure, kindness, rhythm, music, melody, fortune, prosperity, money, security, food, mother, womb, family.

Negative

Venereal disease, syphilis, disappointments in love causing illness, lewdness, lasciviousness, incest, adultery, sloth.

THE MOUNTS OF MARS

Mars rules two mounts on the palm. Traditionally Mars rules two signs of the Zodiac; Aries by day and Scorpio by night. Since the Mars active mount is located on the Solar side of the palm, it has a more Aries quality; while Mars passive, is located on the Lunar side of the palm, has a more Scorpionic quality.

Mars Active Mount: Positive

Power, energy, force, endurance, assertion, drive, esprit de corps, fortitude, gallantry.

Mars Active Mount: Negative

Anger, belligerence, violence, brutality, murder, ferocity, cruelty, rape, venereal disease, obscenity.

Mars Passive Mount: Positive

Courage, resistance, endurance, excitability, desire, sexuality.

Mars Passive Mount: Negative

Lasciviousness, lust, rape, obscenity, vengeance, violence, animosity, jealousy, cowardice, sore throat, bronchitis, laryngitis, blood disorders, haemorrhage, inflammations, rashes.

THE JUPITER MOUNT

Positive

Privilege, justice, equity, religion, faith, goals, aspiration, hope, superstition, ambition, compassion, benevolence, optimism, ideals, pride, liver.

Negative

Austerity, callousness, meanness, sternness, vanity, ostentation, gluttony, apoplexy, lung troubles, biliousness, overindulgence especially overeating.

THE SATURN MOUNT
==

Positive

Patience, concentration, discipline, steadfastness, responsibility, duty, conditioning, caution, structure, solitude, father.

Negative

Repression, fear, selfishness, melancholia, sorrow, pessimism, apprehension, sluggish circulation, haemorrhoids, constipation, rheumatism, biliousness, nervous irritation, paralysis, hemiplegia, trouble with legs, teeth and ears.

THE SUN MOUNT
==

Positive

Illumination, creativity, art, genius, talent, fame, fortune, wealth, dignity, optimism, health.

Negative

Pride, haughtiness, arrogance, extravagance, vanity, heart troubles – especially palpitations, fevers, eye troubles.

THE MERCURY MOUNT
==

Positive

Ideas, intellect, reason, invention, science, learning, study, writing, medicine, business sense, communication, language, speech, eloquence.

Negative

Financial ineptitude, theft, embezzlement, dishonesty, deceit, boasting, gossip, superficiality, forgetfulness, liver disease, nervous irritation, indigestion, accidents to arms and hands.

THE LUNAR MOUNT
==

Positive

Emotions, receptivity, sensitivity, intuition, imagination, dreams, vision, psychic, moods, ambience, mother, nurse, affection.

Negative

Hallucination, illusion, lunacy, sadness, bladder and kidney disease, dropsy, stones, rheumatism, gout, anaemia, lymphatic disorders, female troubles, intestinal disease, diabetes, hysteria, convulsions, paralysis, eye weakness.

The topic of mounts has assumed considerable importance in palmistry books, yet the full-blown formations on the palm worthy of the name 'mount' are today rarely found. When present they can stand up to 1 cm above the plain of the palm. Palmistry books tend to lead the reader to believe that the prominence of mounts is very common when in fact to find a full set of mounts is rare.

Since a full set of mounts is rare, a single mount 'standing out' on the palm is significant. It indicates the predominance of the corresponding Planetary influence within the person. The Planetary influence reflected in the development of particular mounts has also been used as the basis of classification of hand shape according to the Planets. The Planetary hand shapes will be considered in Chapter 15 after lines and fingers, since greater subtlety of detail within hand shapes will then be appreciated.

The most important aspect of mounts is their relationship to the palmar lines. If the lines on the hand are considered to be like rivers, then mounts can be regarded as their mountainous sources. Just as the source of a river powerfully colours the water flowing along it, so, too, a mount colours the energy flowing through a line. This idea will be developed further in Chapter 12 when considering the rulerships of lines.

CHAPTER 11

The Palmar Lines

LINES on the hand are immensely varied, even more varied than people's faces! No two hands are ever alike, even when considering the right and left palms of the same person. One of the most important parts of cheiromantical study is to collect as many handprints as possible specifically to observe the fascinating and wonderful diversity of lineal patterns. The larger the range of handprints taken, the greater the appreciation of their varied formations.

The palmar lines describe how a person experiences the Celestial World. As already explained, the Celestial World encompasses the whole realm of emotional experience. The Etheric vital force in sustaining the structure of the physical body simultaneously constitutes the medium of the emotional experience. It is variations in the flow of the vital force through the body that we experience as different emotional states. Etheric vital force also constitutes the substratum of mental experience, for all ideas and images within the mind are generated out of its substance.

THE FORMATION OF LINES

The lines are formed by the Etheric vital force flowing across the palm, in the same way as a river erodes a channel as it flows across various terrains. Since Ether is linked to the animation of the physical body, the flow of emotions and the formation of ideas, lines are intimately connected with the consciousness of an individual. The lineal patterns on the palm are unique to the individual.

The lines start to develop on the palm after about seven weeks of embryological development and by ten weeks they are fully present. Only after twelve weeks are the muscles in the wrist sufficiently developed to begin the first primitive movements of the palm.[19] This dispels the prevalent idea that lines are creases formed from the mechanical movements of the hand.

The Etheric energy flowing in the lines cannot be directly perceived by the physical senses. However, through using the imagination to cultivate a symbolic awareness, this flow of Ether can be perceived. A skilled cheiromancer can build up an intricate picture of a person's consciousness from the line patterns.

THE INTERPRETATION OF LINES

Planetary Rulership of Lines

The first step towards interpreting lines is to allocate them their Planetary rulers. The seven

Planets – Saturn, Jupiter, Mars, Sun, Venus, Mercury, and the Moon – traditionally rule the Celestial World. In the hand the Celestial World corresponds to the lines, which is why Planetary names are found amongst the palmar lines. Originally in cheiromancy the Planets were allocated to all the lines. The Planetary names such as Saturn, Mars, Apollo (Sun) and Lunar (Moon) still found in palmistry today are a vestige of this allocation of rulers. The specific allocation of rulership to a line is based upon its flow in relation to a particular mount.

Figure 11.1 shows the traditional relationship between lines and mounts. All the palmar lines, with the exception of the head line, start, or flow through or round, or terminate upon, a particular mount. On contact with the mount, the energy in the line becomes coloured by its Planetary ruler. For example the Mars line in starting on the Mars active mount is coloured with Martian energy. Likewise the Saturn line in flowing towards the Saturn mount is coloured with Saturnine energy. An important point to note in relation to all diagrams of the palmar

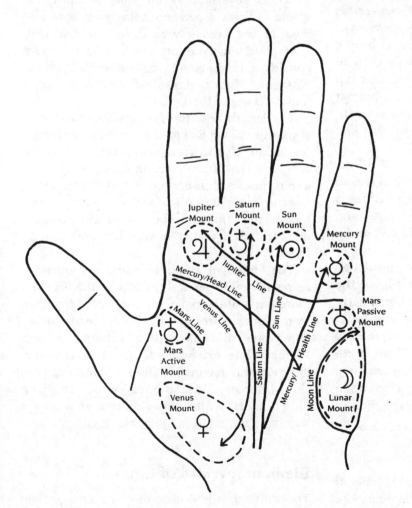

Figure 11.1 The Traditional Relationship of Lines and Mounts

lines is that there is immense variation in the actual patterns found on the live palm. The diagrams are purely representational in order to demonstrate the main principles of lines and their rulership. Doubtless there will be many who find the diagram does not fit with the lines on their own palm. Of this variation, more will be described a little later.

The head line is ruled by Mercury because it does not touch any particular mount. For as already described, the symbolism of Mercury is synonymous with Ether. In one sense Mercury rules all the lines on the hand. However, as soon as a line contacts the Planetary energies of a mount, the latter can be regarded as having taken over rulership or coloured the energy of the line. Though it is possible for branches from the head line to reach several of the palmar mounts, it does not consistently connect with any one mount. Hence the energy in this line remains purely Mercurial.

Once Planetary rulership is given to a line, then the associated Planetary symbolism is used to ascribe meaning to it. Further significance is found in lines from their width, length and markings. These points will be explained in the following chapter.

With the decline of cheiromantic knowledge the significance of Planetary rulership of the palmar lines became obscured. In palmistry other names like 'head line', 'life line' and 'heart line' have crept in to replace the Planetary names. Once this Planetary symbolism is re-invoked these palmistic names will be seen in a new light. This will become more apparent when the Planetary rulership of lines is explained in the next chapter.

Lineal Manifestation

The palmar lines have been described as flows of Etheric energy. In interpreting the lines the analogy of a river is a useful tool for visualizing the energy flows across the palm. The relative length, width, degree of presence, clarity, markings, degree of curvature and orientations are all significant to lineal interpretation. All these features provide specific insights into a person's experience of life.

Length of Lines

The longer a line the more energy flows through it. Hence it reflects a greater range of awareness in that particular realm of the personality which is governed by the line. A short line would indicate a corresponding lack of awareness in the area governed by the line. For example a long Mercury line would indicate a considerable range of the subject's thinking patterns, whereas the short line indicates a limited range of thought.

The length of a line also indicates speed of response. A long line means that it takes longer for an impulse to travel from one end to the other, so that it is slower in function. A short line is quicker in function. For example, a long Mercury line describes a slow, detailed and long-winded thinker, whereas a short Mercury line describes a quick, succinct and snappy thinker.

The length of a line is important in other respects too; in general the longer the line, the more parts of the palm are connected together by it. Hence more connections are made within a person's psychology. For example a long Mercury line extending to the Lunar mount indicates an imaginative thinker. By contrast a short Mercury line stopping under the ring finger, short of the Lunar mount, indicates a lack of imagination to their thinking.

Elemental Width of Lines

The width of a line describes the energy flow along it. There are four relative widths of lines, corresponding to the Four Elements. These widths are demonstrated in Figure 11.2.

The Earth Width

The Earth width line is broad and has a dark colouration. Note the colour of a line can only be seen from the live hand. It indicates a slow rhythmic use of energy that can be sustained for long periods of time. However, this energy flow tends to remain fixed and intransigent when confronted with change.

The Water Width

The Water width line is fine and very pale. It reflects a very subtle delicate energy flow that is highly impressionable and visually expressive. However, this energy flow is highly fickle and lacks sustaining power.

The Air Width

The Air width line is clear and well defined. It does not have a particular colouration other than the colour of the skin. It reflects a focused

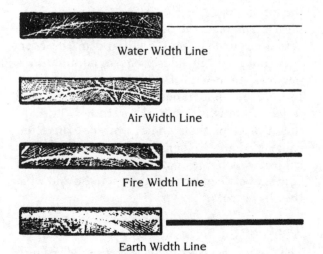

Figure 11.2 The Four Elemental Widths of Lines

Water Width Line

Air Width Line

Fire Width Line

Earth Width Line

and responsive energy flow, though lacking physical strength. It indicates achievement of goals through economy of energy. However it can sometimes be too dispersive to achieve anything.

The Fire Width

The Fire width line is deep and reddish in colour. It indicates considerable strength and intensity to the energy flow, making it highly spontaneous and responsive to change. However, the strength of the energy flow suggests that yielding or relaxation is difficult.

It is quite possible to have different Elemental widths amongst the individual lines on the palm. For example in the same palm it is possible to find that the Venus line has a Water width while the Jupiter line has a Fire width. Even an individual line may exhibit variations between two or even three Elemental widths along its length.

The particular Element shown by the width influences the way the Planetary ruler of a line is expressed. For example a Mars line with its hot and dry Fiery associations will reflect a person with physical power, strength and assertiveness when the line has a Fire width. By contrast a Mars line with a Water width suggests the opposite, a person lacking drive and motivation who dreams about obtaining their goals instead of accomplishing them.

Degree of Presence of Lines

The extent of a line presence on the palm can range from its being completely formed throughout its length to its total absence. When completely formed the line indicates that all the qualities and functions symbolically associated with it are all well developed and integrated in consciousness. In contrast the absent line indicates a deficiency of the qualities and functions associated with the line.

▶ For example a well-formed Mercury line suggests that all the mental processes such as thinking, decision-making and communication are able to function clearly. In contrast an absent Sun line indicates that the person's creative abilities have not been developed.

The complete absence of either the Venus, Mercury or Jupiter lines is very rare. However absence of other lines occurs much more frequently.

The partial presence of a line is commonly found, implying that the qualities of the line are only partially developed. The partial presence is frequently found as a delayed start to a line. For example the Mercury line may start roughly 1 cm across from the thumb side of the palm, indicating that the ability to think and communicate does not begin to develop until approximately teenage – a late developer.

The Clarity of Lines

The clarity of a line is particularly important. The more clearly defined the line is the more easily the Etheric energy flows along it. This harmonious energy flow reflects a person's inner clarity. A clear cut line will usually indicate particularly strong qualities associated with the line present within a person. The clarity enables the person to express these qualities freely. Conversely an ill-defined line indicates it to be an area of weakness within a person, while the lack of clarity detracts from ease of expression.

In assessing the clarity of a line it is important to consider the proportion of the line that is clearly defined in relation to the proportion of line obscured by markings. This indicates how much of the line is functioning well and how much is not. Since markings mar the energy flow and detract from its overall function, it is important to search in the hand for factors contributing to these markings. The

various markings found in lines are considered next.

The Markings in the Lines

This section covers the various markings and features found in the lines. Each marking describes a particular effect upon the energy flow within the line. These distortions of energy flow distinctively reflect the particular experience of the person. The impact of the marking should then be considered in the sphere connected with the line. The various markings are illustrated in Figure 11.3.

The Island

The island describes an obstruction to the energy flow along a line where, as a result, the energy flow splits to divert round the obstruction. The island leads effectively to a doubling of energy flow at the moment in time corresponding to the island's location in the line. The timing of markings in lines will be covered a little later (see page 84). Each path of the island can be seen to repel the other across its ovoid shape, reflecting a period of conflict in a person's life.

In a horizontal line such as the Mercury line, the upper path of the island corresponds to ideals, whereas the lower path is linked to actual circumstances. This island in the Mercury line typically describes a conflict in a person's mind with its subsequent indecision. In the hand of a student, for example, it could reflect dissatisfaction in their studies. Perhaps the subject of their choice was not on offer, causing them to compromise and accept a subject which does not suit them. Hence their conflict between what they want to do and what they have to do.

The Chain

The chain is essentially a series of islands replicated through the length of a line. Each

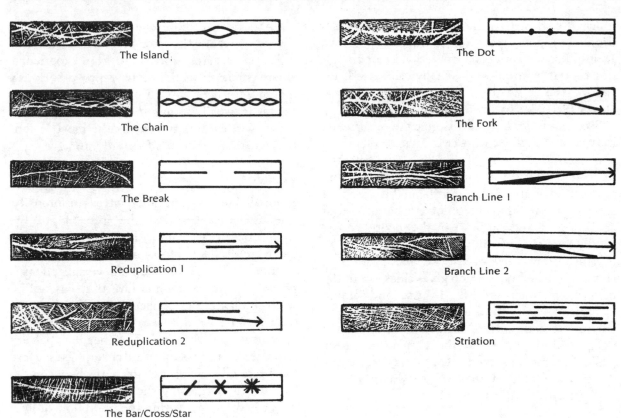

The Island

The Dot

The Chain

The Fork

The Break

Branch Line 1

Reduplication 1

Branch Line 2

Reduplication 2

Striation

The Bar/Cross/Star

Figure 11.3 Markings in the Lines

island composing a link in the chain. The chain formation describes periods of conflict that persist in the person's experience. Though the circumstances may change, described by the different islands included in the chain, the conflict shown by the pattern persists, impairing the function of the whole line. For example a chained Mercury line indicates a prolonged period of indecision and uncertainty as defined by the length of the chained portion. This conflict would additionally detract from the positive development and expression of the person's mental abilities.

The Break

The break is a clear gap in the course of a line. The feature needs to be distinguished from reduplication where there is a definite period of overlap between the two sections in a line. The break is a rare feature. However, when present, it is very significant for it indicates an absence of function in that line. The gravity of such loss of function depends on which line has the break. For example a break in the Venus line can indicate the affect of a coma on the body's vitality. A break in the Jupiter line can show the impact of an emotional trauma causing the total blockage of emotional expression.

Reduplication

Reduplication consists of a distinct overlap between two sections of a line. The feature indicates that the energy flowing through the line during this phase is doubled. This is in marked contrast to the break where there is a distinct gap or blockage to the energy flow. Reduplication reflects a transition in a person's life that is gradual and usually calculated, for before the first line expires the second line starts and gains in strength and autonomy.

For example, reduplication in the Saturn line may well describe a career change; the start of the second section of the line suggests the person taking on a course of study over and above their current work, indicated by the first section to the line. The point at which the first section ends indicates when the second career finally takes over from the original one.

The orientation of the second section in relation to the first section gives clues about the new direction in their life. If the second section is parallel to the first, it implies a similarity to the previous direction. If the second section is tangential to the first section, then it indicates a radical departure from what was previously done. Examples of this are shown in Figure 11.3 – Reduplication 1 and 2.

The Bar/Cross/Star

A bar is a very common feature that consists of a small line cutting across a main palmar line, interrupting its flow. A bar indicates a sudden precipitous blockage to the line's energy flow. Bars are linked to times of stress and commonly denote traumas and accidents. Despite the intensity of the experience it is generally of short duration. For example a bar cutting the Saturn line might indicate an accident at work. A series of bar lines may cut through the main lineal flow so severely as to allow only spasmodic function of the line. This is commonly seen in the Venus line where many bar lines radiating down from the Mars active mount reflects stressful interference with the person's vitality, as in Figure 12.6 – B and C page 97.

More rarely a cross or a star can be found interrupting the flow of a line. Both these features involve more energy being focused at the point where the flow of a line is cut. This indicates greater gravity to the experience, where such an accident may prove seriously maiming or even fatal. For this reason a cross or star is usually found at the end of a line. Of these two features the star is the most serious because more energy is focused into it.

The Dot

A dot also reveals a period of stress or intensity. The dot indicates that the intensity of the experience arises from within, in contrast to the bar which reflects stress arising from external circumstances. A dot can be visualized as a phase of a main palmar line that has a Fire width indicating a focused intensity of energy flow. A series of dots can present as a beaded appearance in the line. The 'beaded' pattern indicates a succession of intense phases. Here the energy flow of a line alternates between the Fire width composing the dots and the Water or Air width constituting the main flow of line, this indicates powerful fluctuations in expression and in constancy of performance.

The Fork

A fork describes a splitting of energy flow in a line. Forks are usually found at the ends of lines. When each branch of a fork is clear and equal in strength it indicates a positive divergence of energy. As well as showing two different orientations in a person's life, the feature increases the length of a line which reflects an increase in the overall perception of the person. If, however, the branches of a fork are uneven and lack definition then the feature shows a dispersal of energy indicating irresolution and uncertainty.

The same principle holds true for assessing tridents, which have the potential of even greater diversity or dispersal depending on the quality of formation.

The Branch

A branch line generally describes an influence that either feeds into or draws from a particular line. To distinguish which is the case, one needs to determine the direction in which the energy of the branch line flows. The simplest way is to recall the arrow sign used to indicate direction. The smallest point shows the focus of direction, while the wider part of the tail indicates where the energy comes from. Branch lines that feed into a main line (Figure 11.3 – Branch line 1), describe influences that colour the energy flow in the line. It is important to see where such branch lines start, as this will provide clues as to the nature of the influence. Generally they will start from mounts or from other principle lines on the palm. It is also important to consider the flow of the main line after the point of union to see what effect the influence has had.

For example, if an influence line feeds into the Jupiter line from the Mars passive mount at which point the Jupiter line changes from a Water to a Fire width, this strongly indicates the awakening of the person's sexual energies within their relationships at the time indicated by the point where the branch line feeds into the Jupiter line. (See page 84 for chronology.) Alternatively a branch line feeding into the Jupiter line from the Saturn line weakening the flow of the 'heart' line, indicates the influence of work pressures blocking the free expression of feelings with others. In turn such an influence suggests a person becoming withdrawn and isolated.

When a branch line flows out of a main line (Figure 11.3 – Branch Line 2), its orientation reveals what the person is directing their energies towards. Once again this is revealed by mounts and lines. Further clues come from noting on which side of a main line the branch emerges. This further depends on whether the main line is horizontal like the Jupiter and Mercury lines or longitudinal like the Sun and Saturn lines.

To illustrate this point, an influence line branching downwards from the Jupiter line suggests the energy flow in the branch line becoming more physically manifest. The influence of a sexual relationship is commonly shown by this feature. By contrast an influence line branching upwards from the Jupiter line suggests that the energy flow in the branch line is becoming more sublimated and idealized. This can indicate the influence of a platonic relationship or the devotion to a spiritual ideal.

Striation

In striation the true definition of a line is replaced by a series of fine feathery lines resembling paintbrush strokes. This dispersed energy flow indicates that whatever is associated with the line cannot function clearly. Striated lines function in a spasmodic and haphazard way.

From the above it will be evident that the ideal line should be clear and free from markings. Predictably, such lines are rarely found.

Ancillary Lines

Where the flow of energy in the main lines is marred by markings, ancillary lines appear on the palm. Just as a blocked channel of a river causes the water to overflow its banks and flood the plains, so, too, ancillary lines appear when the energy flow in the main lines is frustrated, as shown in Figure 15.1, page 149.

Ancillary lines are symptomatic of times of stress and conflict in a person's life. They can appear and disappear rapidly as stresses in life come and go. By noting the Elemental width of these lines and the general direction of their flow, what mounts they flow from and what mounts they flow towards, the nature of the stress can be determined. The flow of ancillary lines across the palm may cause distinct barring of the main lines. The line that is interrupted by the bars indicates the area of a person's life impaired by stress.

THE CHRONOLOGY OF LINES

Markings in the palmar lines frequently reflect events in people's lives. To ascertain when a specific event occurred, what is currently happening and what is likely to happen in the future, the lines need to be divided up to indicate age. These times can then be correlated with an individual's experience.

Figure 11.4 summarizes the approximate times and divisions made in the principal palmar lines. For the Venus, Mercury and Jupiter lines the total span of a line can be taken as roughly seventy years. The midpoint of these lines can be taken as approximately thirty-five years. These two divisions of thirty-five years can be further divided by eye into intervals of five or ten years. It is then possible to determine at what age specific markings occur on a line to within approximately eighteen months either side of an event.

Initially this method should be used quite loosely since it is difficult to give a precise date to a particular experience in a line. With

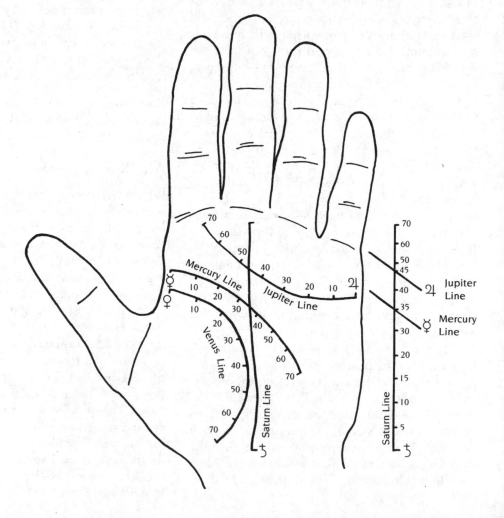

Figure 11.4 The Chronology of Lines

confirmation from the person involved, markings can then be pin-pointed with far more accuracy. For example if an island occurs in the Mercury line between the apparent ages of 10 and 17, it could well lead to the following explanation; 'You had a conflict at school between the ages of 10 and 17.' At which point the person replies, 'Actually it was from 11 to 18.' This then identifies the two precise points of 11 and 18 on the line at either end of the island. The whole line can now be recalibrated to give far more precise timings. With experience the ability to time events accurately greatly improves.

Timing in the Saturn line is much more irregular, as shown separately in Figure 11.4, with the first quarter of the line's length spanning about fifteen years. The scale then increases so that the final eighth of the line spans roughly twenty years. The points at which the Saturn line crosses the Mercury and the Jupiter lines can be taken as approximately 35 and 45 years of age respectively.

The timing on the Sun line, when present, may be considered in parallel to the timing on the Saturn line. The Neptune line can similarly be timed in relation to the Jupiter line. It is not really possible to time events on other lines of the palm beside those mentioned above.

PROGNOSIS OF MARKINGS IN THE LINES

With all markings on lines it is important to ascertain the duration of the associated experience and see what effect the marking has on the general energy flow of the line. This assessment of duration of the experience is most important for islands, chains, breaks, reduplication and branches. There is no need to assess

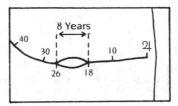

Figure 11.5 The Timing of Markings

the duration for other markings such as the bar or cross since they represent brief experiences. The technique involves super-imposing the chronological scale onto the line to determine at what age a marking starts and when it ends. The difference in the two ages describes the duration of the experience. For example in Figure 11.5 an island in the Jupiter line starts at the age of 18 and resolves at the age of 26, so the emotional conflict described by the island persists for eight years.

It is important to compare the quality of a line before and after a specific marking. If, as in Figure 11.6, the line after an island is weaker than the line leading into the island then it suggests the person has not successfully overcome the period of conflict and recovered their former strength. Figure 11.7 shows the reverse where the line after an island is stronger than the line leading into the island, suggesting that the person has successfully overcome the period of conflict and gained in strength. This assessment of the impact of markings on the energy flow is particularly important for the succinct markings such as bars, crosses and stars, for despite their brief duration they commonly reflect experiences that can have a long-lasting impact on a person's life, such as a car accident.

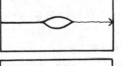

Figure 11.6 Prognosis of Markings – Poor

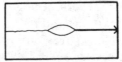

Figure 11.7 Prognosis of Markings – Good

CHAPTER 12

The Planetary Rulership
of Lines

IT is not possible to give a definitive catalogue of all lineal formations and their meanings; that task would be immense and would always remain incomplete. It is only to be expected that as people go through this book (or indeed any other book on handreading) superficially comparing the lines in their own hand with the handprints and diagrams included, they will inevitably find differences between their own palms and the diagrams. This leads to a typical question – 'My Mercury line is different; I can't find it in the book, what does it mean?'

Don't panic. It is precisely these observations of differences that make a skilled cheiromancer. Every time a difference in palmar line is observed, it should lead the reader to ask, 'How is it different?' Then consider all the lineal formations listed under the previous chapter on lineal manifestation in turn to define precisely what the difference is. Is the line longer or shorter? What Elemental width/s does it have? How strong is its presence? Is it absent? Is it clear or marred? What markings are present and at what age do they occur? You should then be able to work out what the difference means. This exercise will teach people far more about lines than merely memorizing line patterns and their interpretations from books. As previously mentioned, it is impossible to cover every line

pattern and variation in a book since they are as varied and different as the people they belong to.

A good way to focus the mind on reading a specific line is to draw it separately on a piece of paper, noting all the markings, features and directions. As you note down the specific observations, use the appropriate Elemental or Planetary symbolism and try to visualize what they mean; then list your ideas.

Another useful technique is to compare each handprint to your own and ask once more, 'How is it different?' Differences here contrast your own experience in life to someone else's. This provides considerable food for thought; not only does it sharpen your perception of other people's lives, but it also makes you more aware of your own. For example, if your Jupiter line is longer than your counterpart's, then it suggests that you have a greater range of emotional expression than the other person. The reverse observation would mean the precise opposite.

This chapter will outline each of the palmar lines in turn, dealing with their commoner features and formations as well as giving a selection of their interpretations. These interpretations are not exhaustive: any meaning needs to be considered relative to the circumstances of each individual. For example, the early section of a line relates to childhood and usually the influence of one's parent/s. However, on an orphan's hand it would describe the influence of the foster care. No matter what reason exists for supplanting a person's natural parents, whether it is due to schooling, travel or religious training, the same section of the line must be interpreted in the context of the school, foreign country or religion respectively.

As you go though all these features and markings, instead of merely learning the interpretations try to understand symbolically how these meanings have been derived. Some of the interpretations are explained in full, others are left intentionally terse, requiring contemplation to understand the association. If the rationale for the interpretation is not immediately apparent, then turn back to the appropriate section on symbolism. Rereading the material should remind you of certain ideas necessary to understand the interpretation. By grasping the underlying principles of lineal interpretation, the novice will gain the skills necessary to interpret lineal patterns found in the populace at large. This should lead beyond the illustrations

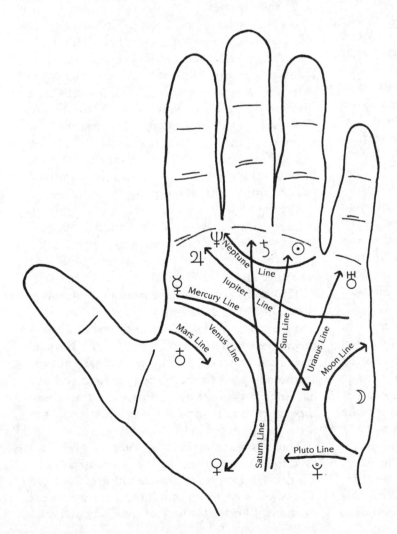

Figure 12.1 The Modern Rulership of the Palmar Lines

in this book to a greater proficiency of reading hands.

The lines will now be described with their modern rulerships as represented in Figure 12.1.

THE VENUS
(LIFE OR VITALITY) LINE (♀)

The Venus line starts about halfway between the angle of the thumb and the base of the index finger. It typically curves down around the base of the thumb towards the Venus mount. The palmistic names of 'life' or 'vitality' line obscure the Venusian rulership. However, on reflection of the relationship between love, mother, womb, birth and life previously explained in the section on the symbolism of Venus, it is easy to see how the energy flowing through this line describes the 'vitality' that sustains the body.

The associations of this line with life and vitality is remarkably confirmed by it being the first to form on the palm, at about seven weeks of embryological development.[20] The formation of the line at this time reflects the enormous thrust of cellular growth that forms the physical body.

In connection with this line recent medical research, based on a hundred autopsies showed a statistically higher than average correlation between the length of the 'life' line and the age at which a person died.[21] The name 'life' line is based upon the loose association between the amount of vital energy and the length of their physical life. This correlation is certainly interesting since it suggests that people die when their vitality runs out. However, the palmistic assertion that the length of the life is shown by the length of the life line should not be taken too literally, for death can occur when a person possesses full vitality.

The line reflects the maternal bond of love and the degree of emotional security experienced in childhood. The quality of childhood, the support and influence of the family or foster care is shown by the line. The degree of nurturing and security experienced in childhood profoundly influences the later ability of a person to love themselves. This in turn affects their sense of self-worth which, in relation to work, relates to the value placed upon their skills and abilities.

If a person has a poor sense of self-worth they will not value themselves or their talents, so undercharge for their services or accept poorly paid work despite their skills and experience. In extreme situations the lack of self-worth may prevent the development of their talents and skills. This results in insecurity, frustration, unhappiness and physical exhaustion through being overworked and underpaid. The pressure of this frustration in work can strain emotional relationships to breaking-point.

By contrast, someone who has a positive sense of self-worth will ensure they earn a just fee for their work. Consequently they will be able to earn the money for maintaining their life structure and responsibilities.

Thus self-value can have profound effects on the ability to earn money, on personal security, and on emotional stability and health. This in turn is reflected in the influence parents have on their own children. So the emotional patterns are perpetuated through the generations. Love has such an important influence on all these aspects of our lives. All these interconnected ideas are reflected in the Venus line.

There is a strong link between this line and food since Venus rules the Zodiacal Earth sign of Taurus. The line describes the eating of food and its assimilation to maintain the constitution of the body. Our first source of food is breast milk given with the love and nurturing of the mother. Psychologists have noted the strong links between the expression of love and the eating of food. A candlelit dinner is a common romantic activity for couples. Similarly mealtimes provide a regular focus for the emotional bonds within a family.

When people are unable to find fulfilment in love they are commonly drawn to overeating, especially of sweet things like chocolate (also ruled by Venus). By contrast, one factor found in anorexia sufferers is often an intense dislike of themselves. They do not want to nurture and care for themselves, so denying their body's need to eat.

In pregnancy the female body undergoes a series of powerful changes leading to a notable increase in weight, not only from the growing baby, but also from the laying down of food reserves as fat. During lactation the food is transferred to the developing infant. In turn the nutriment from the milk becomes the substance of the child's body. The medical name for a pregnant woman is gravida, which comes from the Latin gravis, meaning 'heavy'. This very strongly shows the Venusian principle of drawing energy down into the material world.

Venus Line Keywords

Physical constitution, vitality, love, pregnancy, womb, birth, generation, family, parental ability, self-value, money, wealth, home, security, sensual pleasures, food and digestion, health.

The general procedure for interpreting all lines will now be illustrated in relation to the Venus line.

Origins of the Venus Line

When a line is visualized as a flow of energy, then the beginning section of the line describes how the person's consciousness has come into the world. This section of the line particularly reflects the formative influences of childhood. These influences are shown by what mount or palmar area the line starts from, and by the starting-point of any secondary influence lines that feed into the main line.

Refer to Figure 12.2. The typical start of the Venus line as shown by point (A) in the diagram, is approximately halfway between the angle of the thumb and the index finger, corresponding to the start of the Mercury line. Symbolically the Four Elements composing the body are formed out of the Ether, so it is most appropriate that the Venus line should start from the region where the Mercury line begins. The Venus line may begin from the Mars active (B) or Jupiter mounts (C), or alternatively receive influence lines from these mounts.

The Martian origin (B) injects Fiery qualities into the line, which are often reflected by a naturally strong constitution and outgoing personality. This origin could be descriptive of the person having parents who are linked with the armed services or the child who was trained in martial arts at an early age. Note the quality and clarity in relation to the width of the Venus line, for it will then tell you how this energy is being used. Usually, though not invariably, the Martian influence gives the Venus line a Fire quality width. Additionally in this context, it is important to see if the line is clear, in which case the Fiery energy is well controlled and disciplined, as in a soldier or a sportsperson. If the line is marred, the energy is ill disciplined indicating an aggressive, violent and pugnacious person.

Since Mars is the symbolic opposite to Venus, a Martian influence to the Venus line will naturally compromise the inherent Venusian characteristics, such as caring and nurturing, making a person hard and callous but prepared to die for their mother country.

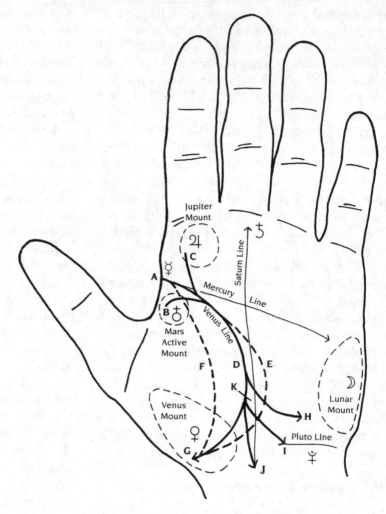

Figure 12.2 Variations of the Venus Line

The Jupiterian origin (C) infuses Airy qualities into the Venus line. Naturally it confers a heightened or expanded opportunity at birth or in childhood. It used to denote a high birth, someone born into a family of wealth and influence. In former times they would have had their life's opportunities enhanced by having their education paid for. In modern times with broader education opportunities this is less of a distinguishing feature, but may still describe someone born to parents of outstanding talents and abilities and who readily absorbed such skills as part of their childhood learning. It may denote an early exposure to and influence of a religious teacher/teaching that has powerfully inspired them in their life. With this broadened opportunity during childhood, the Elemental width and clarity of the line will tell you whether the person is motivated by compassionate humanitarian concerns or worldly greed and ambition.

After determining the origins of the line, it is best to consider the actual flow of energy along it, shown by the line's general orientation and overall Elemental width.

Curvature of the Venus Line

The curvature of the Venus line is descriptive of the degree of loving and nurturing received during childhood. A well-rounded line (D) shows a strong loving influence, which in turn reflects a kind and providing person, who readily shares their own happiness. They would naturally make a good parent. The fullness of the Venusian energy often denotes fertility, which may well be reflected in the number of children they have.

An excessively full curve (E), that cuts across the central vertical division used to divide the palm when drawing up the quadrants indicates sensual overindulgence, which is commonly reflected by an obese constitution.

By contrast, a shallow curved line (F) describes the austerity and hardship experienced through a lack of love. Stern or absent parents are often indicated, which in turn makes it difficult for the person to become a loving parent. Childlessness is traditionally correlated with this formation. It may well denote the imposed austerity of a monk or nun who has negated sensory pleasures. This is typically reflected by an emaciated constitution.

Elemental Widths of the Venus Line

Earth Width

Here we take the symbolism of the Earth Element and apply it to concepts involved with the Venus line. When the Venus line has an Earth width, it reflects a person whose body is robust but not very dynamic due to a sluggish metabolism. Their physical health would be sound, but prone to digestive upsets such as constipation and liver disorders through eating too much. Digestion would be slow, with a tendency towards being overweight. Though distinctly reserved in displaying affection, they would be very loyal and providing to their family.

In earning money they are very unadaptable, preferring work that they can plod along in, happy just to take home their pay at the end of the week. They seldom apply any simple business strategies to get ahead financially. Changing jobs is often difficult since they would prefer to stick at what they have always been doing, rather than learn any new skills. They often have a very strong practical sense, especially when working with natural material like timber and stone. An example of an Earth width Venus line is found in Figure 7.2, page 53.

Water Width

Next take the symbolism of the Water Element and apply it to concepts involved with the Venus line. A Water width Venus line reflects a person with a very delicate constitution and metabolism who often lacks energy. They would be prone to anaemia and water retention. They typically lack resistance and would be prone to phlegmatic conditions like flu and bronchitis. A single bout of flu can leave them low in spirits for a week or more. Healing is slow. Physically they would be prone to allergies and their health is strongly influenced by their emotional state. They love to use their bodies to express feelings through movement, rhythm and dance. They are often very loving and caring, being particularly sensitive to the needs of others. It is easy for them to give too much time and energy if they feel the need to help others, causing them to collapse through exhaustion. In money matters they will range from being completely hopeless to being highly successful. In the first instance they will dream about having money, rather then dealing with the practicalities of actually earning it. In the second, success comes through using their sensitivity to provide exactly what the client needs, which generates further goodwill and personal recommendation. An example of a Water width Venus line is found in Figure 15.6, page 155.

Air Width

Next take the symbolism of the Air Element and apply it to concepts involved with the Venus line. The Air width Venus line reflects a person with a moderately strong constitution and metabolism. The constitution is not as fragile as the Water width line, but still lacks a powerful vitality. They are often rather aloof from their body and can be prone to nervous upsets through too much worry. However, they can be very disciplined in health matters once they set their mind to it. The sensitivity associated with the Air width often describes strong humanitarian concerns rather than the expression of affection in close relationships. They would prefer to maintain a romantic ideal rather than deal with issues that arise in relationships. In money matters they can understand economics well, but are typically lazy when it comes to actually earning it, remaining a financial dreamer. They would be good at work that requires scientific or technological knowledge. An example of an Air width Venus line is found in Figure 15.5, page 154.

Fire Width

Finally take the symbolism of the Fire Element and apply it to concepts involved with the Venus line. The Fire width Venus line reflects a person with a strong constitution and a powerful metabolism generating an abundance of energy. They are seldom ill from infections. However, if they succumb, a high fever will soon burn it out in a matter of days. An inability to relax makes them prone to stress-induced illnesses like ulcers and cardiac problems. In relationships they would be very demanding of affection from others, though poor at returning it. They accept the responsibilities of providing for the family but typically get more involved with doing the work than directing their energies to the family. They can easily become workaholics if their emotional life becomes difficult. Their strong practical sense and abundant energy generally means that they can easily make money. However, their short-sighted economic sense leads to them taking risks rather than considering the situation more fully. This results in either making a fortune or ending in disaster or even both. An example of a Fire width Venus line is found in Figure 7.3, page 55.

Comparison of Origins with Width

It is important to compare the influences feeding into a line with the actual Elemental width. For example in the case of the Venus line starting from the Mars mount, the above description will be truest when the line also exhibits a Fire width. With an Air or Water width this Martian influence will be expressed differently. The Air width would temper this energy and could provide the physical skill to handle sharp instruments. It is a feature that could make a good surgeon (Mars traditionally rules knives and sharp instruments). An engineer might also take advantage of this influence. The Water width makes the Martian influence much more caring and sympathetic. It would be good for a nurse, who could channel this energy into caring for others. They would be likely to have strong pacifist ideals. Paradoxically, you might find the military nurse who risks their life in treating casualties in field hospitals. Alternatively such a line combination could indicate someone who is drawn to physical activities such as dance, swimming and gymnastics that demand flexibility and suppleness of the body.

Terminations of the Venus Line

The end section of a line is descriptive of the person's goals and aspirations. Chronologically, the end section of a line corresponds to the latter phase of their life. Interpretation of the line's end is, once again, done by noting what mount or palmar area the line ends on or branches towards.

The truest ending for the Venus line is on the Venus mount, Figure 12.2 (G). This reflects immense love and support for the family and mother country. Typically this feature would describe someone who will retire to the place where they were born, to be with their family at the close of a long life. The line ending on the Venus mount displays a fondness for music and a love of nature. This ending is also shown in Figure 15.4, page 153.

The Venus line ending towards the Lunar mount (H) by contrast, displays a marked lack of affinity with their home and family. They prefer to explore new horizons overseas and usually retire abroad.

The Venus line ending on the Pluto line (I) shows a marked proneness to sexual indulgence and alcoholism. In a woman's hand it could indicate gynaecological problems. This ending is also shown in Figure 15.7, page 157.

The Venus line ending at the beginning of the Saturn line (J) has a sternness about it. The lack of curve to the Venus line shows little love or attraction to the family, while the lack of orientation of the line to the Lunar mount shows a fear of exploring new horizons. It suggests a long hard struggle for their independence and a notably conservative attitude in what they have achieved.

In palmistry books the short Venus line ending at point (K) is interpreted literally as a short life. In isolation it rarely means this, though the lack of length does indicate a diminished vitality and poor health. The end section of the Venus line is important in other respects, since it reflects how the person grounds or anchors themselves in the material world. The absence of this section indicates someone who puts down no permanent roots. This ending is shown in Figure 7.3, page 55.

It is useful symbolically to compare the influences at the beginning of a line to the indications at the end. For example the strong Martian influence at the beginning of the Venus line (B) typically indicates a violent, aggressive character, but its curving towards the Venus mount (G) suggests a marked mellowing of this tendency as they get older – the nature of Venus being the symbolic opposite of the nature of Mars. This will be confirmed by changes in the Elemental width of the line, classically by the Fire width thinning to a Water width.

One may also interpret the finishing point of the Venus line. The ending on the Lunar mount (H) suggests retiring to a hot climate by the sea, since the Moon is connected to the sea while the Martian influence would like a hot climate. The ending on the Saturn line (J) suggests ending up in prison, since Saturn is linked to walls, restriction and retribution. Again look for confirmation in the line width.

Features and Markings within the Venus Line

Having considered the overall flow of energy along the course of a line, the punctuating effects of the markings can be seen with greater significance. For example take a bar line cutting through the Venus line reflecting a trauma affecting a person's vitality. Additional observations can now be made through noting what Elemental width the bar line has, where the bar line comes from and where it goes to. The width gives clues about the relative intensity of the trauma. A Fire width bar line indicates a very severe and intense experience, an Air width a far more moderate experience, and a Water width a mild experience. Markings of an Earth width are seldom found in bar lines.

Consider, too, the relative strengths of both the marking and the main line as in Figure 12.3. For example in (A) a Water width bar line is not usually going to have much impact upon the

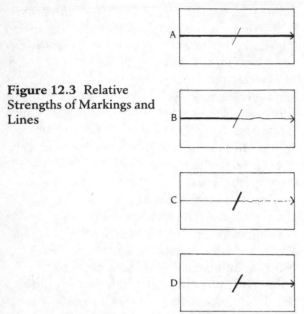

Figure 12.3 Relative Strengths of Markings and Lines

are now covered in Figure 12.4 in a succinct tabulated format. If the suggested correlations do not fit with the experience of the person whose hand you are reading, do not be disheartened. Instead recall the symbolism that is involved in the specific feature and try to work out what it might mean for the person.

Refer to Figure 12.4.

A Island – insecurity/conflict in childhood, poor self-esteem, weak vitality, poor maternal bond/lack of breast-feeding.

B Island with stress lines – emotional rejection/unwanted child, resultant insecurity and low self-esteem, absence of breast-feeding, very poor health.

flow of energy in a Fire width main line. However, it is possible as in (B) that a Water width bar line can extinguish the flow of energy in a Fire width main line. By contrast it is much more likely as in (C) that a Fire quality bar line will shatter the flow of a Water quality main line. However, it is possible, as in (D), that a Fire width bar line has a galvanizing effect upon the flow of a Water quality main line. Check the flow in the main line before and after the bar line for confirmation of its impact and to prognose the most likely outcome of the trauma.

Considering the general ages at which markings occur helps to define the most likely experience associated with the line. Thus a Fire width bar line on the Venus line before 10 years old suggests some sort of break-up to the home, the loss of a parent, the effect of being sent off to boarding school, or an intense childhood fever. Other correlations such as loss of a job, being made redundant, financial worries would be inappropriate here.

The features and markings in the Venus line

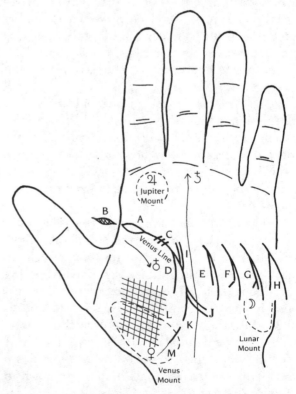

Figure 12.4 Markings and Variations of the Venus Line

C Bars – stresses affecting late teens – Exams? Relationships? Job interviews? Challenges to sense of security, accidents.

Influence lines generally denote influence of relationships. Length of line down Venus mount reflects depth of influence.

D Typical relationship.

E Very close relationship.

F Very close relationship, sudden painful break-up.

G Very close relationship, additional influence of child.

H Relationship that rapidly grows apart from outset.

I Influence lines towards Jupiter mount – ambitions, new horizons, inspirations, religious teachings. See Figure 15.4, page 153.

J Influence lines towards Lunar mount – travel, exploring new cultures, search for inner values. See Figure 7.3, page 55.

K Break – severe illness, coma, possible death.

L Grill on Venus mount – domestic strife, inability to relax, digestive problems; male hand-ulcers, colitis. Female hand – premenstrual tension, gynaecological problems. See Figure 7.3.

M Faded ending – weakening vitality, degenerative illness.

THE MARS (TEMPER) LINE (♂)

The Mars line usually starts on the Mars active mount as in Figure 11.1, page 77. It is located in the angle of the thumb and runs down parallel to the Venus line. Its typical length is about 2.5 cms though its course can run as far as the length of the Venus line. The close proximity of the Mars line to the Venus line symbolically reflects the supply of extra energy to the person's physical vitality. In times of illness the line confers resistance. It provides the abundant energy needed to 'burn off' infections in a fever facilitating a rapid recovery. The well-defined presence of the line denotes considerable strength of the body as evidenced by a powerful musculature.

The Martian energy that the line provides is dynamic and assertive. When positively directed this energy can contribute enormously to the successful accomplishment of tasks and projects. If thwarted or frustrated then anger is very easily aroused. It is for this reason that the line is traditionally linked to violence and palmists have erroneously called it the 'temper' line.

As mentioned earlier, temper is a term that was used to describe the balance of the Elements and humours within a person. Disruption of the Elemental balance leads to 'loss of temper'. The resulting imbalance of the Elements can be perceived in a number of Elemental ways. An excess of Fire leads to anger and aggression. An excess of Water leads to sadness and crying. An excess of Air leads to excessive laughter and hilarity. An excess of Earth leads to sullenness and withdrawal. It is an interesting cultural reflection that 'loss of temper' is thought to be purely the discharge of anger.

Sexual drive and potency are linked to the Mars line. Where the line starts chronologically in relation to the Venus line often denotes the beginning of a sexual relationship. The traditional influence lines running down parallel from the Venus line can also be seen as embodying some of this Martian energy.

In modern times the character of the Mars line has changed from the short truncated line to a profusion of lines fanning out from the

thumb. These formations will be explained
later.

Mars Line Keywords

Physical strength, resistance, assertiveness,
drive, discipline, aggression, anger, sexual
desire, potency.

Forms of the Mars Line

The Mars line needs to be considered in
relation to the Venus line since it supplies extra
energy to it. For this energy to be positively
directed the Mars line needs to have a flow
roughly parallel to the Venus line. Thus the two
lines flow in harmony.

Refer to Figure 12.5. The classic Mars line

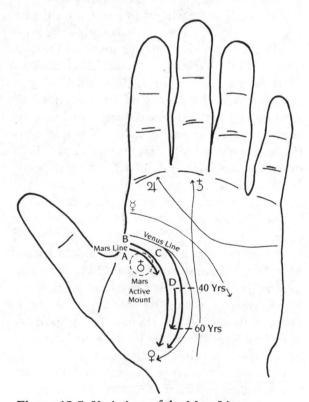

Figure 12.5 Variations of the Mars Line

(A) is a short truncated line mainly spanning
the width of the Mars active mount. This type
of line reflects immense power inside the
person generating muscle and might. The line
indicates a strong fighting spirit with a very
robust constitution.

The contemporary Mars line (B) is more
useful for civilized living; the extra length of the
line reaching down the Venus mount describes
a less intense expression of energy and more
moderate nature. Sometimes referred to as the
'double life' line. This Mars line is also shown in
Figure 15.2, page 150.

Line (C) is an alternative form, where an
influence line from the Venus line has grown in
magnitude to take on characteristics of a Mars
line. It suggests that a relationship is instrumental in bringing out the Martian qualities of
the person. Sometimes it is displayed when a
person takes up sport or commits themselves to
some other form of physical training. It could
indicate a job that places extra physical
demands on them. This Mars line is also shown
in 15.4, page 155.

The incomplete Mars line (D) is a partial
form of (B). When timed against the Venus line
this section of the Mars line augments the
vitality, associated with extra strength and
resistance for the duration of the line, which in
this example is twenty years. This Mars line is
also shown in 19.3, page 188.

Elemental Widths of the Mars Line

The most powerful expression of the Mars line
requires a Fire width. The Air width moderates
the energy flow leading to much of its intensity
being dispersed as nervous energy. The Water
width extinguishes the flow to the point of
physical weakness; there may also be hypersensitivity. The Earth Element is reflected by
the absence of a Mars line and a corresponding
lack of Martian energy. Note this absence of a

Mars line may be compensated for by other lines exhibiting Fiery characteristics.

Negative Features of the Mars Line

Refer to Figure 12.6. Negative expression of Martian energy is frequently shown by a fan of lines radiating down from the Mars active mount, which intercept the flow of the Venus line in a series of bar patterns. This shows that the Martian energy, instead of augmenting the vitality, is antagonistic to it. Each radiating line is indicative of a time of stress upsetting the normal harmony to the Venus line. Anger, frustration and intense worry are typically displayed in this manner. Close inspection of these lines reveals where the tension is inwardly contained (A), where it interferes with the Venus line (B) and where it bursts right through, shattering their vitality (C).

Stress-induced illness is often linked to the grill pattern (D), reflecting a build-up of tension from inner conflict and anger, also shown on the Venus mount in Figure 12.4 (L), page 94. A grill pattern is also shown in Figure 19.1, page 180. Grills will be considered more fully under section on phalangeal marking in Chapter 13.

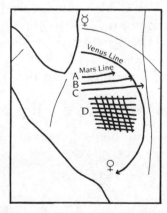

Figure 12.6 Markings and Variations of the Mars Line

THE JUPITER (HEART) LINE (♃)

The Jupiter line, shown in Figure 11.1, page 77, starts under the little finger and traverses across the palm towards the Jupiter mount. Jupiter is linked to the drawing down of the spirit through the heart and giving expression to its inspirations. The curve of the line subtends the fingers which encapsulates the Intellectual World, showing that the line symbolically receives the ideas that descend from it. The palmistic 'heart' line can now be seen in its deeper sense since the heart is considered the gateway to higher knowledge.

In response to the subtle impressions received from the realm of ideas, feelings are generated. The course and direction of the Jupiter line found in a hand is highly descriptive of the way a person expresses their emotions. The length of this line indicates the degree to which that person opens their heart and shares feelings with others. A long line crossing the Saturn line and extending to the Jupiter mount reflects a strong sense of compassion and love for others. In contrast a short line barely extending beyond the Saturn line indicates a lack of love and selfishness.

Jupiter rules the sanguine humour, which is synonymous with the correct temper of the humours within the blood. When the blood is properly composed, the vital force flows freely through it, nourishing the tissues. The Jupiter line is particularly linked with the circulation of blood and traditionally rules the lungs, where respiration occurs. This involves drawing air into the blood so that the tissues can receive oxygen and carry out their vital functions. Note the affinity between Jupiter and the Air Element.

Jupiter Line Keywords

Heart, emotions, feelings, inspiration, compassion, caring, circulation.

Origins of the Jupiter Line

Refer to Figure 12.7. The flow of the Jupiter line, in contrast to the Mercury line, moves from the inner side of the hand outwards. The line typically starts between the Mercury mount and Mars passive mount (A). Energy from either of these mounts can feed into the Jupiter line. An influence from the Mercury mount (B) electrifies the heart line indicating psychic sensitivity. More negatively it reflects a person who rationalizes their emotions so blocking their spontaneous flow and under-

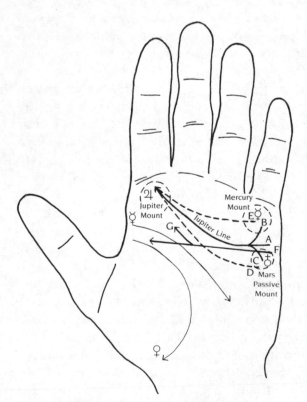

Figure 12.7 Variations of the Jupiter Line

standing. The influence from the Mars passive mount (C) indicates a passionate expression of feelings and a strong physical need for sexual expression.

Height of the Jupiter Line

The height of the Jupiter line across the palm reflects the level at which emotions and feelings operate. A low-set line (D) starting on the Mars passive mount describes a rather coarse level of emotional expression with little sensitivity and refinement. Emotions are largely expressed physically. By contrast a high-set line (E) starting on the Mercury mount describes a much more sublimated emotional expression with far greater subtlety and refinement in the use of feelings.

The level of the Jupiter line is most significant when considering the degree of straightness or curvature in the line. Typically the straight line (F) confines the Jupiter line to the coarse emotional expression described in the low-set line (D), indicating an insensitivity to the needs of others. Where there is a gentle curve as in the high-set line (E), it indicates an evolution of their emotionality from the sensual to the sublime. This indicates someone who develops increasing sensitivity to others in relationships. A sudden curve starting from a straight section of the line (F and G) shows a marked increase in emotional sensitivity and is often linked to the start of a new relationship. Look carefully for any influence lines.

Elemental Widths of the Jupiter Line

Each of the four Elemental widths produces characteristic emotional responses.

Earth Width

The Earth width line describes sluggish emotional responses that are dull and lacking in affection. They are not easily roused, tending to choose a relationship that is plain but secure. They remain faithful to their partner to the end. An example of an Earth width Jupiter line is found in Figure 7.2, page 53.

Water Width

The Water width displays a bright bubbly responsiveness to emotional exchanges. The line indicates someone with a refined sensitivity and whose moods are very changeable. They derive great pleasure from having many friends. They tend to remain very loving and faithful to their partner and children. An example of a Water width Jupiter line is found in Figure 15.6, page 155.

Air Width

The Air width is generally counter-productive to the free expression of emotions. The Air width indicates that emotions would be imagined rather than experienced. As a consequence relationships tend to be idealistic and unaffectionate, typically ending in disappointment. Shared interests and ideals commonly form the basis of attraction for people with an Air width Jupiter line. An example of an Air width Jupiter line is found in Figure 15.5, page 154.

Fire Width

The Fire width displays passion and intensity, especially in sexual expression. A person with a Fire width Jupiter line would be prone to losing their temper if frustrated, and given to extremes of emotional behaviour. They form very strong likes and dislikes. They are seldom loyal to one partner, especially when things become boring and predictable. They enjoy social activities that provide opportunities for new relationships. The excitement of the chase is more important to them than any lasting commitment.

Terminations of the Jupiter Line

The Jupiter line has several possible endings, which encompass various degrees of emotional expression towards others. Each ending is particularly characteristic of the person's emotional behaviour. Referring to Figure 12.8, when the line stops under the Saturn mount at point (A) it shows someone who is emotionally cold and extremely selfish. They have very little appreciation of how others feel and are notably reserved in their emotional expression. This pattern is compounded further when the Jupiter line curves up to the Saturn mount (B). This extra length exhibits a pronounced despondency and pessimism. Such people often take great pleasure in sharing their gloom and apathy with others, quite unaware of the emotional drain

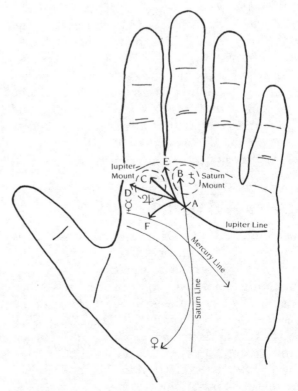

Figure 12.8 Terminations of the Jupiter Line

they cause for those around them. This ending of the Jupiter line is shown in Figure 15.2, page 150.

By contrast, when the Jupiter line extends over to the Jupiter mount (C) it indicates a person who readily shares their feelings with others. When the line is clear and well formed it indicates someone who is very loving, caring and compassionate. They are particularly sensitive to the needs of others. This ending of the Jupiter line is shown by the middle fork in Figure 19.1, page 180. If the Jupiter line is exceptionally long, travelling right across the Jupiter mount (D), then it indicates the opposite extreme of someone who surrenders themselves to the service of others, particularly within charities and religious organizations.

The ending between the middle and index fingers (E) is a blend between these extremes of Saturn and Jupiter respectively; it describes a more moderate balance between restraint and expression. This ending of the Jupiter line is shown by the top fork in Figure 7.2, page 53. When the Jupiter line curves down and touches the Mercury line (F), it indicates someone who is blind in their emotional judgements and frequently unable to understand difficulties arising from their relationships. This ending of the Jupiter line is shown by the lower fork in Figure 7.2.

Markings of the Jupiter Line

See Figure 12.9. Of the various markings afflicting the Jupiter line, the island is possibly the most frequent. The island (A), as well as indicating emotional conflict, can also show weakness of the physical heart. Should the island end in a cross or a star (B) this suggests a heart attack. This illustrates the link between stress, emotional conflict and its effect on the physical heart as reflected in the line. Finding the reasons for this emotional conflict from the hand could suggest ways for overcoming the

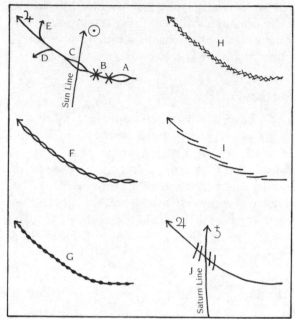

Figure 12.9 Markings and Variations of the Jupiter Line

conflict and thereby avoiding the implications of a heart attack.

One traditional correlation with an island being located as the Jupiter line crosses the Sun line (C), is eyesight difficulties. Since the Sun traditionally rules the eyes (along with the Moon) and the physical heart while the Jupiter line is linked with the circulation, then it suggests that the cause of the eye trouble lies in their blood supply to the eyes.

Influence lines are commonly found leading off the main flow of the Jupiter line and they need to be differentiated as to whether they lead downwards (D) or upwards (E). Lines that flow down from the heart line suggests that their energy is grounded or earthed. Such lines are descriptive of sexual exchange and commonly indicate relationships. The emotional nurturing of a child can similarly be shown. They may also indicate times of work commitments or creative projects that require comparable degrees of emotional involvement.

Energy that flows upwards from the heart line suggests a more idealistic influence. This can range from a platonic relationship to the inspirational influence of a spiritual teaching. Possibly it might indicate the development of a deeper artistic appreciation.

The chained pattern (F), essentially composed of a series of islands, not infrequently affects the Jupiter line. Each island describes a phase in this prolonged emotional conflict. The pattern typically describes someone who starts one relationship that ends through conflict, whereupon they start another that is similarly stricken, and so on, throughout the length of the line. The pattern suggests an ignorance of the factors that cause the conflict, resulting in a series of relationships which repeatedly end in disillusionment. Factors in the hand could, once again, reveal what needs to be understood to change this pattern. An example of a chained Jupiter line is shown in Figure 7.4, page 56.

The dotted pattern seen in (G) produces highly spasmodic emotional expression alternating between intensity and apathy. A single dot can have sufficient intensity to create heart problems.

The criss-cross patten (H) has no clear flow to it and similarly denotes someone who has no constancy of emotional expression. It can indicate hatred of the opposite sex.

Reduplication is often found in the Jupiter line. It is not uncommon to find it forming a series of ladder-like steps up the line (I). The duplication of the line at the overlap may describe conflict, but which is resolved. The ladder-like effect exhibits a prolonged struggle that leads to increasing understanding and subtlety of feelings.

Bar lines generally impede the flow of emotional expression. In particular, when found in the vicinity of the Saturn line (J), they indicate a pronounced fear in sharing feelings with others. This formation is typically linked with disappointments in relationships.

THE SIMIAN LINE

See Figure 12.10. The simian line is such a significant variant from the normal configuration of lines encountered in handreading that needs its own explanation. It is such a pronounced feature that people who have it feel that something is 'odd' about the lines on their hand. A person who has a true simian line instead of having separate Mercury and Jupiter lines, possesses only a single line in their place. A true simian line is quite rare, with approximately one in five hundred having this feature. However, due to it being such an outstanding feature on the palm, people who have it often seek out handreaders to gain an explanation of it, so it may be seen quite frequently.

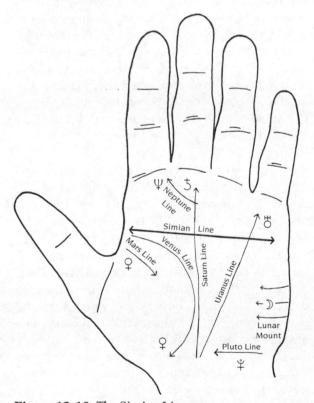

Figure 12.10 The Simian Line

Since the simian line is a fusion of Mercury and Jupiter lines it indicates someone who becomes emotionally involved with whatever they think about, while whatever affects their feelings powerfully colours their mind. With this emotional intensity any difficulty in life tends to get blown out of all proportion. The simian line indicates a person who tends to be very impulsive, lacks patience and finds relationships confusing. Due to this it is quite common to find someone with a simian line, tending to use either their head or their heart. How a person uses their simian line is differentiated by its placing on the palm. A low-set simian line, that largely follows the course of the Mercury line, indicates a person who tends to think at the expense of their feelings. A high-set simian line, that largely follows the course of the Jupiter line, indicates the person who tends to feel rather than use their mental abilities.

With the fusion of Mercurial and Jupiterian energies within the simian line its energy is perceived to flow in both directions. The conflict between head and heart indicated by the line heightens a person's sensitivity shown by the presence of the Neptune and Pluto lines and activation of the Lunar mount, as shown in Figure 12.10.

A true simian line is just one single line without any trace of a Mercury or Jupiter line. It is more common to find a partial simian line with traces of the head and heart lines present. The bearer will still recognize a lot of the characteristics associated with the true simian line. Being unable to discriminate between head and heart is a difficult issue to handle in life. However, the feature can be highly successful in skills that require the precise marriage of feelings and ideas. People with simian lines can be excellent at acting, impersonation, music, film direction and teaching the deaf and dumb to communicate. An example of a simian line is shown in Figure 19.3, page 188.

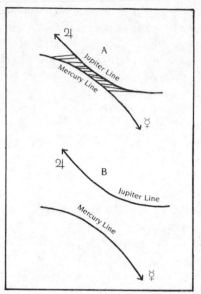

Figure 12.11 The Distance between the Jupiter and Mercury Lines

Refer to Figure 12.11. The principle of the simian line, where head and heart are fused as one, is significant when considering the proximity of both the Jupiter and Mercury lines in hands. The closer these two lines are, the greater the degree of interference between them, as the lines flow in opposite directions. This interference may well be demonstrated by ancillary or influence lines (A) crossing between them. Such lines indicate both emotional upsets generating anxiety and mental worries arousing emotional fears. It is significant that the close proximity of these lines has been linked with hay-fever and asthma. Since Jupiter is the traditional ruler of the lungs, and Mercury is the traditional ruler of the nervous system it is symbolically significant that antagonism between these lines should indicate breathing difficulties. There is a strong physiological link between the speed of respiration and a person's emotional state. Interference between the Jupiter and Mercury lines is shown in Figure 15.4, page 153.

The wider the gap between these lines (B), the more this interference is reduced so indicating a person who is less 'highly strung' and more tolerant. A wide gap between the Jupiter and Mercury lines is shown in Figure 19.1, page 180.

THE SATURN (CAREER OR FATE) LINE (♄)

The Saturn line usually starts at the centre of the palmar base and rises up towards the Saturn mount at the base of the middle finger. As shown in Figure 11.1, page 77, the course of the line reflects the vertical palmar division used in drawing up the quadrants. The Saturn line makes a distinction in consciousness between the outer Solar world and the inner Lunar world – the manifest from the concealed. Saturn is the last Planet in the solar system that can be seen from earth with unaided eyes, thus symbolically it stands on the threshold between the visible and invisible realms. Saturn rules the skin which, while forming a protective barrier around the body, also defines the visible outer aspect of the person from their hidden inner realm.

Under the influence of Saturn the Etheric vital force becomes fixed and solid. The line represents the concentration of will necessary to make ideas, goals and aspirations a reality. This is the very essence of work. The presence of a well-formed line confirms this discipline, enabling the bearer to achieve purpose and success in life. Palmistry equates the line with success, fate, good fortune or even luck. The discipline necessary for creating material order is vital for deriving a livelihood. A person possessing these qualities will usually make a success of their life. In retrospect their particular course in life can be seen as having a definite fate or destiny about it.

Not infrequently the line may be absent indicating the corresponding inability to sustain application, and fickleness of direction. Holding down a job or maintaining a career would be very difficult for such a person and consequently material success is limited.

Saturn Line Keywords

Father, inheritance, concentration, discipline, application, fixity, career, success, security.

Features and Markings in the Saturn Line

Refer to Figure 12.12.

Origins

A Normal beginning – discipline, independence in youth.

B Beginning/Influence from Venus mount – strong family influence over work and career; either through finance or taking over family business, endurance.

C Beginning/Influence from within Venus line – family influence overpowering person's independence.

D Beginning/Influence from Pluto line – emotional rejection, strong influence of opposite sex upon career, healing and transformation skills. See Figure 7.5, page 58.

E Beginning/Influence from Lunar mount – strong use of imagination within career. See Figure 15.2, page 150.

Course

F Well-formed line – successful career, resolute, disciplined, independent. See Figure 15.7, page 157.

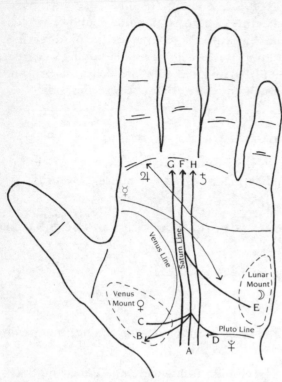

Figure 12.12 Origins and Course of the Saturn Line

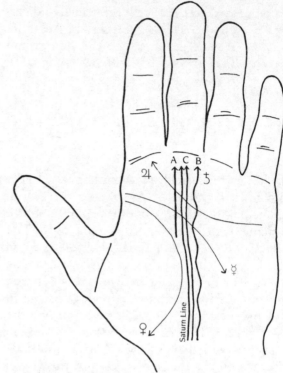

Figure 12.13 Variations of the Saturn Line

G Solar side displacement of line – public employment, communal activities, social prestige and status.

H Lunar side displacement of line – inner vocations, private pursuits, secret work. See Figure 15.2, page 150.

Refer to Figure 12.13.

A Incomplete line – success late in life, time of responsibility.

B Wavy line – fickle, unreliable, inconsistent at work.

C Doubled line – two careers; public and private roles.

Absent line – lacks discipline, unable to hold down job, wanderer.

Refer to Figure 12.14.

A Island – conflict at work; heart not in it/conceals disinterest.

B Break – mental breakdown, redundancy.

C Beginning/influence from Pluto line causing break in line – career/marriage broken through a clandestine affair or prostitution.

D Ending at Mercury line – misjudgement ending career, misfortune.

E Island at start of a wavy Saturn line, inhibiting its flow – illegitimacy, interference with career, inheritance, independence, somnambulism.

F Stress lines from Venus mount – family interfering with career.

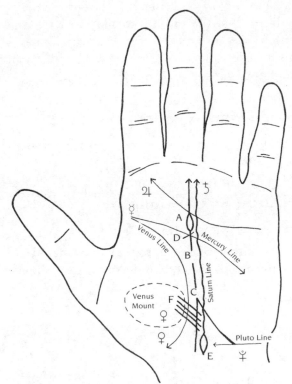

Figure 12.14 Markings and Variations of the Saturn Line

THE SUN (APOLLO) LINE (☉)

The Sun line starts at the centre of the palmar base and rises upwards to the Sun mount at the base of the ring finger, as in Figure 11.1, page 77. This line is sometimes called the Apollo line after the god Apollo, who was the Solar deity of the Roman pantheon.

This line is traditionally associated with fame and fortune. The Solar rulership explains this association, for the presence of the line indicates in a person the ability to draw light and inspiration from their soul through into their work. The line indicates true creative expression, where the artist displays an outstanding brilliance in their work. The brilliance of the work leads to the development of their reputation and the wider recognition of their talents. The success of their work contributes to their personal wealth, hence the general association of fame and fortune.

Someone who contacts their inner light can directly perceive the Light of Creation permeating all things. The artist who is said to have an 'eye' for beauty will be powerfully motivated to reproduce this inner vision in their work. Mythologically Apollo is associated with art and music.

It is noteworthy that the Sun line is seldom found fully developed. However, its partial presence is quite common, in which case it should be considered in conjunction with the Saturn line. The latter describes their work and career while the former indicates the degree of fortune with it.

Sun Line Keywords

Creativity, brilliance, charisma, sense of beauty, artistic sense, refinement, abundant success, fame, fortune.

Features and Markings in the Sun Line

Refer to Figure 12.15.

A Well-formed line – strong creative expression, fame, very successful.

B Wavy line – success/fame waxes and wanes, fickle popularity.

C Incomplete line, starting above Jupiter line – creative ideals but lacks ability to express themselves, hero worship, creativity flows in later life. See Figure 7.5, page 58.

D Island – infamy; private life does not square with public role, obstructed creativity.

Absence of line – lacks creative expression, lacks sense of beauty.

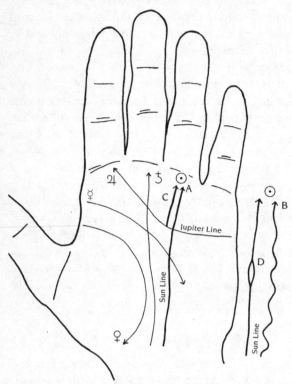

Figure 12.15 Variations of the Sun Line

THE MOON
(INTUITION) LINE (☽)

════

When present the Moon line curves around the mount of Moon, as in Figure 11.1, page 77. The curvature of the line is symbolically connected to the reception of ideas from the realm of spirit. The definite formation of the line describes a well-focused imagination that gives a clear vision of the spiritual world. The line is thus linked to clairvoyance and the development of intuition. It gives the subject an ease of understanding mystical teachings and inner knowledge. It often confers a powerful sense of the deeper motives behind other people's ideas, even before they are spoken. The partially

present or wavy forms of the line usually indicate that the intuitive facility is fickle and unreliable; instead it often causes a nervous disposition. The Moon line is possibly the least common line on the palm.

Moon Line Keywords

Intuition, clairvoyance, mysticism, nervousness, lunacy.

Features of the Moon line

Refer to Figure 12.16.

A   Well-formed line – strong clairvoyant ability, mystical sense, Lunar devotions. See Figure 15.7, page 157.

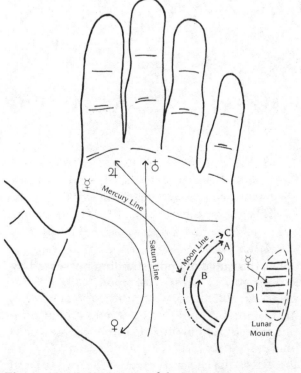

Figure 12.16 Variations of the Moon Line

B Incomplete line – partial development of inner vision.

C Ill-defined line – hypersensitivity, neurotic patterns, inner confusion.

D Striated Lunar mount (absent Moon line) – activation of imagination. Note this energy needs to be accessed via Mercury or Saturn lines to be used productively; otherwise it causes hypersensitivity. See Figure 19.1, page 180.

THE MERCURY (HEAD) LINE (☿)

As shown in Figure 11.1, page 77, the head line makes no consistent connection with any palmar mount so the Etheric energy flowing within it remains uncoloured by any particular Planetary influence. Since Mercury is synonymous with Ether it naturally rules the head line.

The Mercurial energy flowing through the head line is linked to what was formerly called the *Sensus Communis*, or common sense – the unifying factor in which all sensory information is brought together in a common consciousness. When the physical senses are linked to the Four Elements, then touch corresponds to Earth, taste corresponds to Water, smell corresponds to gross Air, hearing corresponds to subtle Air, and sight corresponds to Fire.[22] Ether, their quintessence, corresponds to the *Sensus Communis* which unifies all sensory information.

The length of the Mercury (head) line describes the range of understanding possessed by a person. The word 'understanding' literally means to 'stand under'. Seen metaphorically it describes Ether beneath the Intellectual World receptive to the inspiration from the realm of ideas above. Once the ideas have formed from the substance of the Ether they can be said to be understood. The longer the line, the greater

the flow of Etheric energy within it. This increases their receptivity and understanding. A short line denotes a diminished range of understanding.

The course of the Mercury line traverses the Saturn line, which divides the palm into inner and outer halves. Two sections can now be perceived within the head line. The section on the inner side of the palm can be referred to as the subjective portion, and that on the outer side as the objective portion.

The words subjective and objective when looked at closely share the same word root, from the Latin *jacere* meaning 'to throw'. The throwing here refers to the 'throwing' of ideas through the Air Element of the mind. Communication involves ideas being thrown out to those listening. The inner section of the line is where conception of ideas takes place, before they are 'thrown out' through the outer section of the line. The prefix *sub*, meaning 'below or behind', refers to the area below or behind the throwing. The prefix *ob*, meaning 'to or towards', refers to the throwing towards those who are listening. Thus subjective and objective are different aspects of the same mental process.

Communication is particularly symbolized by Mercury. The word communication needs to be looked at closely for it comes from the Latin *communicare*, meaning 'to make common to many, to share'. The act of making things common refers to the invoking within others the same understanding and so sharing the same 'common sense'.

Speech, being a mode of communication, is connected to the head line, particularly through the Geminian associations of Mercury. Gemini is an Air sign and speech largely consists of air being forced up from the lungs through the larynx. In the larynx the air passes through two vocal cords, analogous to the Gemini glyph (II), which then vibrate, generating the sound of the voice. The sound of the voice is further modified as it passes through the mouth by the tongue and lips. The tongue is traditionally ruled by Mercury. By extension of these ideas, languages are also linked to Mercury and the head line since they are in essence vehicles of communication. The word language comes from the Latin *lingua* meaning 'a tongue'. The head line also describes how a person expresses their ideas in speech.

The orientation of the subjective portion of the Mercury line reveals what interests a person has. Interest contains the Latin word root *ter*, meaning 'Earth', and can literally be translated as 'it matters'. This link with the Earth Element captures symbolically the degree of mental concentration involved in an interest. The mounts and lines which the end of the head line may contact indicate what a person is interested in.

The changeability of Mercury is reflected in the ephemeral nature of ideas, which unless concentrated in the mind, soon evaporate. When the mind is focused, ideas flow like a breath of wind but soon vanish unless sufficient will-power and discipline are applied to make them concrete. The crossing of the Saturn line by the head line provides concentration and discipline to the mind, facilitating the ordering and structuring of ideas. A well-formed Saturn line crossing the head line is a useful asset in subjects such as law and science. However, when negatively expressed, it can lead to a notable lack of free thinking and acceptance of new ideas. Such people become dogmatic in their conservative and orthodox attitudes.

Since Mercury equates with the flow of Etheric energy through the nerves, the head line is also descriptive of the nervous responses in the body. It particularly connects with the somatic nervous system, which is the part under our direct conscious control. An example of a somatic function is the control of our voice. The Mercury line is an important palmar line, since it is through our mental awareness and understanding that things are found out, learnt and evaluated. Thus calculations and decisions are made, goals are formed, and action is planned and co-ordinated. All these processes are vital to individual autonomy. Factors that mar the clear formation of the line detract from this development.

Of all the palmar lines the Mercury line is perhaps the most variable, reflecting the uniqueness of each person's mental make-up. It is correspondingly important to find every nuance possible in the formation of this line to reveal precisely how each person uses their mental abilities and whether they have control over their lives.

Mercury Line Keywords

Common sense, mental abilities, thoughts, ideas, understanding, intellect, interests, decisions, plans, subjectivity/objectivity, communication, speech, languages, nervous system.

Origins of the Mercury Line

See Figure 12.17. When considering the start of the Mercury line its relationship with the Venus line is important. Here two main patterns are found. Firstly, the independent Mercury line (A) which starts about 5 mm above the Venus line and secondly, the connected Mercury line (B) where both lines are fused as one at their beginning.

The independent Mercury line (A), found on about 10 per cent of hands, shows the person's mental abilities coming into their own at a very early age. They are highly independent in their thinking and unrestrained by family and childhood conditioning. They have a very original, individualistic and free-flowing mind. Since they are quick to take initiative, they rapidly gain advantages in many situations. However,

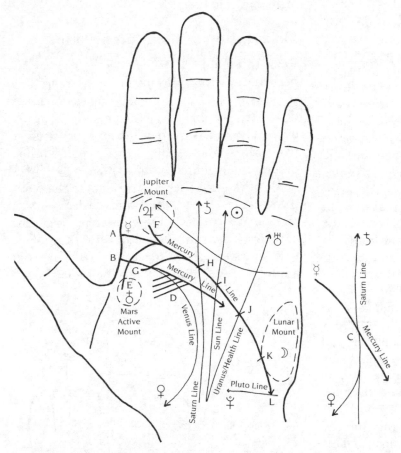

Figure 12.17 Origins of the Mercury Line

their schemes are frequently impractical. This origin of the Mercury line has a reputation of the 'naughty' child whose inquisitive nature is always poking into things, while asking difficult and demanding questions of their parents, seemingly in advance of their years. An example of an independent Mercury line is shown in Figure 15.4, page 153.

The connected Mercury line (B), found on about 85 per cent of palms, describes someone much more restrained in thought. They are slow in waking up to their mental abilities and are particularly cautious in outlook. This type of Mercury line is usually much shorter in length than its independent counterpart. Since the

Mercury line is fused with the Venus line, it shows that the family background, especially the maternal influence, has a powerful impact on the quality and style of thought. Whether this is good or bad is shown by the quality and clarity of the union between these two lines. Generally the Venusian influence makes a person much more practical in their thinking than the independent types. An example of a connected Mercury line is shown in Figure 15.2, page 150.

The point of separation between these lines is important to note, since this is the time when mental independence is gained from the family/mother. When this separation does not occur till near the Saturn line, which often joins in the flow of the Venus line (C), it classically denotes a late starter in life. If the two lines do not have a clear break, this also detracts from mental independence. The latter may be delayed till further clarity emerges in the Mercury line. This is shown in Figure 7.4, page 56. Additional restraint may be shown by stress lines marring the separation of the two lines as shown by (D). In the diagram these stress lines often indicate the family preventing the person from gaining their full independence and the recurrence of dependence/independence issues throughout their life.

Additionally the Mercury line may start from the Mars active and Jupiter mounts, or receive influence lines from these mounts. The line from the Mars active mount (E) reflects an intensity of their thinking. They will form strong opinions on topics, enjoy argument and challenges of wit. If the energy is not channelled well, indicated by a poor quality of line, then it would describe someone who is very irritating and antagonistic in their manner, who is insensitive to others and tactless in whatever they say. Both extremes are noted as 'loud mouths' since they like attracting attention to themselves.

A Mercury line leading from the Jupiter mount (F) can reflect a mind deeply inspired by vision. Such a person has high ideals and is compassionately concerned for others. Negative expression of this influence reflects a person who is arrogant and conceited in their mental attitudes. This may lead to extravagance and ostentation as they display their over-inflated sense of self-importance. This overbearing pride makes them repellent to others.

A Mercury line may start from inside the Venus line (G). It is the beginning of what otherwise would be an independent Mercury line. Here initially the person's independence is severely compromised by the restraints of the family, but once the Mercury line crosses the Venus line the person gains their independence

in no uncertain terms and predictably goes off at a tangent in their life.

Orientation of the Mercury Line

Refer to Figure 12.18. The degree of straightness or curvature present in the Mercury line reveals further distinct mental characteristics. A dead straight line (A) is a powerful feature, especially if it has a Fire width and goes straight to the Mars passive mount. This 'javelin' like line describes someone with a piercingly direct mode of thought that goes straight to the point of an issue. Their speed and decisiveness is awesome to witness as they penetrate the depths of topics. They can become an authority in their field in a very short space of time. They will adroitly argue and defend their very fixed

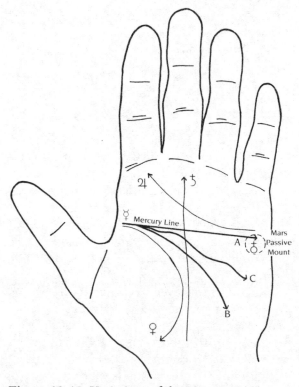

Figure 12.18 Variations of the Mercury Line

opinions. However, one major failing is their difficulty in listening to and accepting other's viewpoints. Consequently they can be severe and lack diplomacy in dealing with others. This negative trait, in conjunction with a short Jupiter line ending at the Saturn line, describes an intensely selfish and avaricious person. A straight Mercury line is shown in Figure 7.5, page 58.

This intensity is markedly softened by a gentle curve to the line (B). The curve indicates someone far more receptive to others' points of view and who can accept them even when directly opposed to their own. Thus it makes a person far more diplomatic and tactful. Though the person will not be as direct as someone with the straight line described above, if their Mercury line is well formed they can convincingly argue and express their points of view. A curved Mercury line is shown in Figure 15.5, page 154.

The opposite extreme is found with a wavy line (C). The meandering course describes someone who is very indecisive and vacillates to the point of inactivity. One day it is yes, the next day no. They are unable to form their own resolutions. They are easily deflected in argument and vulnerable to being swayed by others. Their intentions are easily compromised in relationships, which causes them no end of frustration. A wavy Mercury line is shown in Figure 15.2, page 150.

Elemental Widths of the Mercury Line

The Elemental width of the Mercury line powerfully colours mental performance.

Earth Width

The Earth width Mercury line describes someone whose mental processes are slow and deliberate. They have a remarkable simplicity and clarity, and can accept things without distortion.

Ideas are used very literally – 'a spade is a spade' without any room for abstraction as to what a spade might symbolize. They are very fixed in whatever ideals they uphold. An example of an Earth width Mercury line is found in Figure 7.2, page 53.

Water Width

The Water width Mercury line describes a highly visual, imaginative mind which is very sensitive and impressionable. When the person is inwardly calm they are able to picture things in great detail. Their vision is delicate, for if anything upsets them emotionally it is shattered. Once the ripples start their mind goes to pieces. They do have difficulty in clearly arguing their point of view, especially when directly challenged. Their arguments can easily be swayed and they often end up saying things that they never intended. Their sensitivity, when clear, gives them a ready understanding of psychic and intuitive experience. An example of a Water width Mercury line is found in Figure 15.6, page 155.

Air Width

The Air width Mercury line indicates a philosophical bent, where ideas are expanded and inflated into elaborate and complex theories, schemes and hypotheses. It gives a powerful facility to express and communicate ideas with others, though such people can be long-winded. All aspects of the media interest them. Since they easily become absorbed into their own realm of ideas, they can become quite eccentric and impractical in their daily life. An example of an Air width Mercury line is found in Figure 15.2, page 150.

Fire Width

The Fire width Mercury line describes an intensity and dynamism to mental performance.

There is a marked analytic emphasis, whereby things are taken apart to find out how they work. Those with this width take great pride in reducing a problem to its basic components so that it can be altered. The pragmatic ideas of science have great appeal, while psychic experience is intensely mistrusted. An example of a Fire width Mercury line is found in Figure 7.3, page 53.

Length of the Mercury Line

The course of the Mercury line traverses several lines that can be used as markers to evaluate its lengths.

Refer back to Figure 12.17, page 109. Very rarely a Mercury line is so short that it stops at the Saturn line (at point H). This indicates a very poor range of understanding, limited to objective experience. The Mercury line's failure to cross to the inner subjective side of the palm shows that there is no inner reflection on their ideas. They will have no interests and whatever is communicated lacks any common sense and thus appears quite literally as 'nonsense'. This line is an indication of subnormal mental development.

Once the Mercury line crosses the Saturn line, then increasing degrees of inner reflection unfold. The chronological age at which a person reaches this crossing-point on their Mercury line is significant. It is a time when life is perceived with increased gravity and the search for inner meaning often starts. In most hands this time is typically shown to be sometime between 30 and 35 years of age.

When the Mercury line reaches the Sun line (at point I), this extra length provides a fair degree of inner reflection. However, only one-third of the line is present on the inner subjective side of the palm, which shows there is a tendency to be superficial. The other two-thirds of the line present on the outer objective side of the palm indicates a strong pragmatic sense.

This relatively short Mercury line does enhance a rapid expression of ideas, which is good for people who need to comment spontaneously on situations or promote certain points of view.

The point where the Mercury line crosses the Sun line is also significant. Chronologically this is a time of increasing concern and motivation to find a creative purpose in life. This time is usually shown occurring between 40 and 48 years of age. For those who have previously led their life employed by someone else, this is often when they seek to gain their autonomy and be their own boss. For those that manage to get in touch with their creativity, this can be a time of increased inner fulfilment and self-expression.

When the Mercury line reaches as far as the Uranus line (at point J), this increased degree of inner reflection creates more of a balance between subjective and objective experience. A person has a greater ability to formulate ideas in relation to the material world. This length of the Mercury line is an asset for scientists, economists and philosophers.

The crossing of the Uranus line is again significant. Chronologically this is a time of increased awareness and utilization of intuition, that typically spans the years from 45 to 55. For those that successfully make contact with their intuition, it speaks to them like a voice. Once a person learns to listen to it there is no limit to the knowledge that can be provided.

The extension of the Mercury line as far as the Lunar mount (at point K) indicates a further increase in mental awareness. With this length of the Mercury line the inner subjective part of the mind predominates over objective application. This describes a person who is very introspective. The depth of imagination associated with the mount of Moon is an asset to such people as painters, artists, clairvoyants and diplomats.

When the Mercury line reaches the Pluto line

(L) the extreme degree of subjective development makes a person very withdrawn and
unable to apply themselves to the material
world without considerable determination. This
length of line in a person's hand is sometimes a
direct result of taking drugs like LSD, and experiencing a mind-expanding trip. Their outlook
on life is summed up in the phrase 'far out man'.
An example of such a line is shown in Figure
19.3, page 188. Note that this length of Mercury
line can be present on a hand without the use of
drugs. If the Mercury line extending to the Pluto
line is clear and well formed, it could indicate a
remarkable talent for penetrating the depths of
another person's mind – a skill of immense value
to healers and the caring professions.

Relative Clarity of the Mercury Line

The relative clarity of any line should be
considered in relation to its overall length. Any
section that is marred by markings will detract
from the overall performance of the line.

Refer to Figure 12.19, page 114. If a Mercury
line reaches across the palm as far as the Uranus
line, but its flow is chained on the objective side
of the palm as in (A), this effectively cuts a
person's mental range in half. Additionally this
formation indicates someone who clearly knows
what they want to say, but has great difficulty in
communicating it to others. The feature is
associated with shyness and reticence.

Terminations of the Mercury Line

In addition to the above different lengths of the
Mercury line, it may curve upwards and join the
Jupiter line as in (B), indicating that decisions
and mental clarity are easily compromised by
emotions. If such a person is angry they are
likely to make rash decisions and act hastily. In
the pursuit of love they will sacrifice their
principles to gain affection.

The Mercury line which reaches the Mars
passive mount (C) shows a mind that likes to
seek out hidden knowledge or to find the
deeper motives behind people's actions. They
take great pride in seeking out neglected topics.
It is a useful feature for a researcher or detective. In conjunction with negative features in
the hand this feature can indicate espionage
and blackmail.

There is a rare form of the Mercury line
which apparently fuses with the Saturn line as
in (D) where, as in the simian line, a single line
takes the place of two separate lines. The latter
section of the Mercury line runs down the palm
in the opposite direction to the energy of the
Saturn line. As a consequence the Mercurial
energies are mixed with the dark, heavy re-
strictive energy of Saturn. It is an indication of
chronic depression, where people become trap-
ped in a 'black hole' with no vision of what they
want to do in life. With their motivation depressed such people tend to resign themselves to
their 'fate'. Palmistry has linked the feature to
suicide. This is understandable since such people could very easily decide to give up and take
their life. However, a little reflection on this
feature shows that it does not have to be such
an ominous indication.

Since the Mercury line lacks an inner subjective portion, encouragement to develop their
imagination through some artistic pursuit will
have the effect of 'drawing out' the Mercury
line to the Lunar mount (E). This will help
dissolve the heavy Saturnine influence and
provide an inner perspective on their situation.
Also, since the top section of the Saturn line is
missing, this shows a lack of a clear sense of
direction in their life.

Encouragement to develop work skills to
further a career could provide a much needed
sense of direction and purpose to a person with
this feature and will draw the energy of the
Saturn line towards the Saturn mount (F). In

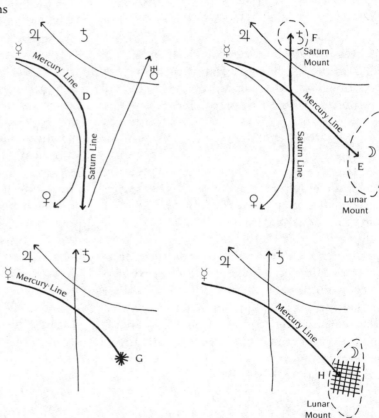

Figure 12.19 Markings and Variations
of the Mercury Line

time such a feature could lead to a person
becoming highly successful.

This feature illustrates the phenomenon of
lineal fusion, where the energies of two normally separate lines are indistinguishable. It
might cause an inexperienced handreader to get
stuck wondering – is it a Saturn line or a Mercury
line? The fusion shows that it functions as both
lines simultaneously. In interpretation both the

lineal rulers can be used to ascribe meaning to
the line.

Forked endings on the Mercury line are
common. There are many possible combinations formed by branches reaching different
areas of the palm described under the different
endings above. A forked ending to the Mercury
line, with one branch leading to the Mars passive
mount and the other to the Lunar mount, on the

hand of a writer could indicate that they write detective stories and espionage thrillers.

The Mercury line ending in a star (G) indicates the sudden termination of a person's life through a fatal head injury or electrocution. The Mercury line ending in a grill on the Lunar mount (H) suggests the clarity of a person's mind dissolving into confusion or lunacy.

THE URANUS (HEALTH) LINE (♅)

Traditionally, in earlier centuries the Uranus line had always been known as the Mercury line or the Health line. But with the comparatively recent discovery of the three outer Planets, and in bringing this knowledge into a contemporary framework, the Planet Uranus is given the modern rulership of this line. When the symbolism of both Planets is applied to the line, it becomes apparent that they are both very relevant.

Refer to Figure 12.1, page 87. The Uranus (health) line flows longitudinally from the centre of the palmar base to the Mercury mount. The Mercury and Uranus lines cross at roughly 90°; their respective flows also symbolically contrast with each other. The Uranus line is located entirely on the inner subjective side of the palm. The line corresponds to a realm of awareness of an entirely subjective nature, in sharp contrast to the Mercury line with its communication to the outside world.

This line is involved with inner projection (L. *pro* = towards + *jacere* = to throw) of ideas over

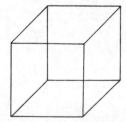

Figure 12.20 The Classic Cubic Optical Illusion

and above those received from without, via the Mercury line. To illustrate this process consider the classic cubic optical illusion shown in Figure 12.20.

As seen by the eye the cube shape is composed of two overlapping squares joined by lines at corresponding corners. It is a two-dimensional outline on the paper. The shape is, however, perceived as a cube in three dimensions. This inner projection of the squares into a shape of a cube can readily be seen by the way it is continually juggled around in the mind's eye.

This mechanism constitutes intuition. Intuition involves the reception of inspiration, knowledge and ideas over and above whatever else their minds are engaged in. Intuition can literally be seen as 'inner tuition', providing the instruction necessary to an understanding of life's experiences, especially personal problems. In this context it is interesting to look at the word 'problem', coming from the Greek *pro* meaning 'before' and *balló* meaning 'to throw'. In other words a problem exists 'before' the necessary ideas for its understanding are 'thrown' into view.

The profound questioning of Uranus pursues the promptings of intuition. In following these lines of inquiry the person is led to new knowledge and technologies. Subsequent innovations bring about radical change. The course of the Uranus line in contacting the base of the Saturn line symbolically shows the flashes of Uranus 'striking' at the 'roots' of Saturn, reflecting the undermining of conventional values that Uranus brings about.

As shown in Figure 11.1, page 77, the 'health' line is traditionally ruled by Mercury through the line contacting the Mercury mount. The health associations come from the Mercurial rulership of Virgo. Virgo is an Earth sign which strongly connects with the body, so the traditional Mercurial rulership of the line strongly connects it with the flow of vital force through the body. The relative harmony or disharmony to this flow corresponds to the state of ease or disease experienced and to our state of health.

Virgo traditionally rules the intestines, the section of the gastro-intestinal tract involved with digestion and absorption of food molecules. Mercury again connects the line to the nervous system, and in particular it reflects the functioning of autonomic nervous system. This controls various bodily functions, like the digestive system, which function automatically without conscious control, reflecting the location of the line on the inner, subconscious side of the palm.

Since the functioning of the digestive system is largely under the control of the autonomic nervous system, the digestive tract can be visualized as symbolically projected onto the health line. See Figure 12.21. The mouth and oesophagus correspond to the upper part of the line (A), above the Jupiter line. The stomach and duodenum correspond to the section of the line between the Jupiter and Mercury lines (B). The rest of the small and the large intestine correspond to the section of line between the Mercury line and the base of the palm (C), the upper two-thirds reflecting the small intestine and the lower third the large intestine. Markings found in these sections can highlight digestive dysfunction within the corresponding areas of the tract.

For example, heartburn can be indicated by heavy striation in section (A) above the Jupiter line. Gastric or duodenal ulcers can be indicated by the line being deeply marked between the Jupiter and Mercury lines in section (B). Inflammation in the small and large intestine can be indicated below the Mercury line (C), in the upper two-thirds and the lower third respectively, by the line being deeply marked. A generally striated appearance to the whole line often evidences what is now commonly described as irritable bowel syndrome.

Other diseases that have been identified reflected in the health line include; asthma, hay-fever, rheumatism, poor memory, bilious upsets and nervous disorders.

The line is also linked with the expression of sexual energy through Mercury being linked to the vital force. In the act of making love the exchange of vital force forms the basis of the experience, and after conception it is the source of the Four Elements that differentiate as the tissues of the newly formed embryo.

From all these apparently divergent associations of the line, links can be appreciated between the use of intuition, nervous tension, sexual expression and physical health. A good clear line generally indicates a positive use of intuition, nervous harmony, ease of sexual expression and sound health. By contrast when the

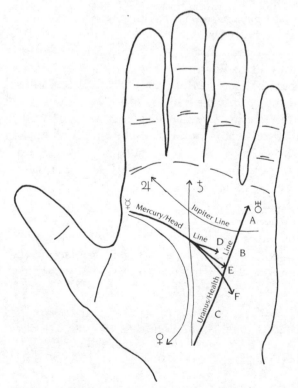

Figure 12.21 Variations of the Uranus Line

line is fragmented and poorly formed it indicates hypersensitivity, sexual anxieties, neurotic patterns and nervous upsets to the body, especially to the digestive system.

Mercury is traditionally linked with commerce, and with its traditional associations with this line on the hand, a well-formed line is an indication of success in business. Commerce depends on a mutual sense of value between the seller and the buyer, without which no exchange can take place. The role of communication in business is to share this sense of value. The exchange of money after goods and services have been provided is referred to as the 'cash flow' – a Mercurial metaphor and the life blood of any business.

This connection with the well-formed line and success in business would stem from the line's further link with intuition. Many who become successful in business do so through following their intuition – usually referred to as 'hunches' or 'instincts'. It is the intuition that provides the ideas to sell various commodities, facilitating links with clients and forging deals with them, while promoting when and where to invest and when to realize assets. Fitting confirmation of this Mercurial association with commerce is shown by caducei being found on the doors of the Bank of England. The caduceus is the wand bearing two intertwining snakes that the god Mercury carries in his left hand. The caduceus symbolizes the Hermetic knowledge that Mercury brings.

Thus the 'health' line is meaningfully interpreted by the symbolism of both Mercury and Uranus.

In assessing how a person uses their intuition it is important to note the relationship of the Uranus (health) line with Mercury (head) line shown in Figure 12.21. Where the Mercury line ends before reaching the Uranus line (D), it indicates difficulty in communicating intuition. Where the Mercury line ends on the Uranus line

(E), it indicates a very restless and fickle mind. Where the Mercury line ends beyond the Uranus line (F) it indicates a strong use and communication of intuition.

Uranus Line Keywords

Inner projection, intuition, health, autonomic nervous system, digestion, innovation, invention, business sense, commerce.

Features of the Uranus Line

Refer to Figure 12.22.

A   Well-formed line – good health, strong intuition, success in business. See Figure 15.1, page 149.

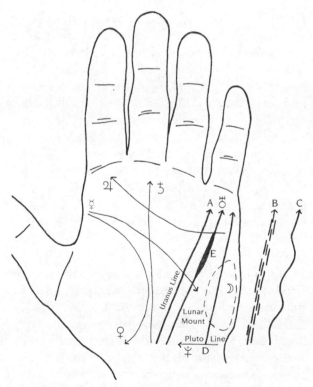

Figure 12.22 Markings and Variations of the Uranus Line

B Striated line – extreme nervousness, fickle intuition, weak digestion. See Figure 7.4, page 53.

C Wavy line – bilious upsets, indigestion, rape trauma.

Absent line – good health, quick mind free from nervousness.

D Course of line runs from Pluto line through Lunar mount – extremely nervous disposition.

E Fire width marking indicating gastric ulcer.

THE NEPTUNE (GIRDLE OF VENUS) LINE (♆)

In the hand Neptune can be very meaningfully used to interpret what is known by palmists as the 'girdle of Venus', shown in Figure 12.23. The course of the Neptune line runs parallel to the Jupiter line. This juxtaposition of the Neptune line above the Jupiter line is symbolically significant, especially if you compare their respective glyphs, (♆) and (♃). Both Planetary glyphs are essentially composed of the Crescent of spirit and the Cross of matter. For Jupiter the Crescent is directly joined to the Cross of matter, bringing the spirit down into the material world. For Neptune the Crescent is separate but linked by a vertical extension of the Cross of matter.

Though the Cross of matter in both glyphs is firmly located in the Elemental World, in the Jupiter glyph the Crescent is located in the Celestial World whereas in the Neptune glyph the Crescent is located in the Intellectual World. The Jupiter glyph shows that the spirit is expressed through the heart whereas the separation of the Crescent and the Cross in the Neptune glyph shows that the spirit is expressed

through the mind. The experience of Neptune can manifest powerful visions but without emotional expression.

Since the emotions provide a link between the mind and body, Neptunian experiences frequently involve detachment of the mind from the body. For the mystic, Neptune describes the sense of their body dissolving away, whereby their consciousness is able to become one with the spiritual world. For the patient, Neptune describes how their anaesthetized body can be operated upon by the surgeon without them being aware of any pain. It is this dual level of Neptunian experience that produces its amphoteric nature: on the one hand vision from the spiritual world, on the other profound insights into how matter is composed.

The importance of the Jupiter line flowing

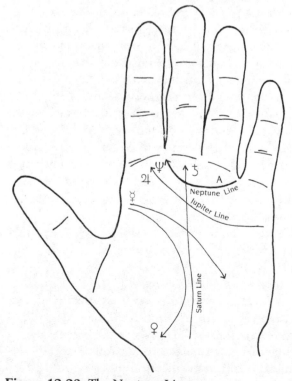

Figure 12.23 The Neptune Line

parallel to the Neptune line is that it provides the emotional link to make the visions and perceptions of Neptune a material reality. Without Jupiter's stabilizing influence, the visions of Neptune cannot be applied, and lead to deception and confusion.

In inner development it is important to resolve emotional blocks and conflicts and to learn compassion before becoming receptive to the spiritual world. Otherwise the experience is likely to lead to the dissociation of mind from body. This is precisely what happens when people become addicted to drugs, causing premature spiritual development before the time is ripe emotionally. Their minds become 'spaced out' making it very difficult for them to handle their material responsibilities in the world. In this vulnerable emotional state addicts often become preyed upon by negative forces in the spiritual world, leading to schizophrenic behaviour or even psychotic breakdown.

With the emotional stability shown by a clear Jupiter line the Neptune line can provide the sublime clarity and illumination of a spiritual vision. Without the emotional clarity indicated by a clear a Jupiter line the Neptune line would be linked to the terror, confusion and deception associated with hallucination.

The presence of the Neptune line usually indicates considerable psychic sensitivity. The bearer is usually very receptive to atmospheres in places, and impressions from people's auras often have a strong visual impact upon them. When the line is well formed it indicates a profound metaphysical awareness in life.

In relation to the emotional expression of the Jupiter line, the Neptune line is strongly connected to a person's emotional ideals and wishes. When markings in the heart line describe conflict and blockage within their emotional life, the presence of a clear Neptune line above it indicates that the person sublimates their thwarted emotional energy and projects it

into this idealistic realm. When relationships cease to work well, people often dream about how it could be, 'if only . . .', hiding in fantasy rather than confronting their emotional disappointments. As a consequence of this dreaming, the Neptune line is often highly charged with the emotional projections of the 'ideal partner' in their life. When the person senses the amorous affections of someone who is attracted to them, who corresponds to their ideals, they will rapidly fall in love. This rings true with the line's palmistic name 'girdle of Venus' with a reputation for denoting someone who repeatedly falls in love or who becomes passionately involved in relationships.

But unless the blockages reflected in the heart line are resolved and the concomitant emotional difficulties overcome, such relationships soon end in confusion and bitter disappointment. Once the ideals fade the partner is seen for who they are. The clear development of the Jupiter and Neptune lines indicates that both areas are working in tandem, and offers the potential of a harmonious emotional exchange and profound spiritual rapport within relationships.

The Neptune line also crosses the Saturn line. Like the head line this division is significant, for it reveals whether the awareness of Neptune applies to inner and/or outer realms. The presence of the line on the inner, Lunar side of the palm indicates an awareness of one's emotional state. The presence of the line on the outer, Solar side provides insights into the material world. When both halves are unified the line describes an awareness of the spiritual world within co-existing with the material world around us.

There is a possibility that the name 'girdle of Venus' alludes to the girdle of Mary. According to a Church legend of the Assumption, when the Virgin Mary came to the end of her mortal life she was carried to heaven by angels. When

St Thomas was informed of this miracle taking place he doubted it. He rushed to witness the spectacle just at the moment she was disappearing into the clouds. Mary saw him doubting the event and dropped her girdle for him to see.[23] The girdle is a symbol of the ability to distinguish between the spiritual and material worlds. The placing of the 'girdle of Venus' on the hand between the Intellectual World of the fingers and the Elemental World of the palm is very interesting to contemplate in the light of this legend.

Neptune Line Keywords

Imagination, vision, romantic wishes, dreams, ideals, sensitivity, hallucination, dissociation, deception, confusion.

Features of the Neptune Line

Refer to Figure 12.23.

A Well-formed Neptune and Jupiter lines – strong spiritual awareness, visionary, metaphysical sensitivity, high romantic ideals.

Refer to Figure 12.24.

A Incomplete Neptune line – sensitivity developing in later life, time of greater emotional fulfilment. See also Figure 7.3, page 53.

B Reduplication – radical change of emotional life, becoming a monk or nun, devotional ideal.

C Well-formed Neptune line and poor Jupiter line – projection of romantic wishes, relationship disappointments, deception, renunciation. See also Figure 7.5, page 58.

D Well-formed line and origin on Mercury mount – erotic fantasy, lasciviousness, deception.

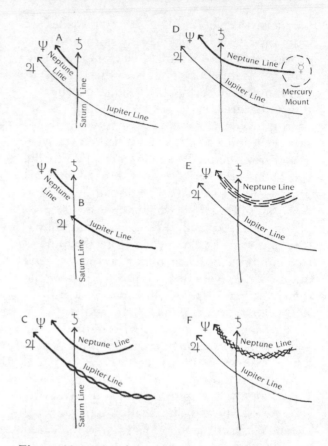

Figure 12.24 Markings and Variations of the Neptune Line

E Striated line – heightened sensitivity, desire to be released from body, prone to addiction to drugs or alcohol, dissociation.

F Criss-crossed line – impact of drugs, hallucinations, dissociation, inner confusion. See also Figure 19.3, page 188.

THE PLUTO (VIA LASCIVIA) LINE (♇)

The palmar line corresponding to Pluto is clearly the Via Lascivia shown in Figure 12.25. The name *Via Lascivia* is Latin for the 'Line of person's hand will be descriptive of how well this energy is expressed.

If a strong Pluto line shows no obvious sign of release or expression through the Uranus line, then it suggests sexual energy becoming pent up within the person. This is where the more omin-ous and degenerate interpretations found in palmistry books comes into play. This build-up of sexual energy colours the mind with erotic desires which, in conjunction with a weak will-power (see Chapter 14 on the thumb), leads people to sexual indulgence. It is this prone-ness to sensuality and vulnerability to intoxifica-tion through alcohol and drugs that has led to the line's association with drunkenness and debauchery. This reputation has been noted to

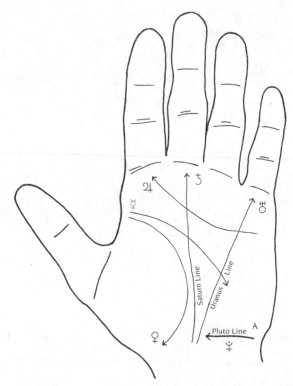

Figure 12.25 The Pluto Line

Lustfulness'. Is it located at the base of the Water quadrant, on the inner subjective side of the palm. It courses from the percussion side of the palm to the Saturn line. The line's location in the Water quadrant suggests it is linked with the expression of emotional energy through the body. When the Pluto glyph is recalled with the 'Lunar' Crescent placed on the Cross of matter, then the presence of the Pluto line below the Lunar mount is also seen to be symbolically appropriate.

As the palmistic name suggests, the line is strongly associated with the sexual energy. Though not always present on the palm, its presence denotes a strong libido. How well this energy is used or expressed depends on the individual. Since the Uranus line is linked with the expression and communication of sexual energy, then the link between these lines in a

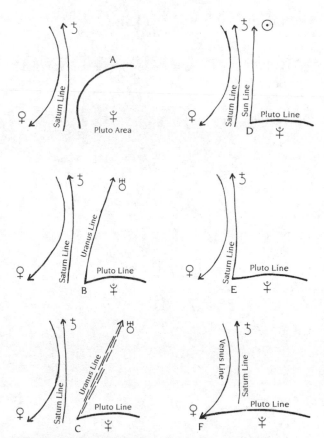

Figure 12.26 Variations of the Pluto Line

be even more sinister in the presence of a strong Neptune line.

However, it needs to be remembered that sexual energy is the powerhouse of the body and when purified and sublimated it rapidly promotes inner growth. When the tendency to self-indulgence is overcome, considerable will-power is freed to heal and transform emotional blocks from the past. Sexual energy can be expressed violently or peacefully.

Pluto Line Keywords

Sexuality, libido, eroticism, physiological sensitivity, allergy, healing, emotional release and transformation, secrecy, debauchery, intoxication.

Features of the Pluto Line

Refer to Figure 12.25.

A Well-formed line – strong libido and sexual motivation.

Refer to Figure 12.26.

A Curved line cutting off Pluto area – repression of sexual energy, celibacy, allergies.

B Contacting Uranus line – strong sexual expression.

C Contacting poor quality Uranus line – neurotic energy from frustrated sexual expression.

D Contacting Sun line – heavy financial losses, obsessive gambling, infamy.

E Contacting Saturn line – career/marriage undermined by prostitution, scandal, blackmail or drunkenness.

F Contacting Venus line – obsessive sexual indulgence, nymphomania, gynaecological problems.

CHAPTER 13

The Fingers

THE fingers describe how a person derives knowledge from the Intellectual World.

THE INTELLECTUAL WORLD AND THE FINGERS

At the outset it is important to clarify and describe what is meant by the Intellectual World, since the term is likely to invoke the inappropriate idea of academic life at a university. To the Hermetic vision the Intellectual World is synonymous with heaven, the source of all knowledge; so implying that a person can only gain knowledge in so far as their hearts are open and receptive to the inspiration from the heavens.

From Fludd's illustration of The Three Worlds (Figure 2.2, page 9), the Intellectual World can be seen as ruled over by the Angels and Archangels. Between the Celestial and Intellectual Worlds is found the name 'Caelum stellatum' or the 'stars in the heavens', which referred to the constellation patterns that were originally seen to constitute the Zodiacal signs.[24] In contrast to the contemporary dry and static astronomical conceptions, the light from the stars was seen to mediate the different types of Intelligences (the angels) from the Intellectual World. Thus the stellar patterns were regarded as 'living beings' of light. The word Zodiac comes from the Greek *kylos zodiakos* meaning 'circle of animals', again reflecting that the star patterns were seen as 'living beings' rather than inanimate objects.

These conceptions are poetically illustrated by Lorenzo's dialogue with Jessica in Shakespeare's *The Merchant of Venice*:

. . . Look how the floor of heaven

Is thick inlaid with patines of bright gold;

There's not the smallest orb which thou beholds't

But in his motion like an angel sings,

Still quiring to the young-eyed cherubins;

Such harmony is in immortal souls;

But whilst this muddy vesture of decay

Doth grossly close it in, we cannot hear it.[25]

With the Intellectual World symbolically connected to the fingers, the Christian prayer position can be see as particularly significant. For as the supplicant prays for knowledge, guidance, inspiration and illumination their hands are clasped together in front of the heart with the fingers pointing upwards to the heavens – the source of knowledge.

In accordance with the connection of the Intellectual World with the fingers, the twelve signs of the Zodiac are used to interpret them. One sign is allocated to each of the twelve phalanges.

The Etheric vital energy within the lines flows upwards from the palm into the fingers, as shown by the palmistic names, Jupiter, Saturn, Sun and Mercury for the index, middle, ring and little fingers respectively. Figure 13.1 shows each finger receiving energy from the corresponding palmar lines; the index finger receives energy from the Jupiter line, the middle finger (medicus) from the Saturn line, the ring finger (annularis) from the Sun line and the little finger (auricularis) from the Uranus/health line. It is a reflection of the decline of cheiromantical

knowledge that the Planets have come to be associated with the fingers rather than the palmar lines, for as has been explained in preceding chapters, the Planets are correctly used to describe the energy in palmar lines, while the Zodiacal signs are used to ascribe significance to the fingers. This explains the inconsistency within palmistry of the number of Planets to the number of fingers.

ZODIACAL SYMBOLISM AND THE FINGERS

The signs of the Zodiac are composite symbols abstracted from the cosmology of the Five Elements. For as already explained in Chapter 3, the Four Elements evolve from the fifth Element, Ether. Since Ether is also synonymous with the principle of Mercury, which embodies the Three World view in its symbolism, each of the Four Elements are visualized as manifesting on each level of the Three World view. From this emerges a cross-ply of symbols, where each Element possesses a cardinal, a mutable and a fixed form in relation to the Intellectual, Celestial and Elemental Worlds respectively (see Figure 13.2).

For the Earth Element, its cardinal sign is Capricorn, its mutable sign is Virgo and its fixed sign is Taurus.

For the Water Element, its cardinal sign is Cancer, its mutable sign is Pisces and its fixed sign is Scorpio.

For the Air Element, its cardinal sign is Libra, its mutable sign is Gemini and its fixed sign is Aquarius.

For the Fire Element, its cardinal sign is Aries, its mutable sign is Sagittarius and its fixed sign is Leo.

This pattern of the Zodiacal signs has come to

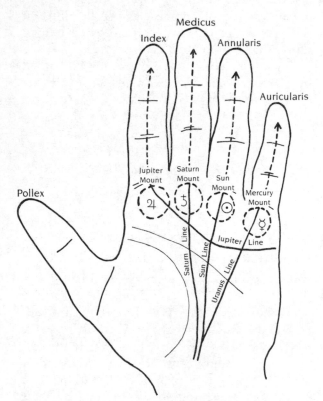

Figure 13.1 The Relationship between the Lines and the Fingers

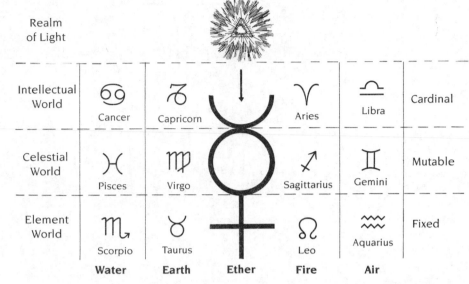

Figure 13.2
The Zodiacal Signs and
the Three Worlds

Realm of Light					
Intellectual World	Cancer	Capricorn	Aries	Libra	Cardinal
Celestial World	Pisces	Virgo	Sagittarius	Gemini	Mutable
Element World	Scorpio	Taurus	Leo	Aquarius	Fixed
	Water	**Earth**	**Ether**	**Fire**	**Air**

be projected onto the constellations in the heavens, with the more familiar sequence of: Aries, Taurus, Gemini, Cancer, Leo, Virgo, Libra, Scorpio, Sagittarius, Capricorn, Aquarius and Pisces. The Zodiacal symbolism enabled the Hermetic philosophers to understand the nature of the influence or knowledge from each of the constellation patterns or *stellata*.

When equated with the Mercury glyph as in Figure 13.2 then it becomes apparent that the cardinal signs, with their link to the Intellectual World, are connected to the formation of ideas, development of goals, ideals, aspirations and the initiation of new projects.

The mutable signs with their link to the Celestial World are involved with translating ideas into action. This is the realm where will-power is applied to make ideas manifest. The extent of their manifestation lies in direct proportion to the amount of will-power directed into them. This realm of mutability encompasses a range of response from intense resolution to total passivity.

The fixed signs with their link to the Ele-

mental world are involved with the grounding and concretion of ideas. This is the realm for understanding the material world. Once compounded, these ideas remain fixed or materialized and endure for long periods of time.

THE ZODIACAL RULERSHIP OF THE PHALANGES

The palmar lines that channel their energies into the fingers colour the Etheric energy flowing through the fingers. As shown by Figure 13.1, the Sun line directs Fiery energy into the ring finger, and the Saturn line directs Earthy energy into the middle finger. The Uranus line, through the Mercury mount, directs Airy energy into the little finger, while the Jupiter line directs Watery energy into the index finger. When the three phalanges along the length of each finger are connected to each of the Three Worlds, the signs of the Zodiac are easily transposed to the phalanges, as in Figure 13.3.

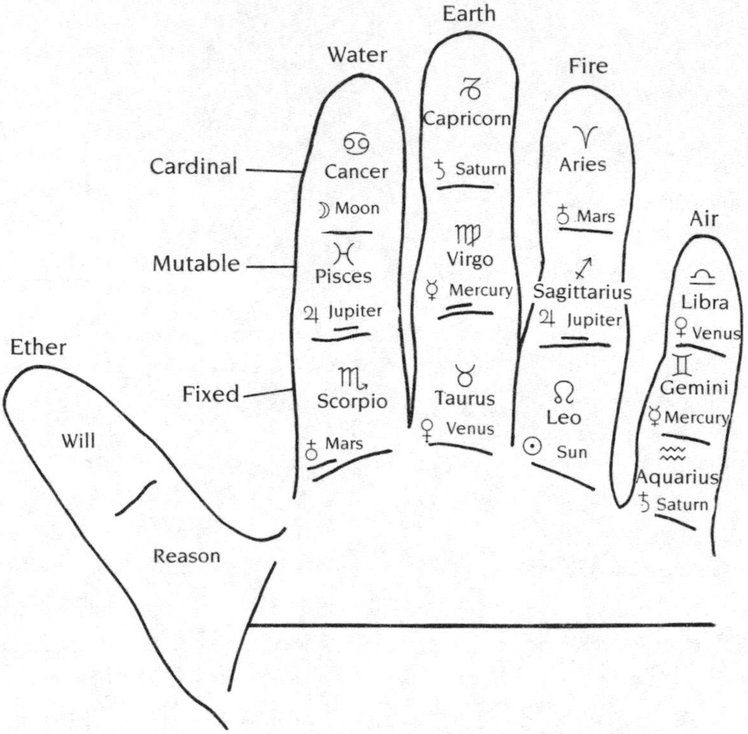

Figure 13.3 The Zodiacal Signs and the Phalanges

Accordingly the cardinal signs align with the top phalanges, the mutable signs with the middle phalanges and the fixed signs with the bottom phalanges.

The top phalanges correspond to the formation of ideas, goals, ideals, wishes and aspirations; the visual part of the mind that generates images allowing understanding to occur.

The middle phalanges correspond to actions, disciplines, skills; the part of the mind linked to the application of ideas, such as ordering, structuring, developing concepts and strategies, together with their dissemination.

The bottom phalanges correspond to the consolidation of ideas, manifested energy, knowledge of materials and sensory experience.

Energy flowing along the length of a finger connects all three phalangeal levels within it. For example, architecture is symbolically described by the Earth or Saturn finger. The top phalanx relates to the conception and design of the building; the middle phalanx relates to the drafting of the design, the administration and the planning permission, and the skills of the builder; and the bottom phalanx relates to the completed building and its materials.

THE ASSESSMENT OF INDIVIDUAL FINGERS

After describing the individual phalanges within a finger, the finger as a whole will then be explained. The energy flowing through each finger is described by both Planetary and Elemental symbolism. In order to avoid confusion each finger will now be called by its traditional name (shown in Figure 13.1) to explain the various associations.

THE INDEX OR FIRST FINGER

Top Phalanx – Cancer (♋)
Ruler: The Moon (☽)

As shown in Figure 13.3, each Zodiacal sign is ruled by a Planet – as you study the functions of each phalangeal section, try to perceive the symbolism of the Planet working within it. The positive or negative expression of each phalanx is assessed from its overall shape, development and markings. The assessment of phalanges will be explained a little later.

The top Cancerian phalanx very strongly connects with the imaginative, visual part of the mind essential to the clear function of intuition. The clear formation of this phalanx enhances the development of a strong intuition. Accordingly the phalanx naturally embraces the religious and spiritual ideals, goals and aspirations of the person. In the absence of higher ideals, it describes the personal goals, beliefs and values upheld. The phalanx does have a link through its Lunar rulership to the maternal bond. Cancer rules the breasts and the Moon is linked to milk, which specifically correlates to the emotional nurturing of the child established through breast-feeding. This is in contrast to the Venusian aspect of motherhood established through the womb (see section on the Venus line, page 88). The symbolism shows the link between the maternal bond and the development of intuition and personal values.

When positively expressed the phalanx reflects a person who has high ideals, strong personal goals and a confident self-image. They are generous and caring for the immediate needs and wants of those around them. They are patient and resourceful in holding a family together. They understand well the value of forgiveness in dissolving emotional blocks. They are deeply sensitive to the needs of others and compassionate towards the suffering of humanity. When the visual part of the mind is clear and reflective it confers the inner vision of a clairvoyant or the communication of a medium.

Negatively used the phalanx reflects a person with confused ideals, poor self-image and a lack of confidence. Here their sensitivity leads to neurotic and irritable behaviour, making them especially concerned about what others think of them. Their imagination generates many phobias that limit and restrict their lives. They hide in their own shell stoically defending their own selfishness. Their closed-minded behaviour leads to snobbery, making them quite oblivious to all concerns but their own. Their inner stagnation leads to religious apostasy or sectarian fanaticism.

Middle Phalanx – Pisces (♓)
Ruler: Jupiter (♃)

The middle phalanx is involved with engaging ideals from the Cancer phalanx in relation to others. It is the area of managerial abilities, of being able to handle relationships of all kinds and command respect. The Water associations of the finger suggest that learning to serve others is the best way to gain their respect and co-operation. Business sense is strongly linked here, since success in business involves listening to one's intuition to know when to buy, sell, invest or realize commodities and assets. Similarly, the success of an organization lies in internal co-operation and service to the customer.

Positive expression of this phalanx describes someone who is successful in business through acumen, the generation of goodwill and the inspiration of confidence. Their open-hearted approach allows them to be creative, innovative and diplomatic, with displays of largess. Their motivation stems from strong spiritual values. Their relationships become immensely pleasurable and naturally fulfilling.

Conversely negative expression leads to a person's failure in business through selfishness and an inability to understand the needs of others. They seek to control situations by imposing their will over others, which in the long run generates ill will. Their relationships are fraught and lack tactfulness. Many, with their potentials locked up within, tend to overindulge in food and drink in the search for happiness, while others try to drown their sorrows in alcohol. They often become quite paranoid about others seemingly conspiring against them.

Bottom Phalanx – Scorpio (♏)

Ruler: Mars (♂)

This phalanx is concerned with emotional power in relation to the material world and is, in turn, linked to social status and investment. Since the bottom phalanx is the manifestation of the two above it, it shows the substantiation of self-worth. There are strong links here to status seeking, with expensive houses, flashy cars and glamorous partners to show off their power and influence. Keen attraction to the pleasures of food, drink and sex are shown in this phalanx.

When the energies are well directed through this phalanx, it reflects a person who seeks to build up relationships over a long period of time, investing large amounts of emotional energy within them through patience and loyalty. They are naturally drawn to healing, giving patients the power to handle and overcome their illness.

The ill-directed phalanx reflects a person who is powerfully egotistical and who, blinded by ambition, seeks to use friends for personal gain. These people seductively lead others into situations in which they can impose their will through blackmail. Intense enmities are generated in this way. In relationships they are very destructive and draw immense emotional energy from their partners, like a vampire sucking the life blood out of its victim. Perverse sexual practices are also not uncommon here.

Assessment of the Index Finger

The index finger receives its energy from the Jupiter line; additionally, Jupiter rules the sign of Pisces, which is associated with the middle phalanx, while it is exalted in the sign of Cancer, associated with the top phalanx. This very strong Jovial association is particularly illustrated by the Papal Seal, the ring worn by the Pope when officiating in Vatican ceremonies. Jupiter is symbolically linked to priests, sages and teachers – those who draw the spirit down from the Intellectual World and thus commune between heaven and earth. In medieval astrology Jupiter was used to describe Jesus, while the fish (Pisces) is a symbol of early Christianity.[26] The significance of the Papal Seal is highlighted when the Pope, after saying the benediction, performs the sign of the Cross. Appropriately the seal is called the 'Ring of Fishes'.

Confidence has a particularly important link with this finger. Fidius was a surname of the Roman god Jupiter – the 'god of faith and truth', while the word confidence comes from the Latin con + fidere, literally meaning 'with faith'. When a person draws down their intuition (Cancer phalanx) they have faith in themselves and become confident to handle whatever situation confronts them.

The word index is Latin for the 'one who points out, a discloser, a discoverer, an informer, a witness'. The index finger is used to point out one's intentions, while in gesture to indicate one's own authority, we use our index finger to point to our heart (Note Jupiter rules the heart line). Other meanings of index describe the process of intuition, for that is how knowledge is discovered or disclosed.

Rings on the Index Finger

Rings generally have the effect of augmenting the vital energy flowing through the finger. The metal of the ring enhances its conduction, so amplifying the energy present in the finger. The placing of a ring on a particular digit usually indicates the need to boost or strengthen the corresponding psychological qualities. A ring on the index finger commonly indicates a lack of confidence and a weak self-image.

Relative Length

The relative length of the index finger shown in Figure 13.4 (A) also describes of the degree of confidence someone possesses. A long finger (A1) implies a very confident person, who is self assured and easily able to assert themselves. A short finger (A3) is the opposite, someone particularly lacking in confidence, with a poor self-image who consequently has great difficulty in asserting themselves.

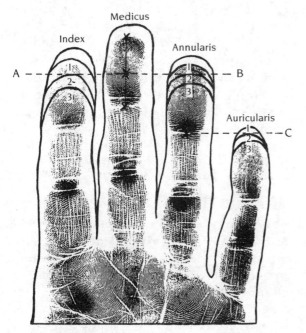

Figure 13.4 Measuring the Length of Fingers

When considering the relative lengths of fingers it is best to compare finger length from the imprint rather than the outline, as shown in Figure 13.4. To assess the relative length of the index finger, divide the top phalanx of the medicus (middle) finger into half as shown in the diagram. Extend a horizontal line out from this point across to the index finger. This point (A2) provides the standard measure of length of an index finger for comparison. If the length of the index finger exceeds this midpoint (A2), it is considered a long finger (A1). If the finger fails to reach the midpoint it is considered to be a short finger (A3). The handprint used in this diagram is an example of a long index finger.

It is important to observe the quality of energy flowing through the digit in relation to its length. For example a particularly long index finger would usually imply a strong self-confidence. However, if the energy is blocked from flowing along the finger (see section on markings, page 137), this would detract from it. Over-confidence would be the result; someone who believes they are confident and who often appears so to others, but who lacks the inner resources to be confident and consequently collapses under pressure.

THE MEDICUS OR MIDDLE FINGER

Top Phalanx – Capricorn ($\zh$)

Ruler: Saturn ($\hbar$)

The top phalanx is involved with the structuring of ideas and understanding the principles of manifestation. The structuring of ideas can manifest in philosophy, logic, the principles of science – especially physics and chemistry – and in law and history. Those interested in communicating their ideas are often found teaching and lecturing in educational institutions.

When the energies of this phalanx are positively used it often reflects a person with a highly calculating mind that very prudently judges when to initiate action. They well understand the need for sacrifice to achieve their goals. They are trustworthy and loyal, and you know exactly where you stand with them. They are naturally good organizers and executives, while their perseverance leads them to high pinnacles of achievement. They value ideas and techniques tested through time. Their immense resources make them very aware of other people's needs. Through concentration and inner discipline they can develop a deep spiritual understanding.

If the phalanx is negatively used an inability to organize their lives makes them selfish and miserly. They demand attention and affection from others in a very dictatorial way. They can be unsympathetic and very patronizing in their criticism of others. Scepticism makes their minds very arrogant. Their inner emptiness makes them insatiable in their ambitions, worshipping position and prestige. Given the opportunity they will selfishly exploit others to try and achieve their goals. Fear limits their range of free thinking, which makes them very conventional in their attitudes, with a slavish adherence to dogma. They are intensely conservative in accepting new ideas, resisting change at all cost.

Middle Phalanx – Virgo (♍)

Ruler: Mercury (☿)

This phalanx is involved with the manifestation of ideas – putting them into action, with a strong sense of timing, order and routine. The energies found here are administrative – in the widest sense of the term. This phalanx translates ideas from the Capricorn phalanx above into service to others.

Positive expression of the phalanx makes a person very helpful, dependable and unselfish in their service to others. They are clear and sharp-eyed, particularly in attention to detail and as a consequence precise and meticulous in their actions. They constantly seek to refine and develop their skills. This analytical mode makes a good researcher or a natural scientist who becomes absorbed in the minutiae of their studies. They are usually calm, unassuming and self-reliant as they go about their duties. They have an innate ability to judge when to harvest the fruits of their actions.

Negative expression of the phalanx makes a person very manipulative and underhanded in dealing with others. They are overly critical, constantly seeking fault in others and blaming them for their own ineptitude. As a consequence they are commonly highly dependent on others to get things done. A lack of decision and discrimination makes them prone to anxiety and worry. They amplify the smallest of problems out of all proportion. The resultant confusion commonly leads to them forgetting where things are. Secrecy enshrouds their highly nervous behaviour, which is often concealed by a veneer of superficiality.

Bottom Phalanx – Taurus (♉)

Ruler: Venus (♀)

The bottom phalanx is strongly connected with the practical activities of Earth; agriculture, horticulture, growing, building, engineering, carpentry, masonry, sculpture, crafts, cooking, pottery, weaving. Material possessions are linked here: houses, land, antiques and jewellery. The phalanx is closely linked to investment in these things as a means of acquiring and conserving wealth while generating security. Investment here is long-term, not the speculative kind, which is associated with the Leo phalanx. The Venusian rulership of the sign confers a strong feeling for the earth, whether it is the 'green-fingered' gardener, the subtlety of a good cook or the sense of taste and refinement in the acquisition of material objects.

The positive utilization of the phalanx makes a person steadfast and loyal, while intensely sensitive to the material needs of others. They are affectionate and generous in sharing their wealth. If they lack money they will provide material support in other ways. They have a strong sensual appreciation of beauty. Their actions are generally productive, fertile and nurturing, providing much-needed security and stability to others.

The negative expression of this phalanx makes a person stubborn without just reason and particularly determined to get their own way. Their feelings can become blocked, making them hard, aloof and insensitive to the needs of others. Alternatively they may become overly emotional, especially if worried about their financial security. They are prone to being greedy and are easily drawn to overindulgence, especially in sexual passions. In relation to others they become rigid and stingy, seeking only material rewards for their actions – 'What's in it for me?'

Assessment of the Medicus Finger

The middle or medicus finger receives energy from the Saturn line. Additionally Saturn rules the sign of Capricorn associated with the top phalanx. The energy flow through the finger connects it to a sense of time. The equivalent Greek deity to Saturn is *Kronos*, from which the word chronology is derived. The finger is also connected to the sense of stability, discipline and concentration.

The name *medicus* derives from the Latin meaning 'of medicine or healing'. Timing was formerly seen to be a very important part of healing. Decumbiture is a specialist form of astrology that flowered in the seventeenth century, based upon the time a patient fell ill and decided to lie down (L. *decumbo* = 'to lie down; to fall'). From astrological charts of these moments physicians made judgements of diagnosis, prognosis and what medication – predominantly herbal – to use. In turn importance was placed upon the best time to gather and administer herbs. A little vestige of this time when medicine was linked to astrology is found in the word chronic, used to describe a cold and dry illness that lasts for a prolonged time (also see section on the symbolism of Saturn, page 103). The effect of chronic illness is that it often causes much long-term suffering in the body. In the struggle to overcome the illness the patient learns much about the healing forces within. 'Only the wounded physician heals' is a traditional medical maxim which shows that understanding the corrupting forces of Saturn is essential to practising medicine.

Relative Length

Excessively long or short medicus fingers are rare. The finger would be considered long if its whole top phalanx stood clear of the tips to both index and annularis fingers. In contrast it would be short if the tip of the medicus finger only just extended beyond the tips of the index and annularis (ring) fingers. A long medicus finger would denote someone who is overly pedantic and a stern disciplinarian, while a short finger denotes someone who lacks concentration and stability, making them extremely fickle. A ring on the medicus finger denotes insecurity and instability.

THE ANNULARIS OR RING FINGER

Top Phalanx – Aries (♈)

Ruler: Mars (♂)

This phalangeal area correlates to the realm of inspiration used for creative expression. This includes artistic ideals, perception of beauty and harmony, initiation of new projects and the galvanizing of others into action.

The positive utilization of these qualities makes someone bold, courageous and charismatic. They will often possess a skill in oratory and rhetoric that profoundly inspires others to follow them. The intensity of their inspirations and the alacrity of their decisions means they always like to take the initiative in any situation and take great pride in leading others out of darkness.

Negatively the phalanx describes someone who is headstrong and arrogant, typically acting without forethought and covering up their mistakes with an egotistical display of bravado. Their thinking lacks subtlety and originality, which commonly leads to the exploitation of other's ideas for their own use at the slightest opportunity, taking the kudos but never acknowledging their sources. They are subject to anger if anyone stands in the way of their ambitions.

Middle Phalanx – Sagittarius (♐)

Ruler: Jupiter (♃)

The middle phalanx is linked to the drawing down of inspiration from the Aries phalanx above and directing it into various activities and pursuits. The phalanx strongly connects to the way a person expresses themselves through their life-style, dress sense and decorum, particularly when in the public eye. Physical activities are involved here, too, like sport, dance, martial arts and cultivation of physique.

When positively directed the phalanx reflects a person who enthusiastically shares their inspirations with others, deriving pleasure in getting them to see the larger issues at hand. They make good judges and conscientious teachers, particularly delighting in the nurturing of students who lack confidence. They are straightforward, magnanimous and generous in their time and energy. They thoroughly enjoy the well-being of a sound mind tempered with a fit body and thrive on challenge and competition.

The negative expression of the phalanx reflects a person who lacks inspiration, and who propagates their own shallow image. They like ostentation and tend to exaggerate their abilities and activities. With their creativity blocked they spend a lot of time criticizing and discrediting other people's achievements. In trying to compensate for their dissatisfaction they are typically drawn to gluttony and overindulgence.

Bottom Phalanx – Leo (♌)

Ruler: Sun (☉)

The bottom phalanx is connected with the manifestation of the creative Solar energy, which can be expressed through a range of artistic skills, especially those that involve performance. On stage their full brilliance shines as they bring characters alive with great vivacity.

Positive expression of the phalanx describes a person who is self-assured, warm and sincere. They are very affectionate in love and protective to those they hold dear. They are cultivated and refined in their artistic expression, and the brilliance of their work is awe-inspiring.

Negative expression of the phalanx describes a person who indulges in pleasures. Their blocked creative energies draw them to seek excitement through taking risks and gambling. They show off in the vain search for inner fulfilment and approbation. Their extravagant and decadent life-style generally attracts notoriety.

Assessment of the Annularis Finger

The ring finger receives Solar energy from the Sun line. Additionally the Sun rules the sign of Leo and is exalted in the sign of Aries. Leo and Aries are associated with the bottom and the top phalanges respectively. The finger, like the Sun line, is connected with beauty and harmony, since the Sun symbolizes the soul 'the source of Light within'. A person who is aware of this Light understands the process of Creation and sees beauty radiating in all things.

The placing of a wedding ring upon this finger is symbolically significant. The Sun traditionally rules the heart, which in former times meant not only the physical organ but also the seat of the soul. Additionally the annularis finger has a definite neurological connection to the physical heart. This is illustrated when people suffer from angina. A classic feature of this syndrome is the radiation of pain down the left arm into the hand, specifically the ring finger.

Traditionally wedding rings are made of gold, the metal of the Sun, so the mutual wearing symbolizes a union of souls. The Latin name *annularis* means 'a ring', which also recalls the annular movement of the Planet Earth around the Sun, giving rise to the further idea of the eternal bond when two souls are properly joined as One.

Relative Length

Figure 13.4 (B), page 129, shows the relative lengths of the annularis finger, measured in the same way as the index finger by division of the medicus finger at the midpoint of its top phalange. This gives the normal length of the finger (B2) from which comparisons can be measured. The length of the annularis finger describes a person's innate sense of beauty. A long finger (B1) implies someone with a strong sense of beauty and the potential to express it. A short finger (B3) implies an absence of artistic sense and creative ability. Again it is important to note the energy flow in relation to the finger, to see how it may become compromised. The handprint used in this diagram is an example of a long annularis finger.

THE AURICULARIS OR LITTLE FINGER

Top Phalanx – Libra (♎)
Ruler: Venus (♀)

The top phalanx is linked to the formation of abstract and metaphorical ideas, theories, hypotheses, languages, music and poetry. The emphasis here is upon Venusian associations of beauty and art. Philosophy in its deeper sense is found here, deriving from the Greek meaning 'love of Sophia' – the goddess of wisdom, implying that the way to knowledge and wisdom is through love.

Positive expression of this phalanx describes a person who is a skilled communicator. They are sensitive, graceful, charming and tactful in all their social activities. They have a refined sense of aesthetics and delight in humorously sharing their ideas with others. Their sensitivity makes them considerate and fair in making decisions, while strongly motivated to establish harmony in as many situations as possible. They are very equitable in relationships and marriage, and enjoy sharing their energies with a partner.

Negative expression of this phalanx describes a person who is coarse and tactless in communication and is notably incapable of making decisions. Instead they try to use others to make decisions for them. In relationships they seek to dominate their partner. However, since they have difficulty in asserting themselves and expressing their views, they do this in a very manipulative and deceitful way. Without the subtlety of the Venusian energy they are drawn to pleasure-seeking and hedonism and as a consequence selfishly exploit relationships for personal gain.

Middle Phalanx – Gemini (♊)

Ruler: Mercury (☿)

The middle phalanx is connected to the execution of ideas, especially the written word, and aspects of communication like broadcasting, promotion, acting, teaching and studying. Finance is reflected here particularly through interest in economics and business studies.

Positive use of the phalanx reflects someone who is light-hearted, cheerful, intelligent and inquisitive. Their minds are very versatile, delighting in a range of knowledge that they can comment upon. They are witty, clear and precise in their thinking and they enjoy responding to other people's ideas.

The negative counterpart reflects someone who is silly and stupid. They like to pretend to be 'super-intelligent' but often get lost in their own words. Their minds flit from topic to topic of which they only have a superficial understanding. They fritter away their nervous energy through idle gossip. They notably lack discrimination.

Bottom Phalanx – Aquarius (♒)

Ruler: Saturn (♄)

The bottom phalanx is connected to the application of ideas; science, technology, especially electrical and electronic, encompassing the whole range of computer and related skills, as well as advertising, buying and selling. The

phalanx also relates to sexuality, procreation and relationships with children.

The positive development of the phalanx reflects someone who is amicable and sociable. Their lives are often fired by strong humanitarian ideals which are expressed in their devotion to a particular cause or ideology. Their electrically fast minds are original, innovative and provocative. They enjoy argument and typically play the 'Devil's advocate' to elicit a counter-response. They are immensely resourceful in solving new problems.

Negative expression of the phalanx reflects someone who is an excessive talker. This time, however, they usually know their subject well. They can be zealous and fanatical in their idolatries, which they tend to impose on others. Their zany plans are typically unrealistic and impractical. Despite their high ideals they are unsympathetic in human relations.

Assessment of the Auricularis Finger

The little or auricularis finger receives energy from the Uranus line through the Mercury mount. Additionally Mercury rules the sign of Gemini associated with the middle phalanx.

The Mercurial associations clearly make this the finger of communication; less obviously it is the finger of sexuality. To understand this, one needs to recall that Mercury is synonymous with Ether – the vital force in the body. When sexuality is projected along the little finger, the Libra phalanx with its Venusian rulership is linked to flirtation, romance and courtship. The Gemini phalanx is linked with the physical act of two bodies coming together and with the exchange of sexual energy. Gemini is a dual-bodied sign ruled by Mercury. The Aquarius phalanx, with its Saturnine rulership, is linked to conception and procreation. Saturn is symbolically linked to the descent of the soul into matter.

The name auricularis comes from the Latin *auricula* meaning 'the ear', an association that is not immediately obvious till seen figuratively to imply 'listening'. The allusion here is the 'listening' to the intuition from within, the basis of Hermetic teachings.

This finger is where the signet ring is traditionally placed. In days when letters and documents were sealed with wax, the signet ring, bearing the owner's crest of arms, was imprinted into the soft wax before it hardened. The wax, in addition to sealing the document, provided further authenticity of the sender. The ring was customarily worn by the owner at all times, which guarded against its fraudulent use. The placing of the ring on the 'Mercury' finger is symbolically most appropriate, since not only does Mercury rule documents and letters, but it is also linked to deception and crookedness.

Relative Length

Figure 13.4 (C), page 129 shows the relative lengths of the auricularis finger. The normal length of the auricularis finger (C2) is measured from the top phalangeal crease on the annularis finger and compared with the height of the auricularis finger imprint. Above this point the finger is long (C1), whereas below, it is short (C3). A long auricularis finger implies someone who is an excessive talker. However, one must look at the quality of markings on the finger to discern whether they are an inspired orator or only an idle gossip! A short auricularis finger implies a reticent or tongue-tied person. The handprint used in this diagram is an example of a short auricularis finger.

It is important to note, additionally, whether or not the auricularis finger is low-set, (see Figure 13.5). A low-set auricularis finger is present when its base is set distinctly below the general curve formed by the phalangeal creases of the other fingers at the palm. Even though the finger may appear to be short by comparison with the normal length of the auricularis finger,

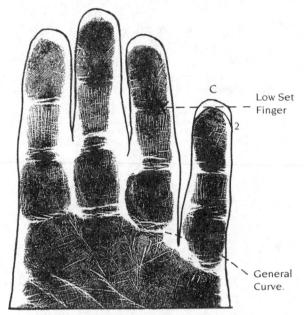

Figure 13.5 A Low-Set Auricularis Finger

if one takes into account the extra length of finger below the general curve it will become apparent that the finger is actually quite long. A low-set finger suggests an inquiring mind, penetrating into the material world symbolized by the palm, showing an aptitude for subjects like physics, chemistry, medicine or pharmacy. If such a finger's imprint does not reach the base of the top phalanx (C2), then it suggests a secretive nature. Such a person keeps the bulk of their knowledge to themselves.

KEYWORDS FOR THE PHALANGES

Index Finger

Cancer phalanx (♋)

Visualization, imagination, intuition, magic, religion, goals, spiritual values, maternal bond, forgiveness, clairvoyance, mediumship, alchemy.

Pisces phalanx ($\mathcal{H}$)

Managerial skills, confidence, acumen, diplomacy, faith, ritual, generosity, truth, authority, self-assurance, deceit.

Scorpio phalanx ($\mathfrak{M}$)

Power, status, investment, politics, prestige, healing, transformation, sexual habits, food and drink.

Medicus Finger
Capricorn phalanx ($\mathcal{Z}$)

Mental structure and manifestation, philosophy, logic, science, chemistry, mathematics, physics, lecturing, history, calculation, law, planning, goals, ambition, convention, dogma, orthodoxy, conservatism, paternal influence.

Virgo phalanx ($\mathfrak{M}$)

Manifestation, timing, order, administration, service, maturation, dependability, refinement, criticism, discrimination, harvest, manipulation, discipline, pedantry, precision, healing.

Taurus phalanx ($\forall$)

Farming, horticulture, gardening, building, engineering, carpentry, masonry, sculpture, pottery, weaving, material possessions, houses, land, estate, antiques, jewellery, investment, wealth, food, security, growing, nurturing.

Annularis Finger
Aries phalanx (Υ)

Creative inspiration, artistic ideals, perceptions, charisma, initiative, desire, anger, courage, bravado, oratory, rhetoric, arrogance, kudos.

Sagittarius phalanx ($\nearrow$)

Artistic activities, self-expression, dance, harmony, dress sense, life-style, decorum,

martial arts, sport, well-being, fitness, challenge, competition, ostentation, gluttony.

Leo phalanx (Ω)

Artistic skills, performance, theatre, pleasures, risks, gambling, vanity, decadence, notoriety, speculative investment.

Auricularis Finger
Libra phalanx ($\triangleq$)

Abstract and metaphysical, ideas, language, music, poetry, culture, books, hypothesis, art, grace, philosophy, theory, communication, charm, sensitivity, tact, aesthetics, humour, sharing of ideas, equality, romance, manipulation.

Gemini phalanx (II)

Execution of ideas, study, documents, written word, media, drama, science, teaching, handreading, finance, economics, versatility, gossip, listening, hermeticism, sexuality, fraud, theft.

Aquarius phalanx ($\approx$)

Application of ideas, science, technology, electricity, electronics, computers, buying and selling, advertising, children, sexuality, procreation, humanitarian concerns, medicine, pharmacy.

ASSESSMENT OF THE PHALANGES

Three main observations of phalangeal shape constitute the basis of their assessment; length, width and profile.

Length

The length of a phalanx, demonstrated in Figure 13.6, indicates the range or depth of knowledge that a person can potentially draw from in the specific area ruled by the phalanx. A long phalanx (A) generally provides a good range of insight and depth of understanding, whereas a short phalanx (B) provides a restricted range of insight and understanding. In considering the length of a phalanx it is important to differentiate between anatomical and functional length. Assessment is based on functional length, which is the distance between the bar lines of the interphalangeal creases as demonstrated by (C) in the diagram.

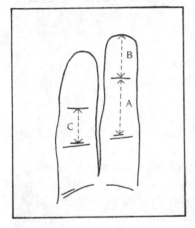

Figure 13.6
The Comparative
Lengths of
Phalanges

Width

The width of a phalanx shows the degree of utilization of the knowledge from a particular phalangeal area. Just as a muscle develops when it is used more, so does a phalanx develop when its abilities are utilized. A wide phalanx suggests a lot of use, whereas a wasted phalanx suggests negligible use. (See Figure 13.7.)

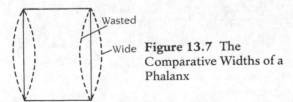

Figure 13.7 The
Comparative Widths of a
Phalanx

Profile

This is the degree of fullness shown in a phalanx when viewed in profile. As Figure 13.8 shows, fullness is usually conspicuous in a handprint by the darker imprint as a 'fuller' phalanx becomes more impressed onto the paper than a 'flat' phalanx. When present, fullness indicates refinement and sensitivity in the corresponding area of phalangeal expression.

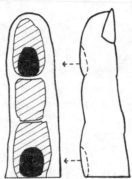

Figure 13.8
The Comparative
Fullness of a Phalanx

Combinations in a Phalanx

It is possible to have any combination of these three criteria on a phalanx. For example, a short Capricorn phalanx that is wide with no fullness could well describe someone with a limited understanding of scientific principles, who none the less may amass a considerable amount of data, though lacking the ability to sift the relevant from the irrelevant.

Phalangeal Markings

Once the shape of the phalanges has been considered, observation of their markings completes the assessment. Since the energy flowing through the lines is linked to consciousness, the various lineal patterns describes how a person is utilizing the knowledge from each phalanx. Longitudinal lines evidences energy being directed into the phalanges and enabling the person to derive the appropriate understanding.

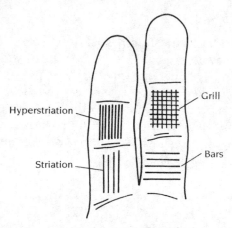

Figure 13.9 Markings on the Phalanges

The markings described in the following sections are shown in Figure 13.9.

Striation

This is formed by longitudinal lines showing activation of a phalanx; up to three or four lines is usually sufficient energy to activate the phalanx and put it to positive use. Striation is also shown within the phalanges in Figure 15.5, page 154.

Hyperstriation

More than four lines shows an excess of energy focused into the phalanx. The resultant over-activation may well be the result of stress, and can indicate areas where excessive demands are placed upon the person. For example someone who is holding down a full-time job, putting energy into a relationship, looking after children and taking on part-time study. Hyperstriation is also shown within the phalanges in Figure 15.1, page 149.

Bars

Horizontal lines cut across a phalanx contrary to the flow of energy through the finger, indicating areas of blocked energy. They evidence where fears operate in a person's mind, causing various inhibitions. The blocked energy prevents a person from clearly understanding and utilizing that particular area of knowledge. Bars are also shown on the middle and lower phalanges of Figure 15.4, page 153.

Grills

Grills are a composite pattern of both striation and bar lines. They indicate conflict from the struggle to overcome the limitations of the blocked energy. Grills highlight areas of knowledge that a person has great difficulty using. Grills are also shown within the phalanges in Figure 15.3, page 152.

In all these lineal patterns it is important to consider the Elemental widths of the lines – that is, whether they are of a Water, Fire or Air width. The Elemental width shows the relative intensity of the phalangeal utilization. For example three or four Fire width lines on the Taurus phalanx could indicate that a person was actively involved with building their own home whereas, if instead there were only two or three Water quality lines present, it would suggest they only dream about having their own home. Earth width lines are seldom found on phalanges.

Interphalangeal lines

The interphalangeal creases can be considered as bar lines but, rather than blocking the flow of energy through the phalanx, they act to define one mental level from another as the energy passes along the finger. Generally the inter-phalangeal creases are found in two main forms: single or multiple.

Single interphalangeal creases provide the sharpest distinction between the phalanges and least amount of resistance to the energy flow along the digit. This allows the most spontaneous use of ideas, an asset for people who need to provide impromptu responses, such as politicians, salespersons or sports commentators.

Multiple interphalangeal creases cause increasing resistance to the energy flow, depending upon the number of lines present. This slowed energy flow causes greater concentration of energy at each phalangeal level. It indicates someone who is far less spontaneous in their ideas, but more attentive to detail – an asset for such people as architects, designers or composers.

Absent markings

It is not uncommon to find an absence of lines on a phalanx, which indicates a lack of energy being directed into it. Though a person may utilize such a phalanx, shown by the width and profile, there is a notable absence of free thinking in relation to this area of knowledge. The person expresses the qualities of the phalanx according to their conditioning, rather than using their own independence of thought. If ability and talent are shown by a good length, width and profile to a phalanx, then an absence of lines may well show the arrogance of someone who takes their talents and skills for granted. They have yet to manifest the full potential of the phalanx.

Fingertip Shape

The assessment of the fingers is not complete without consideration of the fingertip shape. The tip of the finger is significant in two respects. Firstly it is where the Intellectual World of the fingers receives illumination from the Realm of Light, so the tip shape is linked to quality of reception to their inspiration. Secondly the tips are where the Etheric vital energy flowing along the fingers is expressed out into the world. The fingertip shapes describe how we express ourselves, especially our ideas, to others.

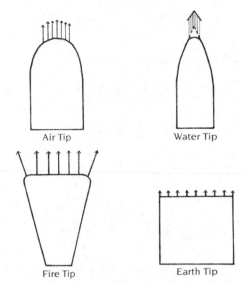

Figure 13.10 The Four Elemental Fingertip Shapes

To aid the understanding of how energy is expressed through the various tip shapes, they can be visualized as a type of nozzle. Once again the tips are classified using the Four Elements which colour the various types of energy flow. Figure 13.10 shows the comparative fingertip shapes, exaggerated so the characteristic features of each are more apparent.

Water Shape Fingertips

The Water tip shape is pointed and conical, causing the energy flowing through it to be direct and focused. Water shape fingertips indicate a person with single-minded concentration who when they direct their energy to the Realm of Light can derive powerful visions of the spiritual world. Water shape fingertips are most commonly found on clairvoyants and mediums. When directed towards other people, the Watery tips are very sensitive and receptive to others. Such a person is usually very good at listening to others and is perceptive of other people's problems. Their energy expression, however, lacks strength, which consequently makes assertiveness difficult, though where possible, expression is refined and graceful.

Fire Shape Fingertips

The Fire shape tip is spatulate, causing the energy flowing through it to be radiated widely. Fire shape tips indicate a person who is practical and dynamic in their self-expression. They enthusiastically delight in getting their ideas across to others. This force of communication makes it very difficult for them to be receptive and listen to other people. They tend instead to provoke responses through insensitive argument. It is very difficult for them to direct their restless minds towards the Realm of Light and consequently they are often quite cynical about spiritual beliefs, preferring instead the practical reality that they know well.

Air Shape Fingertips

The Air shape tip is rounded, causing the energy flowing through it to be moderately concentrated. It is not as focused as the Water tip or as dispersed as the Fire tip. When the energy flowing through the Air tip shapes is concentrated well it indicates a person who is good at communicating their ideas to others and who freely enjoys entering a deep and prolonged discussion. When the energy flowing through the Air shape tip lacks concentration, it indicates a person who is vague and weak in communication. In relation to the Realm of Light, the less concentrated energy flow of an Air tip shape reflects an eclectic approach to the different beliefs rather than a strongly defined personal faith as in the Water tip. They often pride themselves on a personal philosophy that is in fact a synthesis of many philosophies.

Earth Shape Fingertips

The Earth shape tip is square in shape, causing the energy flowing through it to be restricted by the blunt ending of the finger. The lack of free

energy flow associated with the Earth shape tip indicates a person with a dull mind that is limited in expression. Their mental qualities largely remain nascent. The physical strength to achieve their tasks is their forte in contrast to their poor communication which causes them to remain rather isolated. In relation to the Realm of Light the blocked energy flow prevents deep illumination of the mind, leading to a blind adherence to dogma and a literal interpretation of Scripture.

When considering fingertip shapes it is quite possible to find two or more Elemental shapes on the same hand.

EXAMPLES OF PHALANGEAL COMBINATIONS

In order to demonstrate how to assess the phalanges a number of examples are included, illustrating how to combine and interpret all the aspects of a phalanx.

Refer to Figure 13.11.

1. A long, wide Taurus phalanx with pronounced fullness and a good number of activation lines indicates someone who has a refined taste and puts a lot of energy into collecting items such as antiques and jewellery.

2. A long, wasted Gemini phalanx covered by a grill indicates someone who has difficulty expressing their ideas in writing; who has conflicts in dealing with money, and poor business sense. There is a need to check for other features, especially the Mercury line, which might indicate the source of this conflict to help its resolution.

3. A short, truncated Leo phalanx with pronounced bar lines indicates someone who lacks artistic expression. They are selfish,

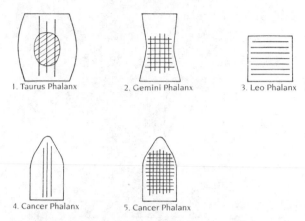

1. Taurus Phalanx 2. Gemini Phalanx 3. Leo Phalanx

4. Cancer Phalanx 5. Cancer Phalanx

Figure 13.11 Markings and Variations of Phalanges

uncaring and unable to enjoy pleasures. They are parasitic on other people's resources. There is a need to check for other features, especially the Sun line, which might indicate the source of this inhibition to help overcome it.

4. A pointed, clear, well-developed and strongly activated Cancer phalanx indicates refined spiritual ideals, strong goals and psychic perception.

5. A pointed Cancer phalanx which is moderately well developed but covered by a grill indicates someone who has confused spiritual ideals, and who is hypersensitive and easily duped. They are desperate to be loved and nurtured. There is a need to check for other features, especially the Lunar mount, which might indicate the source of this conflict to help heal it.

GESTURE

Gesture continually demonstrates the flow of energy through the hands and again the Elements are used to interpret these movements. Earth is apparent by slow, rather heavy movements, as if the person was too weak to move their limbs. Overall the degree of movement is limited and gesture often takes the form of practical demonstrations, like showing how to use a screwdriver. Water is apparent by circular, graceful movements, particularly animated by emotions where the hands are usually held in close proximity to the heart. Air involves wide spatial, wing-like stretching of the arms and hands, accompanying outbursts of ideas. Fire is shown by intense sharp angular movements, where the arms make quick sword like thrusts, often acting out commands of intent.

The relative positions of fingers to palm composing the gesture are particularly significant, since this reveals how energy is flowing through the hand at the moment of observation. Where the fingers are clenched as in a fist, the energy is restrained and held back with a corresponding withdrawal of psychological expression. Where the hand is completely open with fingers outstretched, energy flows freely with corresponding psychological expression.

Between these two extremes of restraint and expression, all the intermediary hand positions can be considered. Thus a single digit outstretched while the others are clenched would highlight all the qualities of that one digit. For example, the index finger outstanding very much emphasizes the person's ideals, intent and self-authority as they point out their directions. By contrast if it was clasped inside the palm by their fingers it would indicate a lack of self-confidence and vulnerability.

SPACES BETWEEN THE FINGERS

See Figure 13.12. The spaces between fingers are also significant. The habitual finger placement visible when taking handprints is particularly revealing. This is why it is important when taking handprints to capture the natural placing of the person's hand on the paper, rather than a contrived and enforced position.

The greater the degree of space surrounding a finger, the more freely the energy flows along it and consequently the fingers' qualities gain in strength of use. By contrast the more the fingers are held together, the greater the restraint of the energy flow and resultant lack of expression of the finger's qualities. Since the fingers have already been covered extensively, the spaces between the fingers can now be explained.

Angle between the Index and Medicus fingers

See Figure 13.12 (A). The Saturnine energies flowing through the medicus finger link it with structured thought, conventional ideals, dogma – ideas that are largely conditioned through childhood and early education, whereas the Jovial energies flowing through the index finger are linked to self-image, personal goals, aspirations and ideals. The angle separating these fingers indicates the degree of independent thought – the greater the angle the greater the independence of thought, due to the person following their own intuitions, questioning conventional ideas and seeking an identity separate from society's norm. By contrast, where the fingers are tightly held together it indicates a marked lack of free thinking leading to unquestioning support of conventional ideals and acceptance of conditioning from childhood.

Angle between the Medicus and Annularis fingers

See Figure 13.12 (B). The Solar energies flowing through the annularis finger link it to creativity and self-expression, so the more the finger stands apart from the medicus finger, the more freely a person can use their creativity and

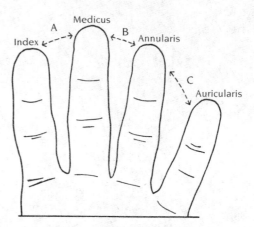

Figure 13.12 Spaces Between the Fingers

express themselves. By contrast, the strong holding of the annularis finger to the medicus finger shows a marked restraint of creative expression. This tied placing of the medicus and annularis fingers commonly describes someone who depends upon a partner to act out their deficient creative expression.

Angle between the Annularis and Auricularis fingers

See Figure 13.12 (C). Since Mercurial and Uranian energies flow through the annularis finger, the wider the angle between the annularis and auricularis fingers, the greater the degree of communication expressed by a person. The tight placing of the auricularis finger next to the annularis finger indicates a lack of communication, reticence and uncertainty of ideas.

BENDS IN THE FINGERS

In time the flow of energy through the fingers can produce distinct bends or disfigurements in their length. The significance of these bends comes from noting what fingers are involved and at what phalangeal level the bend occurs. Also note in what direction, whether to the Solar side of the hand or to the Lunar side, the finger or phalanges lean. Finally note whether, as a result of the bend, two phalanges are brought into proximity or the space between two fingers is increased. There are many possible combinations arising from bends in the fingers. The following is a simple example of how interpretation is made.

If the Aries phalanx at the top of the annularis finger bends at its top joint so that it leans towards the Capricorn phalanx, then it suggests that as the bend is towards the Solar side of the hand, the person in projecting their artistic ideas out into the world encounters resistance and obstruction (Saturn) towards acceptance of their talent.

Blockage to the energy flow at the interphalangeal creases leads to swelling of the joints. The blockage usually causes the proximal phalanges, those closest to the palm, to become enlarged, while the distal phalanges, those furthest from the palm, become atrophied and wasted. Correspondingly, the proximal phalanges indicate overuse, while the distal phalanges indicate neglect.

CHAPTER 14

Pollex or Thumb

THE thumb is intimately connected with the control and flow of Etheric vital energy within a person. In contrast to the three distinct phalanges of the fingers, the thumb has only two. The 'missing' bottom phalanx can be correlated to the Venus mount on the palm, in which case the energy flowing down the thumb can be seen to supply the vital force of the body – the very basis of human existence.

PHALANGEAL DEVELOPMENT

The Etheric rulership of the thumb links with all the lines on the palm – the Celestial World. Of the two phalanges, the upper one is connected to will and the lower one to reason; both these qualities determine how the Etheric energy flows through the lines and, in turn, the fingers. This link between will or volition and the lines is the reason why anatomists refer to the lined surface of the palm as the volar aspect of the hand.

As already seen, the Celestial world is located between the Elemental World and the Intellectual World and, similarly, the thumb performs an intermediary role between these two realms. The base of the thumb is firmly anchored in the Elemental World of the palm, while the tip can reach up to the Intellectual World of the fingers. The thumb can be seen like a rudder, enabling a person to steer a path through life.

Cheiromantically, will can be described as that infinite power that we can draw from, enabling our ideas to be made manifest and our objectives to be achieved, thereby determining the course of our lives. The degree to which will-power is seen to determine the outcome of future events is reflected by the word 'will' being used as an auxiliary of the future tense – as in 'I will win,' revealing the intention of the person's volition.

In order for will-power to flow well and achieve positive results, it needs to be directed and given a definite purpose. Reason provides this control over will-power, enabling a person to work out a particular objective and how much energy is needed to achieve it.

SETTING

The height at which the thumb is set into the side of the palm is significant, for it determines at what level this Etheric energy is manifested. The

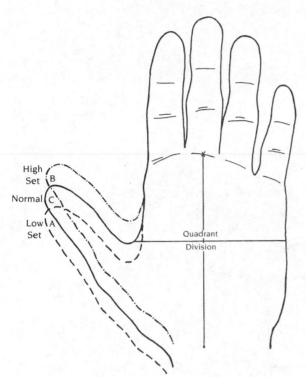

Figure 14.1 The Setting of the Thumb

page 58. Figure 14.1 (C) shows the normal setting of the thumb.

ASSESSMENT OF THE THUMB

The length of the phalanges composing the thumb gives depth to both will-power and reason, while their relative widths indicate the degree to which these faculties are used. A strong thumb enables people to take control over their lives. To assess whether a person has a strong thumb, first ask whether it has a good length so that it can reach up to the fingers. If so, then symbolically it is able to draw down knowledge and wisdom as to the best course of action or behaviour. Secondly, both the phalanges need to have a moderate width, implying that expression of will-power is well tempered by a strong reason. If there is a disproportionate width between the upper and lower phalanges, then one of these faculties predominates over the other.

Most commonly the upper phalanx of will is more developed than the lower one, which suggests a lack of reason to direct the expression of will. As a consequence such people tend to push ahead stubbornly and do things before considering what effects their actions will create. An extreme form of this imbalance is found as the so-called 'clubbed thumb' where the upper phalanx predominates over the lower one like the tip of a drumstick. In palmistry books this has acquired the additional ominous label of the murderer's thumb. Whilst it needs to be pointed out that very few people who possess such a thumb commit murder, it is quite easy to see how they could be goaded into acting recklessly. A clubbed thumb is also a pathognomic sign of Down's syndrome (along with the simian line), which undoubtedly contributes to their impetuous behaviour.

horizontal line of the quadrant division can be used as a point for assessing this feature. A low-set thumb, as in Figure 14.1 (A), indicates a powerful physical vitality which makes a person very pragmatic and determined in achieving their goals, though commonly their will is directed towards materialistic objectives. A further example of a low-set thumb is shown in Figure 19.1, page 180.

A high-set thumb, as in Figure 14.1 (B), indicates someone who lacks physical strength. Instead their Etheric energy is much more easily sublimated towards spiritual objectives. Their strength of will-power is more changeable, volatile and notably lacking in resolution unless they have clear spiritual goals. An example of a high-set thumb is also shown in Figure 7.5,

Rarely the lower phalanx of reason predominates over the upper phalanx; here a person can work out precisely what they need to do but lacks the will-power to achieve their objectives.

Longitudinal striation markings evidence the flow of Etheric energy down the thumb and reflecting the expression of will-power. Horizontal bars block the flow of Etheric energy, which reflects the frustration of will-power.

The benefit of a strong thumb should not be underestimated, which is shown in its Latin name *pollex*, which is connected to the verb *polleo* meaning 'to be strong, to be powerful, to flourish, to thrive, to be able, to prevail'.

Rings are very occasionally found on the thumb. It is never a good sign for it indicates a deficient will-power and a lack of vitality. It is most frequently observed on those people who have lost the will to live, like terminally ill patients or those who have lost their spouse.

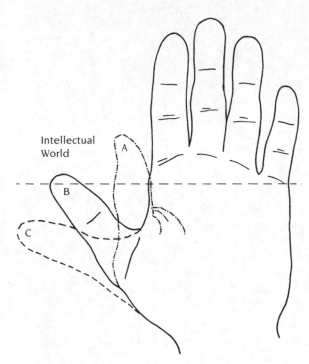

Figure 14.2 The Angle of the Thumb

THE ANGLE OF THE THUMB

In both gesture and in a handprint, the angle of the thumb reflects the degree of will-power flowing through the person. Increasing amounts of will-power are expressed as the angle between the thumb and the side of the palm increases.

See Figure 14.2. Where the thumb in gesture is held inside a clenched fist it is an indication of giving up the will to carry on, of surrendering to the situation, even giving up the will to live. Clinically it has been observed to precede an epileptic fit just before loss of consciousness. It is a sign of extreme vulnerability.

Where the thumb is held close to the side of the palm, as shown in the diagram by (A), the will is cautiously restrained. However, with the tip held up against the Intellectual World of the fingers, it suggests prudence (L. *prudus* = 'foresight, providence' – that is, 'seeing before') before engaging their will-power. This indicates waiting for inspiration before acting. Appropriately this is how the thumb is placed in the Christian prayer position.

As the angle of the thumb separates from the side of the hand, so the will-power increases in strength and assertiveness. This increases to an optimum position of about 45 degrees shown by (B). Beyond this point the tip of the thumb no longer reaches the horizon at the base of the fingers (C). Consequently their will is no longer guided by higher inspirations. After 45 degrees the will is expressed recklessly to achieve their desires and ambitions while, acting without higher conscience, it is often very destructive to others.

THE THUMB AND
WILL-POWER

Perspicacious readers should have already worked out the simple but profound implications of the thumb being connected to both will-power and the lines on the palm. That is – *lines change*. As obstacles in life are confronted and overcome so the lines alter their patterns as conflicts are resolved.

Simple changes to lines can be observed quite easily by taking one person's set of handprints at roughly yearly intervals. By comparing sets of handprints subtle differences can be found, such as slight lengthening or shortening of main lines, changes in Elemental width and clarity of lines, alterations in intensity of stress lines and general clarity of the palm. These simple alterations reflect changes in our personalities as they adapt to new situations within our lives.

By contrast radical positive change is very rare. It usually takes considerable adversity to provoke people into creating major changes in their lives. By using the strength of their will, people have resolved immense inner conflict and gained enormous wisdom; correspondingly whole line patterns have changed, with some negative lines entirely disappearing, while positive new lines have appeared in their place. Such triumphs of the human spirit are astounding to witness! The example used in 'A Study of Change shown in the Hand' in Chapter 19 is one such change.

Cheiromantical evidence strongly suggests that while everyone has will-power to a greater or lesser extent, very few people have the freedom of will and the resolution of spirit necessary to create such transformations. For the vast majority their will is not free but, as their palmar lines indicate, blocked by fears, confused by mental uncertainty, obstructed by emotional issues, debilitated by poor health, restrained by work pressures, family responsibilities and financial concerns. It requires immense courage and strength of spirit to integrate the spiritual world within the mundane, thereby bringing concord to all areas of one's life; but it remains the potential within all people to find this harmony, if they direct their will toward such a goal.

For this reason the fatalistic ideas found in palmistry books should be seen in a completely different light. If a marking on a line suggests a negative experience, such as the breaking up of a relationship in two or three years time, it should lead the skilled cheiromancer to ask such questions as – Why is this going to happen? What is going wrong in their emotional behaviour? What does the person need to learn from the situation? Such a line of questioning leads to a much more positive resolution of the experience. Indeed by careful examination it is possible to gain enough insight into the problem from the hand to enable a person to free their will and change a situation for the better.

CHAPTER 15

Hand Shape
Part 2

PLANETARY INFLUENCES ON HAND SHAPE

Now that all the main aspects of cheiromancy have been covered it is possible to appreciate how the subtle influences of the Planets are reflected in the structure of the hand. The following sequence of Planetary hand shapes is intentionally arranged to highlight the contrasting Planetary qualities of Saturn and Jupiter, Mars and Venus, Sun and Moon.

The following descriptions of Planetary hand shapes are classic examples and not always fulfilled by every feature and detail in a hand. You will be able to spot variations in the example hand shape diagrams and the descriptions given. These descriptions should serve to help identify possible ways in which the influence of a particular Planet can appear in the hand.

THE SATURN HAND SHAPE

An example of a Saturn-shaped hand is shown in Figure 15.1. The Saturn hand shape is long and thin with the prominence of the Saturn mount. The strong influence of Saturn is additionally highlighted by the presence of a strongly defined Saturn line. The Saturnine influence reflects a marked restraint of love and severe austerity in the person's life. The lack of nurturing is reflected by the prominence of the bones in the whole hand, especially in the fingers. In particular, their lower phalanges, connected to sensory experience, are notably wasted, implying a lack of sensual pleasures. Saturn rules the bones. Furthermore the phalanges may be covered by a profusion of bar lines reflecting the inhibition of mental development by fear. The thumb is often high-set and held very rigidly, indicating their strong determination to fulfil their goals and ideals. The Jupiter line may well show a marked restraint in its flow as it crosses the Saturn line. The line may be short, stopping at the Saturn line or even terminating on the Saturn mount. The shortness of the Jupiter line reflects an emotional coldness and a lack of sharing of feelings with others, while the ending of the line on the Saturn mount indicates a marked pessimism and despondency. Alternatively several bar lines may cut the flow of the Jupiter line as it crosses the Saturn line, indicating disappointments in relationships.

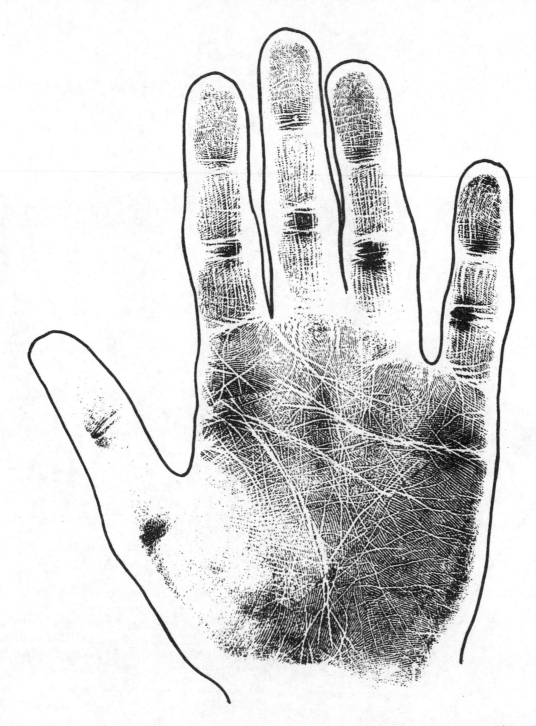

Figure 15.1 The Saturn Shape Hand

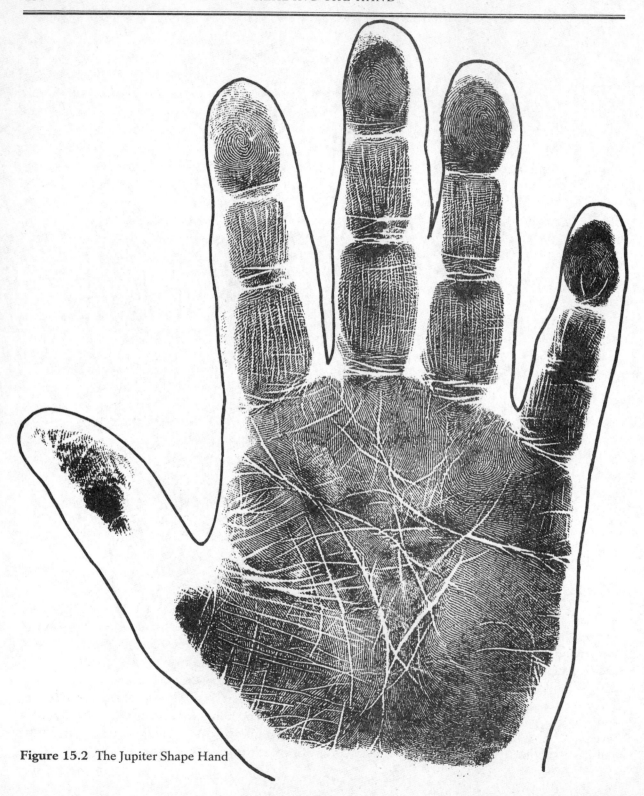

Figure 15.2 The Jupiter Shape Hand

THE JUPITER HAND SHAPE

An example of a Jupiter-shaped hand is shown in Figure 15.2. By contrast to the emaciated appearance of the Saturn hand the Jupiter hand is large and podgy with a well developed Jupiter mount. The influence of Jupiter is further reflected by the Jupiter line rising well up onto the Jupiter mount. The long heart line reflects the open-hearted nature of the influence of Jupiter that enjoys the sharing of feelings with others. Jupiter delights in sensory pleasures, which is reflected in the podgy appearance of the hand. The lower phalanges are correspondingly well developed and specifically the lower phalanx of the index finger, that receives the energy from the Jupiter line, is often substantially formed. In contrast to the Saturn hand the phalanges are generally much better developed and relatively free from bar lines. The phalanges reflect a much greater unfolding of their mental abilities. The thumb is well formed and moderately set on the palm. Its substantial character suggests a strong will-power when the person needs to apply their determination, though the lower setting suggests the tendency to overindulgence in sensory pleasures.

THE MARS HAND SHAPE

An example of a Mars-shaped hand is shown in Figure 15.3. The Mars hand shape is a compact, oblong and pointed palm. The palm has a well-developed mid ridge containing both Mars mounts that may even cause a slight bowing of the lateral edges. The Mars active mount, inside the angle of the thumb, is usually the most developed of the two mounts. In a good hand a well-developed Mars line shows an abundance of available Martian energy. The thumb is moderately low-set which in combination with the Martian energy describes a very practical hand of immense physical strength. More commonly a profusion of lines radiating down from the Mars active mount suggests the thwarting and frustration of this energy, highlighting inner stress and tension. The pointed, pugilistic shape to the whole hand, formed by the fingers held tightly together, suggests a definite thrust of the Martian energy up through the fingers. The phalanges additionally evidence this thrust of energy by the Fire quality activation lines present upon them. Note that the energy within the Mars glyph rises upwards.

THE VENUS HAND SHAPE

An example of a Venus-shaped hand is shown in Figure 15.4. The Venus hand shape is typically a large slender hand with a broad, well-developed base. A large, well-developed Venus mount is the most prominent feature of the whole hand. Accompanying the mount a strong Venus line reflects a powerful vital energy. The marked development of the Venus mount in relation to the slenderness of the rest of the hand, especially the fingers, suggests that the energy is drawn down from the rest of the palm and concentrated in the mount. Note that in contrast with the Mars glyph the energy within the Venus glyph falls downwards (see Chapter 4, on Planetary Symbolism). The slender fingers denote a strong sensual refinement and appreciation which in combination with a moderately set thumb suggests a gentle, graceful and nurturing expression of energy.

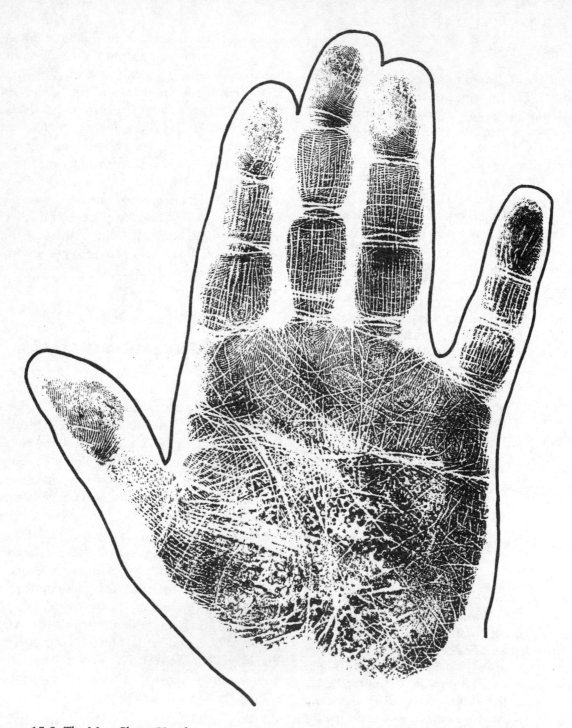

Figure 15.3 The Mars Shape Hand

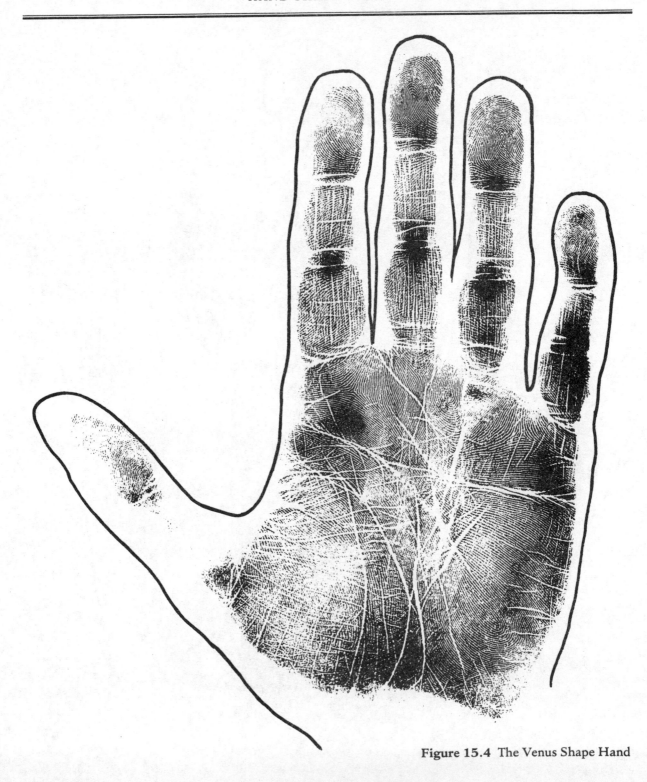

Figure 15.4 The Venus Shape Hand

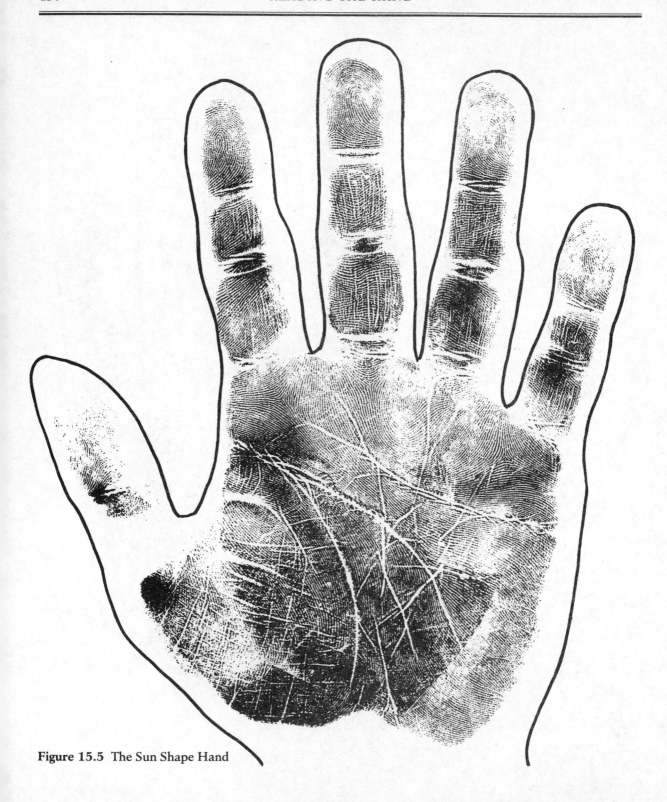

Figure 15.5 The Sun Shape Hand

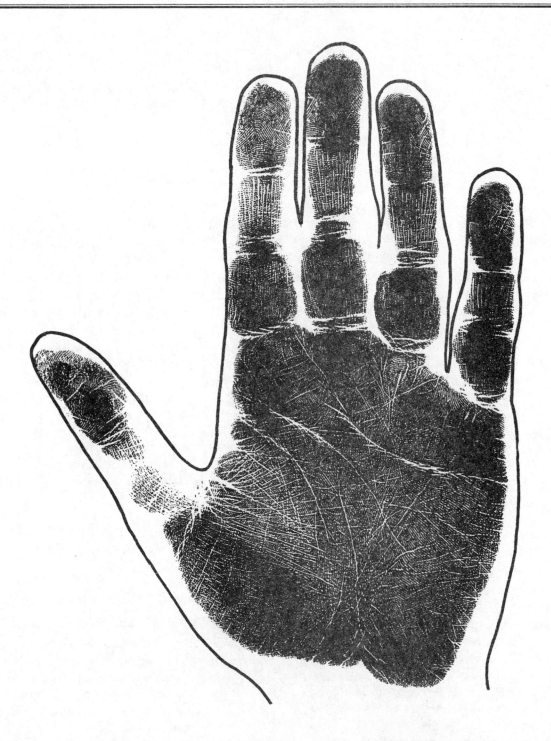

Figure 15.6 The Moon Shape Hand

THE SUN HAND SHAPE

An example of a Sun-shaped hand is shown in Figure 15.5. The Sun hand shape is an expansive, oblong hand. The prominence of the Sun mount is accompanied by a well-formed Sun line. The fingers are well developed and wide-set while the lines supplying the fingers – Jupiter line, Saturn line, Sun line and Uranus (Mercury) line – are all well formed and generally of a Fire width. In combination these features suggest a free flow of energy through the fingers, indicating that their psychological abilities are easily expressed. The moderately low-set thumb held at an angle of 45 degrees in a confident position indicates someone who is self-assured and in touch with their Solar nature. From the placing of the hand it is possible to visualize the illuminating Solar energy radiating out of the hand through the fingers.

THE MOON HAND SHAPE

An example of a Moon-shaped hand is shown in Figure 15.6. The Moon hand shape is a curved oblong hand, especially associated with a very spongy Water quality skin texture. The Lunar mount is strongly developed, projecting out from the percussion side of the hand. Rarely it is accompanied by a Moon line. In the absence of this line, the Mercury line commonly compensates, extending into the heart of the mount, indicating the person drawing upon their imagination. The lines on the palm are often of a Water width. The restrained, tightly held fingers indicate a reticence in expressing their ideas. The high-set thumb indicates a marked sensitivity to spiritual ideas. Its angle is frequently held fairly close to the edge of the palm, indi-

cating a cautious quality. In contrast to the Sun hand shape, the placing of the thumb and fingers on the Moon hand shape displays a marked lack of confidence. Figure 7.5, page 58, also shows a Moon hand shape; in particular the curvature is pronounced.

THE MERCURY HAND SHAPE

An example of a Mercury-shaped hand is shown in Figure 15.7. The Mercury hand is slender and notably lacking in width. A pronounced Mercury mount causes the auricularis finger to stand displaced. There is an accompanying development of the traditional Mercury (health) line, now ascribed to Uranus, directing its energy up to the auricularis finger. The Mercury (head) line is typically well formed. Water or Air widths prevail in the palmar lines. All these features facilitate communication, which is so strongly connected with Mercury. The high-set thumb with a lack of width to the hand reflects a very nervous and sensitive person with a changeable, chameleon-like nature. They are typically very chatty and sociable though lacking a resolute will-power.

COMBINATION HAND SHAPES

It is common to find hands that contain the pronounced characteristics of two or even three Planets, in which case the blending together of their symbolic qualities will help contribute to the picture of the person. When considering the astrological chart in relation to the hand these Planetary patterns should become clearer. This perspective will be covered at length in Chapter

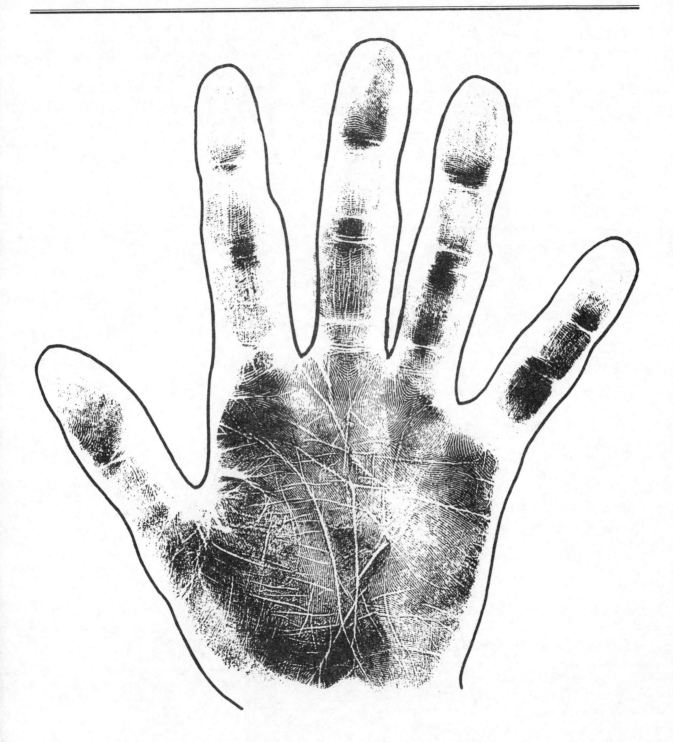

Figure 15.7 The Mercury Shape Hand

18 on astrological connections. A skilled cheiro-mancer should be able to identify the connec-tions between the strength of particular Planets in the birth chart and their patterns in the hand.

Having identified a particular Planetary pat-tern in the hand shape, next consider its re-lationship to the Elemental hand shape. How will it be expressed? For example if a Mercurial hand shape is also a Fire-shaped hand it suggests someone who spends a lot of their time and energy expressing their ideas. The opinions will be strongly formed and they will enjoy argument. By contrast the Mercurial hand shape which is also a Water hand shape suggests the opposite: someone who is shy and reserved with their ideas. Their ideas will be most readily expressed through poetry, art or music.

PART THREE

—

SYNTHESIS AND APPLICATION OF CHEIROMANCY

—

CHAPTER 16

Synthesis

HAVING covered all the symbolism and dealt with the main aspects of the hand, it is now time to connect the various parts of the skill of handreading together so that students can really enter into the 'flow' of reading the hand.

In Fludd's preface illustration (Figure 2.1, page 8.) Man is depicted standing between heaven and earth. In the hand this perspective is shown by the relationship of the Three Worlds: the Elemental World (including hand shape, skin texture and palmar quadrants), the Celestial World (embracing the lines and their length, width, relative clarity and markings, with the thumb) and the Intellectual World (including fingers and phalanges with their formations and markings).

This relationship of the Three Worlds in the hand can be visualized with the following analogy. The Elemental World describes the type of vehicle we are born into, through which we experience the physical world; the Celestial World describes how we drive this vehicle in our emotional relationships with others; and the Intellectual World describes the goals we steer towards, the driving skills used to guide one's life and the knowledge learnt from experience.

By looking at the relative strength and weakness of each of these realms within the hand and seeing how they interact with each other, it is possible to deduce how successfully a person can use their lives according to the resources available to them. For example if the hand reveals strong lines and well-developed fingers but the shape of the palm is poor then, despite having a strong will and a lot of knowledge, they may well lack the physical capacity to achieve anything of lasting value in the material world. Alternatively the fingers and palm may both be well developed but the lines poor, in which case, despite having a lot of knowledge and the physical strength, their emotional blocks may deny them sufficient willpower with which to fulfil their aspirations. A strong palm with clear, well-formed lines but lacking development of the fingers may well describe someone who is physically strong and healthy, emotionally happy but without any inspiration and sense of direction regarding what they should do in their life.

THE ELEMENTAL STAGES OF HANDREADING

In contemplating the symbolic ideas throughout the previous chapters, students will hopefully have been inwardly relating to the material, visualizing processes occurring within themselves and within other people. The extent of this inner connection can now be found out by using the Elemental symbolism as a means of self-diagnosis. Here the Elements are used to represent stages in the process of reading a hand.

Earth – Observation

Earth represents the observation of the shape and structure of the hand and, in turn, being able to recognize nuances of shape that help define and differentiate one hand from another. This ability is largely derived by observing as many hands as possible, particularly through taking handprints and building up a library which eases their comparison. The more hands seen the greater the appreciation of each individual shape. Recognizing differences in shape trains the handreader to see what is particular to each person's hand.

Water – Visualization

Water represents the visualization of the appropriate symbolism to these nuances of shape and formations. Water describes the emotional energy flowing around a person; in reading a hand you enter an emotional rapport whereby your own emotional energy coalesces with the other person. This fusion of emotional energy colours the whole dialogue between you and the person whose hand you are reading. Here each symbol used in defining every observable aspect of the hand becomes like a seed which, when watered by the subject's emotional energy, rapidly grows, forming images within your mind. This mental facility needs to be allowed to grow naturally, like seeds which a gardener plants, waters, and leaves, confident that in the fullness of time they will bear forth fruit. Any forcing of symbolic understanding is generally counter-productive.

Sometimes it is difficult to get the symbols to work for you. Try reading the appropriate symbolic associations to spark off some new ideas and images for you. In reading these lists you should start to get a 'feel' of the most pertinent words for the person whose hand you are reading.

The particular images induced in your mind are highly relevant to the experience of the person. For example, if you are contemplating the Fire Element in relation to the person's vitality, if the image of a raging bushfire comes to mind, then this would vividly describe an immensely powerful vitality. Such an intense vitality particularly needs to be constrained and directed, since there is a real danger that they will burn themselves out through an inability to relax. If, instead, an image of a spluttering candle comes to mind, then the person's vitality is at a very low ebb and needs to be strengthened. It is important to have faith in the images that come to mind.

Air – Communication

Air embraces the symbolic understanding of these images and their translation into words, so enhancing the successful communication of this knowledge to the other person. To this end, developing a rich and colourful vocabulary is immensely useful. Looking up words, especially the Elemental symbols, in a thesaurus, is a simple way of expanding your ability to articulate the meaning of these images. If you have the time it is also useful to look up the roots of the words in a good dictionary, for you will commonly find links to the Latin or Greek names of the Elements:

	Latin	Greek
Earth	Terra	Ge
Water	Aqua	Hydor
Air	Aer	Aer
Fire	Ignis	Pyr

Fire — Activation

Fire is the energy required to read someone's hand. When this energy is put into the observation, application and visualization of the symbolism, the necessary understanding of the hand is sparked off and can then be communicated to the person. Explaining to them what the various palmar formations mean results in confirmation of this knowledge.

It is common for people to find it difficult to initiate a handreading, saying that they need to study more about it first before they have the confidence. However, it is only in the act of giving a reading that the cheiromantical art is learnt. There are understandable reasons for this reluctance to begin, since everyone who reads hands is automatically expected to possess some sort of transcendent vision which enables them to astound the subject by revealing the intricate and compelling details of their lives. Naturally most students don't feel up to it. In reality very few handreaders ever reach that degree of intuitive development, which often takes a decade or more of diligent practice and experience to cultivate.

The simplest way of dealing with this situation is to admit to the person concerned that you are simply studying handreading and that you want to gain experience of looking at hands. In this more relaxed situation people are usually more than willing to oblige by allowing you to take handprints and/or read their hand. It is important to respect people's wishes if you do find someone who is unwilling to let you read their hand. Even if, as is to be expected, the student feels daunted about doing a comprehensive handreading, then responding to such simple questions as – 'What does that fork on the end of my head line mean?' – often provides a wonderful opportunity to explain the appropriate symbolism.

It is precisely at this point of explanation that the student can become deeply inspired through their symbolic understanding. Henceforth the creative spark rapidly fires the imagination as to the potential of this knowledge. It is often much easier to learn cheiromancy by doing 'live' handreadings, since the other person present generates energy, stimulation and the opportunity for dialogue. Such readings can very easily reveal intimate details about a person's life. It is also important to respect people's privacy and keep any personal details that they entrust you with in strictest confidence.

By contrast, studying cheiromancy from handprints, unless done in a group, is often rather dry and distinctly lacks the stimulus from the other person. In this situation the student will need to generate the 'missing' energy to read the handprint. This requires discipline, and the best way to engage this energy is to have a formal structure for reading the hand. Though there are many ways to approach a reading, the following list of questions will provide a useful framework. It will train you to make your observations and apply the appropriate symbolism. The list should enable you to spot the symbolic patterns throughout the hand. As you contemplate the features write down or make rough notes of the images that come to mind and what you understand by them. Think about how you would communicate your understanding if the person were present.

A SCHEDULE FOR READING THE HAND

The Elemental World

What Element rules the hand shape? Can any other Elements be found in the hand shape? What is the general temperament and character of these Elemental patterns?

What Element rules the skin texture? How does this describe the person's relationship to their environment? How does the Element skin texture interact with the Element of the hand shape?

What is the Elemental sequence of the quadrants? What temperamental pattern is expressed with this quadrant pattern? How do the 1st and 3rd Elements interact? How do the 2nd and 4th Elements interact? Do they concord with the Elements already found in the hand shape and skin texture?

The Celestial World

Are there any developed mounts on the palm? Do they show any particular Planetary energy to be strong? What qualities do they encapsulate?

Are the palmar lines clear or hazy? What is the prevailing Elemental width of lines? How is the person generally expressing their energy in the palmar lines? How does this fit with the predominant Elements in the palm?

Which are the strongest lines? Which are the weakest? What Planetary qualities do they indicate to be strong? What Planetary qualities do they indicate to be weak, and what does this imply?

The Mercury Line

How long is it? What Elemental width is it? How clear is it? How does the line originate, orientate and end? Are there any distinctive characteristics in its length? Is it clearer on the subjective or objective side of the palm? What markings are present? Are there any influence lines? How do the characteristics of this line reflect the pattern of Elemental expression of all the quadrants, in particular the Air quadrant?

What implications do all these formations have for the person's ability to think, plan and make decisions, their range of understanding,

their skills in communication, their style of speech and the functioning of their nervous system?

The Venus Line

Length? Width? Clarity? Origins? Endings? Distinctive characteristics? Degree of curvature? Markings? Influences? How do the characteristics of this line compare with the order and expression of the Earth quadrant?

What implications do all these formations have for the person's vitality, maternal influence, emotional security, ability to express love, self-worth and ability to earn money?

The Mars Line

Degree of presence? What form of line is present? Width? Clarity? Proximity to the Venus line? Is the energy of this line well defined? How do the characteristics of this line compare with the order and expression of the Fire quadrant?

What implications do all these formations have for the person's physical strength, resistance, assertiveness, expression of anger and sexual expression?

The Jupiter Line

Length? Width? Clarity? Origins? Endings? Distinctive characteristics? Degree of curvature? Level of setting? Markings? Influences? How do the characteristics of this line compare with the order and expression of the Water quadrant?

What implications do all these formations have for the person's expression of emotions, understanding of feelings, capacity for relationships, ability to derive inspiration and their degree of compassion?

The Saturn Line

Degree of presence? Degree of lateral displacement? Length? Width? Clarity? Distinctive characteristics? Markings? Influences? How do the characteristics of this line compare with the order and expression of the Earth quadrant?

What implications do all these formations have for the person's discipline, concentration, application, degree of success in their career, paternal influence, inheritance and independence?

The Sun Line

Present/absent? Length? Width? Clarity? Distinctive characteristics, Markings? Relationship to the Saturn line? How do the characteristics of this line compare to the order and expression of the Fire quadrant?

What implications do all these formations have for the person's creative expression, sense of beauty and refinement, inner fulfilment, and degree of fame or recognition?

The Moon Line

Present/absent? Length? Width? Clarity? Markings? Relationship to Mercury, Saturn, Uranus and Pluto lines? How do the characteristics of this line compare to the order and expression of the Water quadrant?

What implications do all these formations have for the person's imagination, metaphysical perception, intuitive ability and degree of clairvoyance?

The Uranus Line

Absent? Degree of presence? Length? Width? Distinctive characteristics? Markings? Relationship to the Mercury line? Links to Venus, Saturn, Sun, Pluto, Jupiter and Neptune lines? How do the characteristics of this line compare to the order and expression of the Air quadrant?

What implications do all these formations have in terms of the person's intuitive ability, sexuality, communication, degree of innovation and invention, health and business sense?

The Neptune Line

Absent? Degree of presence? Length? Width? Distinctive characteristics? Markings? Relationship to the Jupiter line? Links to the Uranus, Sun and Saturn lines? How do the characteristics of this line compare to the order and expression of the Water quadrant?

What implications do all these formations have for the person's romantic ideals, visualization skills, perception and spiritual vision?

The Pluto Line

Present/absent? Length? Width? Markings? Relationship to the Uranus line? Links to the Saturn, Sun and Venus lines? How do the characteristics of this line compare to the order and expression of the Water quadrant?

What implications do all these formations have in terms of the person's sexuality, emotional expression, transformation and healing ability?

What Planetary influence is most evident in the hand shape? How does this compare with the predominant lines? How does the Planet interact with the Element found in the hand shape? Are they compatible?

The Intellectual World

Are the fingers long or short in relation to the palm? What implications does this have for mental range? How does this compare to the formation of the Mercury line? Do they tell the same story?

What phalanges are the strongest/weakest? At what phalangeal level, if any – cardinal, mutable or fixed – does the person predominantly lead their life? How does this compare to the Three Worlds in the hand – palm, lines and fingers?

What Elemental width composes the phalangeal lines? How does this describe how a person is using their overall mental abilities? How does this compare with the prevailing widths of the palmar lines and the Elemental energies predominating in hand shape and quadrants?

Which is the strongest finger (shown by length, width, profile and positive markings)? The second strongest? The third strongest? The weakest? What Elemental order does this sequence describe? What implications does this have for psychological expression? (Use the principle of Elemental manifestation to interpret this Elemental pattern explained in the section on interpreting quadrants.) How are the Elements of the fingers expressed in relation to the Elements in the quadrants? What implications does this show in their mind–body relationship?

Are there any distinct spaces between the fingers? What mental qualities are accentuated? Which are inhibited?

Note the length, width, profile and markings of the phalanges of all fingers. For all top phalanges, note tip shape, how each is functioning, and what this implies.

The Index Finger

Is the finger long or short? Is its width consistent throughout? Is there any fullness in profile along its length? What phalangeal level is the clearest? Are there any bends in its length? Does the Jupiter line or any other line supply it with energy? Is the supply strong or weak?

What implications do all these features have for the person's confidence and self-image?

Cancer phalanx

Compare the functioning of the Cancer phalanx to the Lunar mount. Does the Mercury or Saturn line contact the Lunar mount?

Pisces phalanx

Compare the functioning of the Pisces phalanx to the Jupiter line.

Scorpio phalanx

Compare the functioning of the Scorpio phalanx to the Mars active and passive mounts, as well as the Mars line.

The Medicus Finger

Is the finger long or short? Is its width consistent throughout? Is there any fullness in profile along its length? What phalangeal level is the clearest? Are there any bends in its length? Does the Saturn line or any other line supply it with energy? Is the supply strong or weak?

What implications do all these features have for the person's self-discipline and sense of security?

Capricorn phalanx

Compare the functioning of the Capricorn phalanx to the Saturn line.

Virgo phalanx

Compare the functioning of the Virgo phalanx to the Mercury lines.

Taurus phalanx

Compare the functioning of the Taurus phalanx to the Venus line.

The Annularis Finger

Is the finger long or short? Is its width consistent throughout? Is there any fullness in profile along its length? What phalangeal level is the clearest? Are there any bends in its length? Does the Sun line, if present, or any other line supply energy to the annularis finger? Is the supply strong or weak? What implications do all these features have for the person's creativity and self-expression?

Aries phalanx

Compare the functioning of the Aries phalanx to the Mars active mount, as well as the Mars line.

Sagittarius phalanx

Compare the functioning of the Sagittarius phalanx to the Jupiter line.

Leo phalanx

Compare the functioning of the Leo phalanx to the Sun line.

The Auricularis Finger

Is the finger long or short? Is its width consistent throughout? Is there any fullness in profile along its length? What phalangeal level is the clearest? Are there any bends in its length? Does the Uranus line or any other line supply it with energy? Is the supply strong or weak? What implications do all these features have in terms of the person's sexuality and communicative ability?

Libra phalanx

Compare the functioning of the Libra phalanx to the Venus line.

Gemini phalanx

Compare the functioning of the Gemini phalanx to the Mercury lines.

Aquarius phalanx

Compare the functioning of the Aquarius phalanx to the Saturn line.

The Pollex

Note the height of setting on palm. What level does the will-power/vital energy operate on? How developed is the thumb? Which phalanx is the stronger? Implications?

Upper phalanx

Note length/width/profile/tip shape/markings. What is the quality of will-power implied?

Lower phalanx

Note length/width/profile/markings. How clear is the person's reason? Note the angle of the thumb. How is their will-power flowing?

From all these observations on the thumb assess what potential the person has to change.

From going through this list of questions it should be possible to build up a picture of how a person should best direct their energies. From the Elemental World the weakest Elements describe what a person should focus upon physically. From the Celestial World the weakest lines reveal what areas a person should develop emotionally. From the Intellectual World the most deficient phalanges reveal what areas of knowledge they should most concentrate upon.

Ether – Entering the Flow

Ether symbolizes the 'flow' to handreading, in which observation, application of symbolism, interpretation and communication become a continuous process – in other words where all the elements of cheiromancy are brought together. With practice it is soon possible to experience a few moments of this 'flow' where a profound rapport develops between you and whoever is the focus of the reading. This is the moment when cheiromancy truly comes alive.

Using the Elements to represent each stage of reading a hand, the student should honestly look at each Element within themselves to consider where the weakest part of their skill lies. For by developing and working on the weakest Elements of the practice, the flow of cheiromancy is enhanced. The honest student should also be able to spot the correlation between the stages of handreading and the expression of Elements in their temperament. For example someone who has difficulty understanding symbolism and trusting the images from their imagination is weak in the Water Element. This in turn suggests that they will have relationship difficulties stemming from an inability to express and understand feelings.

CHAPTER 17

Right and Left Hands

THIS topic has been intentionally left till after the synthesis chapter, for unless there is confidence in reading one hand, reading both will be twice as confusing!

Between both hands there exists a definite polarity of energy, making one hand 'active' relative to the other 'passive' hand. It is necessary to enquire at the outset of a reading whether the person is right- or left-handed. The majority of people are right-handed. There are a few who say they are ambidextrous, but simple questioning will reveal that they do most of their manual activities using one hand rather than the other. Whatever hand is used the most, this is taken to be the active hand. Only a very small minority are truly ambidextrous and can use either hand with equal ease.

Where there is any uncertainty in deciding which hand is active, then simple inspection of the thumbs can decide the matter. The hand with the most developed thumb indicates that it has the most vital energy flowing through it and as a result can be taken to be the active hand.

This polarity of the hands has important diagnostic significance; the active hand with the greater energy flow within it undergoes change in its development and lineal formations that reflect the immediate present in a person's life. By contrast, the passive hand with the least

energy flow undergoes minimal change. Hence the features and formations reflect the person's past.

In symbolic terms the active hand can be seen to be more Solar in nature, and the passive hand more Lunar. The passive hand very faithfully records the experience of childhood and particularly shows the parental influence. It is quite common to find the psychological patterns of one parent, usually the more dominant, 'stamped' onto the lines on the passive hand. Rarely, where both parents have equal influence, the lineal patterns may well be descriptive of their emotional relationship. When considering parental influence in the lines, the formation of the Saturn line describes the paternal influence while the formation of the Venus line describes the maternal influence. The experience that is 'stored' in the passive hand can powerfully colour the person's behaviour in a largely unconscious (Lunar) way.

The active hand very strongly shows a person's search for self-identity (Solar). The physical development of the palm and lineal patterns shows the degree to which this evolution has taken place.

The comparison of active and passive hands tells the story of where a person is in their own evolution. They may have overcome the traumas and inhibitions from the past and gained in strength of character. Or they may still be a victim of past circumstances, largely unaware of their potential to change.

In practice it is best to take the active hand first, since this reflects what is currently happening in their lives, then to contrast its features with the passive hand. As you consider each feature in the active hand, glance at its counterpart in the passive hand. For example if there is an island on the Jupiter line in the active hand at the person's current age, then it indicates that they are going through a time of emotional conflict and uncertainty. Is there a corresponding island in the Jupiter line in the passive hand? If one is present, then it suggests that the cause of the person's difficulty has come from their past experience unconsciously influencing the present. A successful resolution to the conflict would need to address the traumas and fears from the past. Alternatively the absence of an island in the Jupiter line in the passive hand shows that the conflict has been generated by more immediate behaviour and recent events. If the person is honest about their feelings and sensitive to the feelings of others this will do much to identify and remove the source of their conflict.

The reverse situation, where the island is present in the passive hand but not in the active one, suggests that the emotional conflict from the past has been overcome. This additionally means that the person will have gained in strength and inner awareness, knowledge that can potentially be used to help other people going through similar emotional conflicts.

The divergence in hand shape and palmar quadrants between active and passive hands strongly reflects changes in physical constitution and basic temperament. Divergence in lineal patterns reflects changes in emotional experience and expression: divergence in phalangeal development reveals changes in mental attitudes, ability, expression and knowledge.

In general when a handreading reveals that a person is at a time of confusion and uncertainty in their lives, then you will need to consider the comparison of the hands very carefully, for confusion is usually created through ignorance of how the past is influencing the present. Experience gradually teaches how information from both hands is to be equated.

Modern neurology has identified the right hand as being connected to the left side of the brain where the speech centre is located, while the left hand is connected to the right side of the brain where the spatial centre is located. The right hand has come to be linked with the more rational structured mode of thought, while the left hand has come to be linked with the more imaginative and intuitive mode of thought. Cheiromancy confirms such observations. On the right hand the Mercury line is much more likely to terminate where it crosses the Sun line, whereas on the left hand it is much more likely to extend through to the Lunar mount. Once again this reflects the Solar and Lunar polarity between the right and left hands.

CHAPTER 18

Astrological Connections

As previously mentioned the history of cheiromancy has been strongly associated with astrology. This is particularly highlighted by the fact that many of the people who have contributed to its history have also been astrologers. Paracelsus, Agrippa, Saunders and Wharton have already been mentioned. Other astrologer-cheiromancers include Jerome Cardin (1501–76) and Johannes Rothmann, whose text *Cheiromantia* was translated by Wharton. A quick glance at Fludd's preface illustration (Figure 2.1, page 8), explained in Chapter 2, shows astrology (genethlialogia) also included in his ring of microcosmic arts along with cheiromancy.

Central to the fascination between the astrological chart and the hand was the Hermetic idea that 'Man was made in the image of the heavens'. Much of the symbolism is common to both disciplines: Elements, Planets and Zodiacal signs. So after looking at a map of the heavens, inspection of the hand was made to see just how this pattern manifested on earth.

Those who are unfamiliar with astrological ideas may find this chapter a bit of a challenge. For ease of study most of the astrological terms used are listed in the Glossary at the end of the book.

THE SYMBOLIC UNIVERSE

The Hermetic universe is based on a system of symbolic correspondence, whereby the heavens above influence the earth below. Mercury 'the messenger of the gods' provides the link through which this concordance is brought about, for Mercury is the Celestial counterpart to Ether on earth. In the heavens Mercury symbolically embodies all the other Planets, while on earth Ether is the quintessence of the Four Elements. Each of the remaining six Planets possesses a temperament from the four combinations of hot, cold, wet and dry in turn. The temperaments of these six Planets resonate through the Ether and influence their Elemental counterparts below. Saturn is cold and dry, which has an affinity with the Earth Element; the Moon and Venus are both cold and moist, having an affinity with the Water Element; Jupiter is hot and moist, which has an affinity with the Air Element; while the Sun and Mars are both hot and dry, having an affinity with the Fire Element. This cosmology is summarized in Figure 18.1.

Descending from the Realm of Light, the diagram shows the Planets above in the Celestial World resonating with the Elements in the

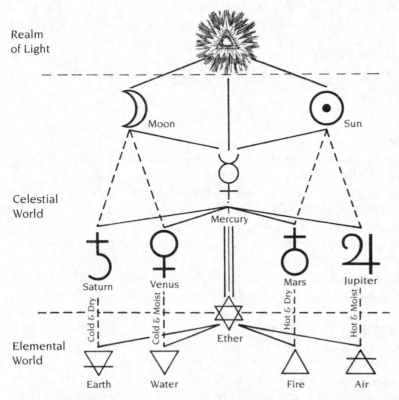

Realm
of Light

Celestial
World

Elemental
World

Moon

Sun

Mercury

Saturn   Venus   Mars   Jupiter

Cold & Dry   Cold & Moist   Ether   Hot & Dry   Hot & Moist

Earth   Water   Fire   Air

Figure 18.1 The Relationship
between the Planets the Elements

Elemental World below. On the right of the
diagram is the Sun, the Universal Father, which
has dominion over the masculine Elements Fire
and Air, while on the left is the Moon, the Universal Mother, which has dominion over the
feminine Elements Earth and Water. In the
middle the synonymous relationship between
Mercury and Ether mediates the influence of
the Planets on the Elements. On the right the
hot and moist nature of Jupiter influences the
Air Element, and the hot and dry nature of Mars
influences the Fire Element. On the left the cold
and dry nature of Saturn influences the Earth
Element, and the cold and moist nature of Venus
influences the Water Element.

Since Mercury is symbolically linked to the
Etheric energy of the palmar lines, the fundamental relationship between astrology and
cheiromancy is found between the Planets in the

heavens and the formation of the lines on the
palm.

The astrologer-cheiromancers implicitly
believed in the relationship between the astrological chart and the hand. An illustration after
one from the 1652 translation of Johannes Rothmann's *Cheiromantia*[27] (Figure 18.2, page 174)
demonstrates this.

Rothmann's illustration draws attention to
one very important point about the juxtaposition of cheiromancy and astrology. Since the
seventeenth century when they were meaningfully brought together, astrological practice has
changed significantly both in technique and
interpretation, while cheiromantical knowledge
has largely remained dormant. Despite the
popularity of astrology today it has lost the
knowledge of the symbolic significance that it
possessed until the seventeenth century. This

symbolic detail is essential when comparing the astrological chart with the hand to find all the correspondences. To rediscover the link between the two disciplines, it is important to go back to the traditional aspects of astrology.

Of the many changes to astrological practice, Planetary rulership of the houses is significantly different from contemporary astrology.

Regiomontanus was the preferred house system used by astrologers in the seventeenth century and it was also in use long before Regiomontanus put his name to it.

In interpretation, astrologers in earlier centuries placed emphasis upon ascertaining the relative strength or weakness of each Planet (called its essential dignity) from its placing in the chart. The strength and weakness of a Planet is ascribed on the basis of Zodiac signs, exaltations, triplicities, terms, faces and mutual receptions, particular houses, speed and direction of motion, along with legions of other technical details. This provides a picture of the most influential Planets in the astrological chart. Space in this book does not permit a thorough exposition of essential dignity, since this is one of the major domains of traditional astrology.[28]

SYMBOLIC CONNECTIONS BETWEEN HAND SHAPE AND THE ASTROLOGICAL CHART

===

There is a strong correlation between the Planet that rules the Ascendant (called in traditional astrology the horoscope) or a Planet present in the 1st house of an astrological chart and the Planetary hand shape. This is because the sign at the Ascendant and the 1st house of the chart describe the health, vitality and shape of the physical body. The Planetary hand shape may also be found reflected by the Planet that rules the 3rd house cusp or by a Planet present in the 3rd house. This is because when each of the houses is correlated with the different parts of the body the 3rd house corresponds to the arms and hands.

If there is no correlation between the rulers of the 1st or 3rd houses and the Planetary hand shape, this suggests that these Planets may lack dignity. In the absence of any connection here, any Planet that has dignity in the astrological chart may well correlate with the shape of the hand.

In studying the Planetary hand shapes illustrated in Chapter 15, astrologers may wish to consider studying the correlations between the 1st and 3rd houses and hand shape. There is a list of birth data at the end of the chapter from which you can draw up the corresponding natal charts.

Before examining Rothmann's illustration in detail another important principle needs to be addressed. To quote Rothmann:'*Whether we must judge by the Right Hand or the Left?*' That is, which of the two hands most reflects the astrological chart? As Rothmann explains:

It is certain, that in one Hand the lines, and other Signatures, are very often more manifest, and by their Featnesse [neatness] *more perspicuous, than in the other, as well as in Man and Woman; wherefore a Question hence arises, whether in both Sexes the Right or Left hand is to be taken; or whether the Right Hand in a Man (as some teach) and the Left in a Woman only?*

To which Rothmann answers:

That Hand (in both Sexes) which shows and exhibits the Lines thereof most clearly, and abounds with a Series of Characters and Signs: Yet so, as that the other whose Lines are more obscure may pay its contribution. If in both hands they consent and appear to be faire and comely, they declare a constancy of Fortune and Health. The cause of which diversity is this: He who is borne in the day time, and hath a Masculine planet [the Sun, Saturne, Jupiter or Mars] Lord of his Geniture, beares the more Remarkable Signs in his Right Hand, especially when the Signe Ascending is also Masculine. The contrary befalls those that are born by Night, so oft as a Feminine planet predominates, and the Signe Ascending if Feminine. If both Hands agree, it must needs be, that in a Day – Nativity the Feminine Planets Rule: or that there falls out a Mixture of Masculine and Feminine. So in the Night by the contrary Reason: which Diversity must necessarily be observed.

From this quote Rothmann makes it apparent that you judge the hand that has the most clearly defined and prominent lines and markings (*Signs*) on it.

He explains the '*diversity*' of lines between hands through the right hand being masculine (Solar) and the left hand being feminine (Lunar). So when a person is born during the day – a masculine time – with a masculine Planet, such as the Sun, Saturn, Jupiter or Mars as chart ruler, this predominantly masculine influence is reflected by the right hand possessing the most defined and prominent lines. This is especially true if the sign at the Ascendant is also masculine (Fire or Air signs) as this gives the hand a further masculine influence.

Conversely, when a person is born during the night – a feminine time – with a feminine Planet, such as the Moon or Venus as chart ruler, this predominantly feminine influence is reflected by the left hand possessing the most defined and prominent lines. This is especially true if the sign on the Ascendant is also feminine (Earth or Water signs) as this gives the hand a further feminine influence.

In these descriptions it is important to appreciate that in Rothmann's era the day started at dawn, at 'day break', rather than at midnight.

If both hands have equally strong and defined lines, then for someone born in the daytime this suggests that the feminine Planets rule the chart. Alternatively in a night-time nativity this suggests that the masculine Planets rule the chart. At first glance this may seem contrary to what you might expect, but on deeper reflection this principle makes sense. Take the case of a person born in the day. This being a masculine time, you would expect to find this reflected by the most defined and prominent lines being found in the right hand. However, in this case, where both hands have equally strong and defined lines it suggests feminine Planets rule the chart, from the predominance and strength of feminine influence reflected in the hands at this otherwise masculine time.

Finally Rothmann mentions that where both hands have equally strong and defined lines, this can be attributed to a '*Mixture of Masculine and Feminine*' influences, such as when a feminine Planet rules a daytime chart.

In Figure 18.2, an illustration from Rothmann's *Cheiromantia*, the right hand has the more defined, clear lines. Note that the hands shown here are from a woodcut so the right hand as seen in the diagram is actually the right hand and not the reverse as in a handprint. The chart is timed at 4.00 a.m. on 24 April 1589, in Thuringia. This was taken to be a daytime chart since dawn was imminent. Aries, a masculine sign, is at the Ascendant of the astrological chart, while Mars, a masculine Planet and ruler of Aries is the chart ruler. This is also reflected by the Mars line only being found in the right hand. If you examine Figure 18.2 closely you will be able to see the Mars line present on the right hand, curving around where you might expect to find the Venus line. The Venus line is actually the next line out, beginning from the bar line on the Mars line and then fusing with the Saturn line.

This illustrates Rothmann's principle; here is a person born at dawn with a masculine Planet, Mars, as his chart ruler and a masculine sign,

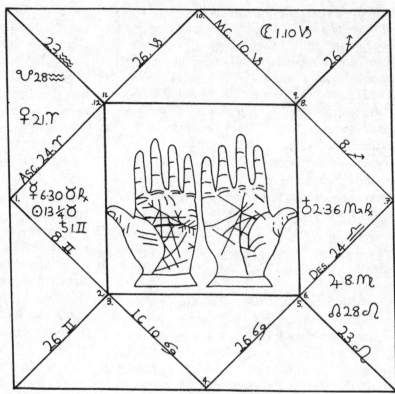

Figure 18.2 After an illustration in Johannes Rothmann's work *Cheiromantia* (tr 1652)

Aries at the Ascendant, showing his right hand to contain the clearer, more defined lines, so reflecting his astrological chart.

Rothmann primarily examines the hand:

In his Right Hand the Epatica [head/Mercury line] *is visible, but passeth not the concave* [the centre hollow of the palm] *thereof. And therefore it shows his shortnesse of Life; especially, because a certain line is transversely let fall from the Vital* [Venus line], *to the end of the Epatica, as it were inter-rupting the Progress thereof.*

Rothmann is clearly concerned by the relatively short Mercury line on the right hand, ending abruptly with a bar line that leads towards the Venus line, which he perceives as indicating a short life. It is interesting that he saw death reflected in this line rather than the life line:

With other cheiromantical observations he looks for correlations in the astrological chart as well;

The vitall [Venus line] *of the Left Hand, receiveth a Line arising from the Tuberculum* [mount] *of Saturne. The Place of the Vitall, thereby touch'd and almost broken, appertains to the 25. yeare of his Age, or thereabouts, wherein without Doubt the Horoscope comes by Direction to the Body of Saturne. Indeed Venus is present but in a strange sign: Whence the native shall then very hardly escape.*

This comparative observation between the left hand and the chart shows that Rothmann was specifically interested in the influence line from the Saturn mount weakening the flow of energy in the Venus line. Having previously drawn the conclusion that the native is likely to die young, Rothmann is clearly looking for other signs in the hand to confirm this. With Saturn naturally signifying death, and this influence line from the Saturn mount weakening his vitality, Rothmann would have regarded this as very ominous. Noting the age of 25 to be the time of this Saturnine influence, Rothmann then turns to the chart for confirmation of this. Using standard Ptolemaic primary directions it is possible to get the degree of the horoscope (Ascendant) to contact the 'Body of Saturne' at exactly 25 years of age, confirming Rothmann's observation in the left hand. Furthermore he notes that Venus, ruler of the 'vitall' line in the hand, in the astrological chart is weakened by its placing in Aries, the sign of its detriment – a further indication of the vulnerability of his life at this time.

Having considered the placing of Venus in the chart in relation to the Venus line, he then looks at its placing in the heavens in more detail:

But although Venus (in the very cusp of the Horoscope) doth produce no slow Ingenuity: yet being in the House of Mars, or a Forraigne Signe, shee will encline the Native to all manner of wickednesse [Petulancy, Lasciviousness, Inconstancy, etc]. Mars Lord of the Geniture (Venus participating) afflicting Mercury (in Taurus and Retrograde) by an Angular Opposition, the same. Therefore hee denoteth, or rather maketh him Contentious, Disobedient, violent unfaithfull, etc. All which are manifestly seen by the Evill Disposition of the Lines in his Hand.

He comments on Venus' placing in the horoscope (Ascendant) at 21° Aries. The Ascendant of the chart is shown at 24° Aries. A Planet placed on the Ascendant, called the rising Planet, has a powerful influence in the native's chart. However, Venus' placing in Aries, 'the House of Mars', the sign of its detriment, indicates that the loving Watery nature of Venus is compromised in the Fire sign of Aries. If, by

contrast, Venus had been placed in Libra, the sign of its dignity (the opposite sign of the Zodiac to Aries) then Rothmann might have given a much more positive description of the Planet; temperate, loving and faithful. The description that Rothmann provides 'Petulancy, Lasciviousness, Inconstancy, etc', gives prominence to the more negative side of Venus in this person's character.

Next he turns his attention to Mars, the Planet that rules Aries and in this astrological chart is the chart ruler ('Lord of the Geniture'). The principle aspect of Mars that Rothmann sees in the chart is its opposition from Mercury. Clearly Rothmann perceives in this opposition a struggle between the native's strong physical energy, symbolized by Mars, and the expression of his ideas, symbolized by Mercury. Hence the description 'maketh him Contentious, Disobedient, violent unfaithfull, etc.'

For comparison Rothmann starts by looking for the presence of Mars, shown by the Mars line, in the hand;

Mars hath a Sister appearing in the Right Hand; but none in the Left. This begetteth wrath, and incites the Native to Warlike Arts, as to be an Engineer, or a Gun-smith, making Warlike Armes and Instruments of all kinds:.

The Mars line on the right hand is described as being a 'Sister' of the Planet in the heavens. In Hermetic philosophy the heavens were regarded as masculine and the earth as feminine. From a cheiromantical perspective the prominence of such a strong (possibly Fire quality) Mars line indeed 'begetteth wrath, and incites the native to warlike arts, as to be an engineer, or a gunsmith . . .', though the idea of the engineer is also likely to have come from the Sun being placed in the 1st house in the fixed Earth sign of Taurus in his chart.

Rothmann returns to the astrological chart to further consider the position of Mars.

Only this when Mars is not Angular, and in his own House (sign), you shall find no Effects of him in the Hand: yet being retrograde hee possesses Men with unhappy Malice, and threatens some Adversities especially in Old Age. And therefore when he neither shows a Proper line in both hands, nor exhibits in one a line that is decently drawn, you may safely adjudge his Decrees, and lesse Prosperous.

From the astrological chart Mars is angular by its placing in the 7th house (the angles in a chart are the cusps of the 1st, 7th, 4th and 10th houses) and in its own sign of Scorpio which it also rules. Mars is strongly dignified (strengthened) by this placing in the chart, which is how Rothmann accounts for the strong Mars line in his right hand. Rothmann clearly perceives that the dignity of Mars is weakened by its retrograde ($\mathrm{R_x}$) (backward) motion, giving rise to the idea of adversity. From the strength of Mars' placing in the chart the direct or forward movement of the Planet would normally have indicated the freedom to express its dynamic energy in a powerful way, yet here its retrograde motion significantly frustrates this expression, further supporting the idea of adversity.

Rothmann then considers the influence of Mercury and Venus in the hand:

The Cephalica [health/Uranus line], *increasing the strength of his Wit, wherewith the Tuberculum* [mount] *of Mercury agreeth, though slenderly, because it is marked with two Incisures* [lines], *at the Heart, in the utmost part of his Hand.*

Rothmann perceives the bars on the Mercury mount of the left hand to detract from the strength of the traditional Mercury (modern Uranus) line, since the line is prevented from reaching the Mercury mount. Though Rothmann does not mention it, this is an indication of Mercury's retrograde motion in the astrological chart.

Venus presents three sufficiently clear Incisures [lines] *in her Region: the rest I found Incult* [rude].

Rothmann perceived these three lines radiating down from the Mars mount to the Venus line on the left hand as indicating rudeness and lack of refinement. Venus is symbolically connected with culture and refinement, so he saw this interruption to the flow of the Venus line as indicating a lack of these qualities. Elsewhere Rothmann comments further on the same feature:

A treble Crosse about the vitall, by the Place of Mars: But in Uxorious matters, it argues Crosse Fortune, and a bad Belief. In the Nativity, Venus is shrewdly suspected for her positure, especially for that her Dispositor is resident in the West Angle.

These incisures cause Rothmann to question this person's sexual morality and attitude towards women. Again he sees this feature as correlating with Venus' affliction in Aries in the astrological chart, where also Venus is disposed by Mars. This disposition symbolically indicates the power of Mars over Venus.

Of the Saturn line he observes firstly from the right hand:

The Saturnia descending by an unaccustomed Path, plainly showes a Corrupt Nature.

The traditional path of the Saturn line starts at the centre of the palmar base and rises up towards the Saturn mount. The distinctly displaced path of the Saturn line in his right hand Rothmann interprets as showing 'a Corrupt Nature'.

The same line passing above the Restricta [lines of the wrist], *to the Region of the Moone, is also a sign of Adversities, and Secret Enemies. And verily there is almost nothing observed in this Geniture, that disposes to a Prosperous Fortune.*

This placing of the Saturn line from the Lunar mount can indicate emotional rejection from the family, which could possibly be how Rothmann perceived the line indicating adversity.

Astrologically, Saturn is fairly strongly placed in the chart. It is in an angular house and in its own triplicity. The Moon by contrast is weak, since it is placed in Capricorn, the sign of its detriment, where it is also disposed by Saturn, the sign's ruler. Since the Moon rules the 4th house of fathers, the Moon in such poor dignity in the 9th house suggests the rejection of a father who was away travelling. Since Saturn rules the 10th house of mothers, the placing of Saturn in the 1st house while disposing the Moon suggests the dominant influence of his mother during childhood.

The idea of *'Secret Enemies'* could also have come from Mars, the chart ruler, being placed in the 7th house of open enemies. However, since the Planet is placed in the secretive sign of Scorpio this colours the interpretation to *'Secret Enemies'*. Additionally since the Ascendant of the chart is 24° of Aries, then Mars ruling Aries also rules a significant portion of the 12th house, which is linked to secret enemies. The retrograde motion of Mars strongly suggests someone getting their own back.

Rothmann found correlations between the Lunar mount in the left hand and the placing of the Moon in the astrological chart:

The two lines in the Tuberculum [mount] of the Moone, premonstrate Journeys: as doe also the Moon in the 9. and Mercury in the first House.

Lines on the Lunar mount have been taken to indicate journeys. In a chart the 9th house is traditionally linked to long journeys and the 3rd to short journeys. Mercury, a natural significator of communication, rules the 3rd house of the chart, while the Moon is placed in the 9th. Thus Rothmann concludes that the native will do a lot of travelling.

Next he considers Jupiter in both the chart and the hand:

Jupiter is most dejectedly Collocated: yet he hath adorned his feate [Jupiter mount] with a little line. This makes a triangle in Earthly Signs, the Moone shining by a Sinister Aspect unto him, the Sun and

Mercury by a Dexter. Wherefore he asswageth and strangely declineth all Misfortune, especially such as appertaine to the Impediments of the Mind.

The adorning of his *'feate'* refers to the bar lines present on the Jupiter mounts in both hands. Jupiter distinctly lacks dignity in this chart, for it is located in Virgo, the sign of its detriment, separating from a square aspect to Saturn. However the Sun has a trine (120°) aspect to Jupiter, and the Moon a dexter trine to Jupiter as part of a grand trine in Earth signs. It is important to note that in traditional astrology Planets had their own orbs. The orb of the Sun was 17° and that of the Moon 12° 30'. Thus the Sun and Moon do have a trine aspect between them, whereas in modern astrology this would not be the case. This contact between the luminaries and Jupiter, the greater benefic, provided Rothmann's unusually favourable judgement.

Finally Rothmann looks at the Sun;

The Sun is Angular, and Riseth exactly with the Pleides in a trine to Jupiter. And therefore you see a smalle Crosse under his Mount, notifying, that this Man shall not altogether live obscure.

The Sun is dignified in the chart from its placing in the angular 1st house and having a trine aspect to Jupiter. This he contrasts with the *'smalle Crosse under his Mount'*, an ending of the Sun line which traditionally indicates success and recognition through the help and goodwill of others. However, the dignity of the Sun in the chart is blighted by its conjunction with the constellation of the *'Pleides'*. The fixed star Alcyone within the constellation is associated with sorrow and suggests that his life ends in tears. This explains Rothmann's less favourable interpretation of this feature.

Having covered all the Planets in the astrological chart and looked at the corresponding formations in the hand, Rothmann further contributes observations made solely from the hand:

In the Left Hand the Epatica [head/Mercury line] *is wanting, and two lines (almost parallel) are let fall from the vital to the Mensall* [heart/Jupiter line]: *which argue the weakness of the Liver, and an evill composure thereof: likewise a Pravity both of Wit and Behaviour.*

In the left hand the course of Epatica [head/ Mercury line] is fused with the Venus line. Hence it is described as '*wanting*'. The two parallel lines traversing across the palm essentially fuse the energies from the Venus/Mercury line with the Jupiter line.

The liver is ruled by Jupiter, which is responsible for maintaining the balance of the humours in the blood and ensuring the vital force (Mercury) flows properly through it. Rothmann perceives these parallel lines as indicating weakness of the liver, which in turn causes an imbalance of the humours in the blood: '*an evill composure thereof*'.

It is interesting to note that Rothmann has a contrary labelling and interpretation of the two traditional Mercury lines. The head line he calls the Epatica, meaning the 'liver' line, while the health line, described above, he calls the Cephalica, meaning the 'head' line.

Having perceived from his left hand a predisposition to liver weakness, Rothmann then looks at his right hand in more detail to find when such weakness is likely to be expressed:

In the Right Hand, the vitall is variously touch'd: wherefore number yea so many Future Diseases, about 7, 14, 25, 32 etc. yeare of his Age.

There are four strong bar lines radiating from the Mars line on the right hand, cutting through the Venus ('*vitall*') line at these ages. The strong Fiery nature of these lines interrupting the flow of vital energy suggests powerful fevers breaking out at these times.

In conclusion Rothmann sums up his interpretation with:

This Diversity of Lines in the Hands, floweth from a troubled Imagination of the Macrocosm,

The lines on the hand were considered to be the microcosm, whereas the Planets in the heavens were considered to be the macrocosm. Rothmann clearly attributes the pattern of lines in the hand to be an expression of Planetary influence.

Birth Data

Saturn Hand Shape (Figure 15.1): 16 Dec. 1959. Time given 6–7 a.m., rectified to 04.00 a.m. GMT; Long. 36E48. Lat. 01S17.

Jupiter Hand Shape (Figure 15.2): 6 Aug. 1933. Time given 03.00 a.m. BST; Long. 01W34. Lat. 53N48.

Mars Hand Shape (Figure 15.3): 20 Aug. 1948. Time given 06.30 a.m. BST; Long. 01W15. Lat. 51N46.

Venus Hand Shape (Figure 15.4): 30 June 1945. Time given 03.30 a.m. DST (Double Summer Time), rectified to 01.18 a.m. GMT; Long. 01W22. Lat. 54N54.

Solar Hand Shape (Figure 15.5): 4 Oct. 1947. Time unknown, rectified to 23.00 p.m. GMT; Long. 00W00. Lat. 52N32.

Moon Hand Shape (Figure 15.6): 20 Dec. 1962. Time given 01.00 a.m. GMT; rectified to 01.12 a.m. GMT, Long. 08W37. Lat. 42N52. This example is found as 'A Study of the Astrological Correlations in a Hand' in Chapter 19.

Mercury Hand Shape (Figure 15.7): 26 Sep. 1936. Time given 00.35 a.m. BST; Long. 00W01 Lat. 51N30.

Example Handreadings

A CHEIROMANTICAL ASSESSMENT OF A HAND

—

See Figure 19.1. This is the right 'active' hand of a 34-year-old male. Though this reading is primarily a cheiromantical reading of the hand, astrological observations are included at the end of certain sections in square brackets based upon the following birth data; 7 Sept. 1956. Time given 01.00 a.m. BST: Long. 05W00 Lat. 53N35. This cheiromantical reading follows the sequence described under the 'Schedule for Reading the Hand' in Chapter 16.

The Elemental World

The large, expansive square palm with long, well-developed fingers identifies the hand to be Air shape. The basal portion of the palm, particularly under the Earth quadrant, is also well developed. Primarily the hand indicates that he is a thinker who spends a lot of his time absorbed in his ideas. The development of the palm in the region of the Earth quadrant compensates for the aloofness that can be associated with the Air shape hand and provides much-needed grounding of his ideas. It indicates that he is a practical thinker with a wide range of interests to do with the Earth such as geology, geography, botany, ecology, nutrition, herbs and healing.

The strength of the Earth influence here benefits him in other ways, for the pure Air-shaped hand typically describes someone who has a lanky frame and a weak constitution who is often highly strung. With the influence of the Earth the constitution is much more robust and his nervous state is more composed. Outwardly he appears to others as solid as a rock.

The Air-shaped hand is complemented by an Air skin texture. The skin texture indicates that he is particularly receptive to the exchange of ideas around him. This combination of the hand shape and skin texture suggests that he enjoys work involving the exchange and communication of his interests, such as educating people to be more aware of their environment, teaching botany or explaining the effects of nutrition on health.

Refer to Figure 19.2.

The Elemental sequence of the quadrants is:

1. Largest – Earth.

2. Second Largest – Water.

3. Third Largest – Air.

4. Smallest – Fire.

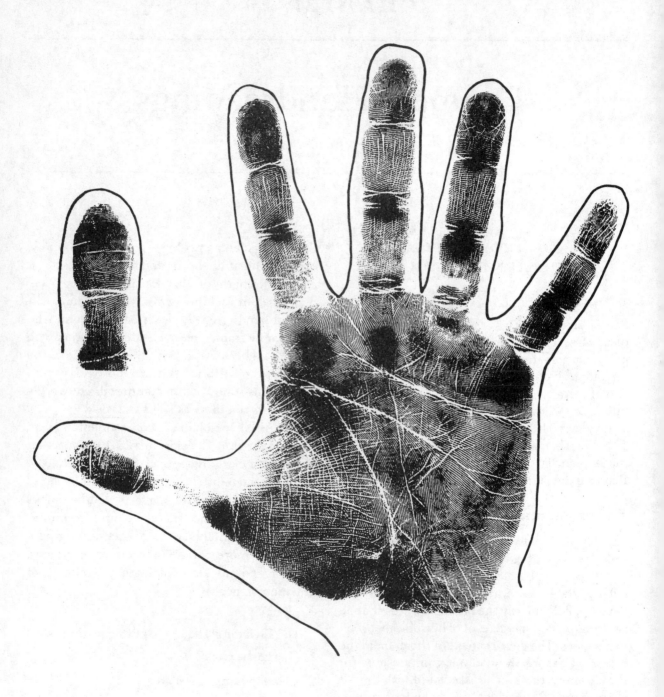

Figure 19.1 Handprint 1 at 75% – A
Cheiromantical Assessment

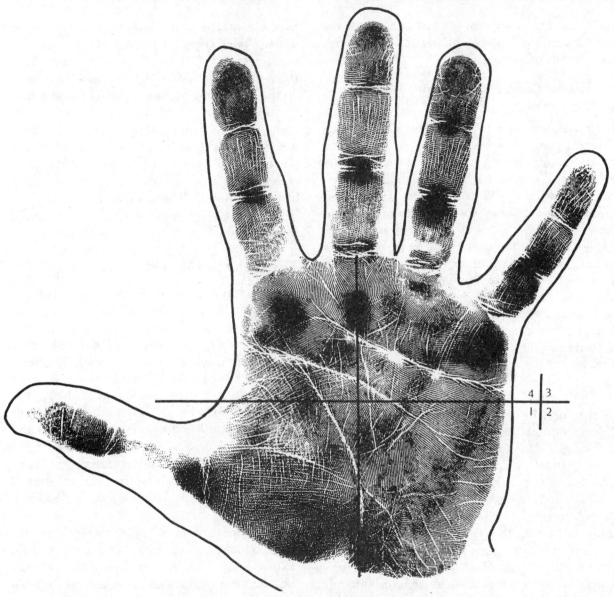

Figure 19.2 Handprint 1 – Showing the Palmar Quadrants

1. Largest Quadrant – Earth

With Earth the predominating Element in the palm, he will strongly identify with a need for a base, placing much importance upon security and stability in his life. He will have a profound love of nature, expressed in such pastimes as gardening (growing unusual plants – Air-shaped hand), walking (especially through mountains and wide open spaces – again Air-shaped hand) and other outdoor activities. He would like routine work so that he can order his life in a regular pattern. He has an aptitude for administration and would patiently deal with tiny details of his work.

2. Second Largest Quadrant – Water

With Water the second largest quadrant, this is the missing Element. This suggests that he has difficulty in expressing feelings and being aware of the feelings of others. As a result his relationships tend to be disappointing. Symbolically when the Water Element is placed on an Air hand it tends to evaporate rather than flow as liquid. This shows that he rationalizes his feelings. Rather than being aware of how his feelings actually are in a situation, he will tend to imagine how they should be. An interest in art is shown here as a means of contacting his feelings. For someone with an Air hand, music is typically the most accessible artistic medium. Fishing and sailing are other watery pastimes that he will find emotionally rewarding.

3. Third Largest Quadrant – Air

With Air the third largest quadrant, this Element describes his resources. This indicates a strong ability to communicate his ideas. In combination with the Air hand shape and Air skin texture, it indicates a particularly powerful facility to share his knowledge on a larger scale as in lecturing or broadcasting. In combination with the first Earth quadrant it indicates that he can skillfully structure ideas before communicating them to an audience. By contrast, personal instruction would be much more difficult for him to give, since this would require qualities from the Water quadrant. This combination of Air and Earth quadrants shows he will naturally plan his actions thoroughly before doing anything.

4. Smallest Quadrant – Fire

The smallest quadrant describes the Element that is least developed. A deficiency of the Fire Element means he lacks energy to get things done. Considering the strength of the Air Element in his hand, there is a tendency for him to think rather than act or to find himself exhausted through trying to pursue too many interests. Procrastination is likely to be one of his shortcomings. The Fire quadrant, in combination with the Water Element in the second quadrant position, indicates that he has difficulty in asserting his point of view. He can be secretive of his intentions. He has a strong need to express his energy through sport or martial arts to avoid inner tension.

The Celestial World

The handprint shows that the Venus, Jupiter, Saturn and Mercury mounts are developed. The Venus mount is perhaps the most dominant, which indicates that he enjoys material pleasures, he is good at earning money, he has a strong love for his family and he has a powerful sense of rhythm, especially in music. The Jupiter mount indicates that he is ambitious in fulfilling his ideals and is concerned for the rights and well-being of others. The Saturn mount indicates he can be very concentrated and disciplined. The prominence of the Mercury mount confirms his communicative nature and his enjoyment of studying.

The palmar lines are predominantly an Air width, which concords with the hand shape, skin texture and strong Air quadrant and confirms the prevalent expression of energy through his mind. Despite the strength of the Air Element within the hand, the lines are not as clear as they could be. Their general fuzziness indicates that he does not express his ideas as clearly as he could. There is also a waviness that can be seen in some of the lines, especially the Mercury (head) line, indicating an uncertainty and lack of resolution in his life.

The hand displays a notably long Mercury line

spanning the full width of the palm and augmented by the fork present over the mount of Moon. Its Air width enhances his ability to communicate ideas, though there are several features that detract from it. The line has a tied beginning with the Venus line which is chained until about 21 years of age, when a clear separation is made. The general clarity of the line is poor on the objective side of the palm. By contrast the Mercury line is clearer on the subjective side of the palm. All of these features indicate he is introspective and cautious in expressing ideas. The waviness of the line shows an indecisiveness, while the pronounced fork on the mount of Moon shows a strong imagination. The latter features suggests that he spends a lot of time dreaming rather than being resolute. [Moon conjunct Mercury.]

A very clear influence line from the Jupiter mount feeds into the Mercury line at about 18 years of age. The influence coincides with the start of the separation from the Venus line. It indicates perhaps the influence of a teacher inspiring the unfolding of his mental abilities. The predominance of the Mercury line concords with the emphasis on the Air Element throughout the hand.

The strongest line on the palm is the Venus line. It is long and at times it has a Fire width, indicating that he has a strong vitality. However, the Water width in the line until the age of 21 indicates that he was prone to illness during his childhood and teenage years. The line is marred by many thin Water width stress lines radiating down the Mars active mount until the age of 34. This suggests the build-up of anger from his childhood weakening his vitality. When under pressure this anger makes him prone to tension. An influence line is shown at 34 after which these stress lines stop cutting through the Venus line. This suggests the positive influence of a relationship helping him release the anger from the past. After the start of the influence line

the curvature of the Venus line becomes subtly more pronounced. This shows the relationship causes him to be more outgoing and expressive with his love. In turn this describes a greater sense of fulfilment in his life. [Venus rising Planet.]

These positive changes in the Venus line also reflect a gaining of security in his life. As has been seen from the Earth quadrant, security has been a dominant issue in his life. The length of the Venus line reflects how his sense of security has evolved. The chained early section of the line indicates that he experienced insecurity during his childhood and teenage years. In combination with the dominant Earth quadrant, this points to an intense search for security in his life. The many stress lines between the ages of 21 and 34, cutting through the Venus line causing dots to appear in its flow, show his struggle to achieve security, accompanied by many financial worries. Though after 34 the Venus line shows greater security, many little islands detract from the clarity of the line and point to the persistence of his anxieties. [Venus trine Saturn and square Neptune.]

The Mars line is not well defined. The bulk of the Martian energy radiates down from the Mars active mount towards the Venus line. This hyperstriation pattern in combination with Fire being the 4th quadrant confirms his poor expression of energy. As already mentioned it is associated with anger from childhood and a poor resistance in times of stress. [Mars is retrograde in Pisces.]

A moderate length Jupiter line crossing the central division of the palm indicates an openness of heart and a strong wish to share his feelings with others. Several factors shown in the Jupiter line, however, conspire against his free expression of feelings. The line has an Air width, confirming his tendency to rationalize feelings described by the Water quadrant being in the 2nd position. The childhood and teenage years are shown in the line as a spiky islanded pattern, once again reflecting his unhappiness in childhood. Between the ages of 20 and 35 the Jupiter line has several phases of doubled thickness, reflecting emotional conflict and blocked emotional expression. After the age of 40 the flow of line distinctly improves, indicating greater ease to his emotional expression. The clarity of the Jupiter line beyond its crossing of the Saturn line, extending to the Jupiter mount, indicates a definite spiritual yearning in his later life. [Jupiter is combust (very close to, and consequently weakened by, the Sun) and in detriment in Virgo.]

A Water width Saturn line is clearly formed on his palm. The Water width indicates he has sensitivity and diplomacy when dealing with others, an asset for the caring professions. The line starts at the age of 15, suggesting that this was when he started to gain his independence. An island at the age of 42 indicates a future career conflict. The fact that this island coincides with the presence of a small segment of a Sun line crossing the Mercury line at the age of 42 suggests that this conflict is about becoming independent and being his own boss. Despite the strength of the Earth quadrant the relatively weak Saturn line shows that his sense of independence is still frail. [Venus trine Saturn in Scorpio (a water sign), Saturn square Pluto.]

A small section of the Sun line is present between the ages of 30 and 50, indicating that this twenty-year period in his career is largely successful, and is a time when he will gain significant recognition for his work. This middle portion of the Sun line indicates a strong wish to be more creatively expressive within his work, though currently lacking the resources to express his creativity more fully. Again the weakness of the Fire quadrant is reflected by the poorly developed Sun line. [Sun at IC, Sun opposite Mars, Sun conjunct Jupiter.]

Despite the absence of a Moon line, a number of clear activation lines are present on the Lunar mount. These, in combination with the forked ending of the Mercury line penetrating the Lunar mount, show that he utilizes his imagination. However, he does not use it as perceptively as he would do if a Moon line were present on the palm, confirming the weak placing of the Water quadrant in the 2nd position. [Moon, chart ruler, is conjunct Mercury, poorly placed in Libra though in mutual reception with the Venus.]

A clear section of an Air width Uranus line is present crossing the Mercury line, indicating intuitive perception. However, since the line lacks any definite grounding by contact with the Saturn or Venus line, it indicates that his inspiration remains largely unsubstantiated through lack of action. [Mercury sextile Uranus.]

The Neptune line is poorly represented in the palm. A small section can be found above the Jupiter line at about 60 years of age, indicating that he will become more perceptive of the spiritual world then.

There is no clear Pluto line in the palm, though several activation lines mark the lower area of the Water quadrant suggesting a frustration of his sexual energy. The most significant activation of this area is a strong, clear branch line that delves down into the Pluto realm from the Venus line at 50 years of age. The accompaniment of this branch line by some stress lines radiating down from the Mars active mount to the Venus line suggests a major change in life direction leading to him doing healing work.

The poor definition of both the Neptune and Pluto lines also reflects the weak placing of the Water quadrant. [Saturn is square Pluto, Saturn trine Venus, Neptune sextile Pluto.]

The hand shape is a composite pattern of both Jupiter and Solar hand shapes. Though these Planetary energies are compatible with the Air Elemental hand shape, the corresponding Jupiter and Sun lines are not fully developed, indicating he has yet to achieve his fullest potential. [Sun conjunct Jupiter.]

The quadrant order shows his need to develop the Water and Fire Elements to create greater balance of the Elements. This pattern is reflected in the poor development of the Lunar, Neptune, Pluto, Mars and Sun lines associated with the Elements respectively.

The Intellectual World

The long, confidently placed, relatively well-developed fingers demonstrate his capacity for significant mental development. The fingers complement the long Mercury line. There is an evenness to the overall development of the phalanges indicating an ease in manifesting his ideas in the world.

The phalanges are activated by Water width lines, which in contrast to the weak emotional expression of the Water Element, indicates that the bulk of his mental energy is expressed in a dreamy contemplative and reflective way. This complements the fork on the Mercury line penetrating the Lunar mount.

We will now assess each finger in order of dominance.

- Dominant – medicus.
- 2nd most dominant – index.
- 3rd most dominant – auricularis.
- Least dominant – annularis.

Dominant Finger – *medicus*

The dominance of the medicus finger emphasizes the structuring and organization of ideas. It shows his powerful ability to concentrate and apply his mind to a task.

2nd most dominant Finger – *index*

The weak expression of the index finger accentuates his lack of confidence and the tendency to put himself down. It indicates that he underestimates his own abilities.

3rd most dominant Finger – *auricularis*

The strong expression of the auricularis finger amplifies his communicative skills. It indicates that he will be regarded by others as a good communicator.

Least dominant Finger – *annularis*

The limited expression of the annularis finger weakens his creative expression and ability to assert himself. It is an indication of frustration.

Note how the order of the fingers is also reflected by the quadrant order.

The average-length index finger is consistently well developed throughout its length. There is a slight bend towards the medicus finger at the middle phalanx. Despite the finger being well developed it does not receive any significant energy flow from the Jupiter line.

The length, width, fullness and clarity of the Cancer phalanx indicates that he maintains strong ideals and principles. It shows that he places importance upon spiritual values in life. The Air tip shape shows that he is able to express his ideals freely. Since the Moon rules the sign of Cancer the strength of this phalanx reflects the strong Lunar ending of the Mercury line. [Cancer Ascendant.]

Though the length is comparable to the Cancer phalanx, the Pisces phalanx is not quite as wide. The striation indicates that he is using his abilities to direct others. However, a slight grill pattern on the Lunar side of the phalanx indicates that he is not entirely comfortable in handling others. Since Jupiter rules this phalanx, this probably stems from a lack of confidence. [Mars is retrograde in Pisces.]

Despite the strong personal ideals indicated by the Cancer phalanx, the hint of wasting and grill patterning on the otherwise strongly developed Scorpio phalanx indicates conflict in the substantiation of his self-worth. It suggests he feels ill at ease in situations of power. Since

Mars rules the Scorpio phalanx, the grill reflects the tension associated with the hyperstriation of the Mars active mount. [Mars is retrograde in Pisces.]

All in all, the index finger shows he upholds strong refined ideals, though the bend shows that they have been compromised and frustrated in their expression. The lack of a clear energy supply from the Jupiter line detracts from the strength of the finger, indicating that he appears to be more confident than he actually is.

Relative to the other fingers the medicus finger is slightly short. Despite this it is well-developed, with a slight bend to the Lunar side at the middle phalanx.

The good length and width of the Capricorn phalanx is marred by diffuse striation and bar lines. The marring indicates that he can be imprecise in the logical structuring of ideas and selfish when making decisions on behalf of others. Since Saturn rules this phalanx it reflects the wavy Water width Saturn line. [Saturn in Scorpio.]

The good length and width of the Virgo phalanx is well activated by striation lines. It shows he has considerable administrative skills, and is good at organization and the execution of commands. It is the most activated phalanx. The Mercurial rulership of this phalanx is complemented by the strength of the Mercury line. [Sun in Virgo.]

The Taurus phalanx is the clearest of the whole finger. Its good length, width, fullness and activation indicates that he has a very refined appreciation of material things such as gemstones and plants. The development of this phalanx shows he can patiently attend to the intricate details of physical objects, like constructing models. The Venusian rulership of the Taurus phalanx corresponds to the strength of energy in the Venus line. [Venus is the rising Planet.]

The dominant position of the medicus finger

is complemented by a moderately strong Saturn line flowing towards the finger. The strengths of the finger indicate that he can be resolute and disciplined when he needs to be, though the slight bend suggests a reluctance to accept authority.

The annularis finger is of an average length. The Aries phalanx is long and of a good width though slightly marred by the diffuse marking present on it. The phalanx indicates that he has good artistic perceptions, though the markings suggest this is neglected. With Mars ruling the sign of Aries, the marring of this phalanx is once again linked to the hyperstriation of the Mars active mount. [Mars retrograde in Pisces, though otherwise strong in the 10th house.]

The middle Sagittarius phalanx is the clearest. It is long, of good width and well activated, indicating his enjoyment of sport and other physical activities. The Water width activation lines show he is very particular about the way he dresses. The Jupiterian rulership of Sagittarius links the phalanx to the expression of energy in the Jupiter line. [Jupiter is combust the Sun, in its fall in Virgo at the IC.]

The Leo phalanx is long and displays fullness at the top, though the bottom is distinctly wasted. The phalanx suggests that his artistic expression would be subtle and refined should he use these talents. The Solar rulership of Leo connects the phalanx to the deficient development of the Sun line. The supply of energy from the Sun line, is weak indicating that the potential is there for him to express his creativity. However, the current development of the finger reveals that it is barely being used.

The auricularis finger is very long with many activation lines running throughout its length. There is a slight bend at the top phalanx.

The Libra phalanx is long, of an adequate width and well activated, suggesting that he is loquacious. A hint of fullness can be seen at the base of the phalanx, showing that he is sensitive and tactful in expressing ideas. A keen interest in philosophy is shown. The Venusian rulership of the Libra phalanx connects it to the strong mount of Venus and Venus line. [Venus rising Planet; Mercury, Moon and Neptune in Libra.]

The Gemini phalanx is long, very wide and well activated. The phalanx reflects the fact that a lot of his energy is directed into writing and studying. A slight grill present indicates that he finds it harder to communicate ideas in writing than by the spoken word. [Mercury conjunct Moon.]

The Aquarius phalanx is long, wide and clearly activated. The top of the phalanx has a hint of fullness, while the lower section does have a grill across it. All in all, the phalanx indicates that he is good on the application of ideas, especially of a scientific nature. The strength of the phalanx, especially in conjunction with the strong Venus mount, suggests that he passionately enjoys making love. The grill indicates blockage to the free flow of sexual energy that he has yet to resolve. The fact that the Uranus line does not flow consistently into the auricularis finger confirms this blockage. He does, however, have a good ability to communicate with children. [Saturn in Scorpio in 5th house, Venus, Lady of the 5th house, rising in Cancer, Uranus in Leo in the 2nd house.]

The auricularis finger reflects his strong ability to communicate ideas, though the bend suggests that they can lack directness.

The thumb is strong and low-set on the palm, confirming his strong physical vitality. Its angle is such that its tip does not reach the horizon of the Intellectual World at the base of the fingers. This indicates stubbornness and an inability to change direction once he has embarked on a particular course in life. The upper phalanx is the most developed of the two, indicating that his will-power is stronger than his reason. However, the long lower phalanx has relatively clear activation lines on it, indicating his good use of

reason which balances the strength of the upper phalanx. The upper phalanx is marred by a few Water width bar lines crossing it. These suggests there are emotional blockages subtly restraining his will-power. [Mars retrograde in Pisces, Sun at the IC.]

Throughout the reading there is a recurrent theme of growing spiritual awareness, highlighted by such features as the clear ending of the Mercury line on the mount of Moon, the clear section of the Jupiter line beyond its crossing of the Saturn line, the small section of the Neptune line at about 60 years of age and the Plutonian branch from the Venus line at 50 years of age. There is also a remarkable astrological confirmation of this inner potential shown by a mutual reception between the Lord of the Ascendant, the Moon, and the rising Planet Venus. If their positions are reversed, the Moon moves to an exact conjunction of the Ascendant while Venus moves to the exact conjunction of Neptune.

A STUDY OF CHANGE SHOWN IN THE HAND

See Figures 19.3 and 19.4. This pair of handprints belong to a Scandinavian who became a monk in an Indian tradition. The first print (19.3) was taken shortly after taking his vows to become a monk, the second (19.4) six years later after he had done a significant amount of yoga and meditation.

Insecurity was a prominent feature of his early life. He had an unhappy childhood, his parents broke up and in his early teens he ran away from home. During this time he became involved with drugs, in particular LSD. Most of his teenage years were spent with no fixed abode, with little money, searching for the next supply of drugs.

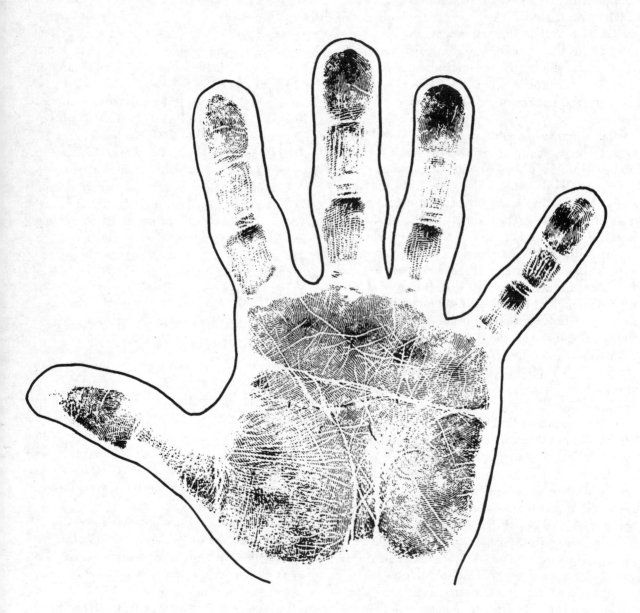

Figure 19.3 Handprint 2 at 78% – A Study of

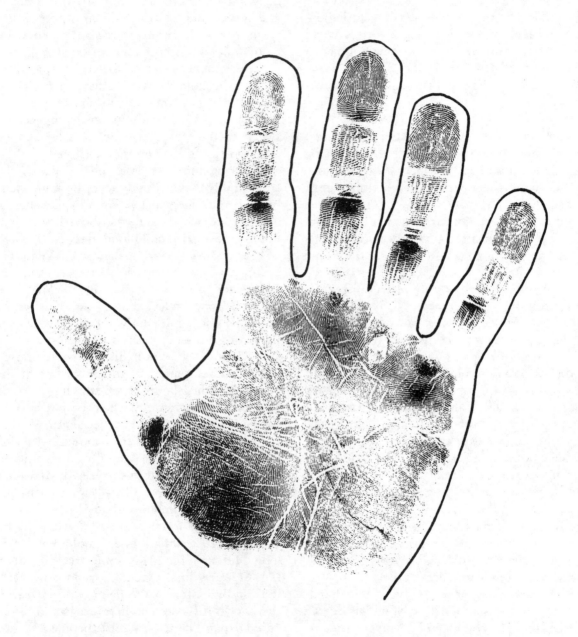

Figure 19.4 Handprint 3 at 78% – Six Years Later

In his early twenties he heard about a particular yoga teacher who was specifically using yoga and meditation to counter drug addiction. His teaching acknowledged that drugs could induce certain spiritual states, though, unless a person was inwardly prepared, these spiritual experiences could be psychologically destructive. He used yoga to generate the necessary inner strength with which to handle these spiritual states while providing the opportunity to experience them at will rather than being dependent on a drug. The Scandinavian, after being drawn to this yoga teacher, became one of his disciples.

This marked a major turning point in his life. After his unstructured existence during his teenage years the yoga and meditation became the foundation of his daily life. On becoming a monk he became further committed to this discipline as part of the ashrama's daily schedule.

Daily life at the ashrama started at 3 a.m. to be ready for an hour of meditation at 4 a.m. This was followed by an hour of hatha yoga till breakfast at 6 a.m. Work started at 6.30 a.m. and carried on until 6 p.m. with breaks only for refreshments, lunch, and a time for personal instruction with the teacher if required. Specifically the monk was instructed to do hard manual labour on the farm which provided food and income to the ashrama. When work was over there was an evening meal at 6.30 p.m. followed by another hour of meditation and/or darshan (audience with the teacher at which the spiritual teaching were explained). After 8 p.m. the monks were free to do as they pleased within the strictures of the ashrama's rules.

In the six years between these two handprints the monk assiduously kept up this degree of discipline. The change in his personality during this time was momentous as can be seen by the difference between the two prints.

In the first handprint (Figure 19.3) the hand displays a taut and enforced position. Many of the lines present have a jangled and confused appearance. There are many stressful features and the general clarity of lines is poor. Numerous little ancillary lines are scattered over the palm indicating emotional tension.

A prominent simian line is very conspicuously seen on the palm. The line, a fusion of both head and heart lines, shows from its uneven width and lack of clarity his inability to distinguish between thoughts and feelings, which undoubtedly contributed to his inner tension.

The beginning section of the Venus line (regrettably the beginning section cannot clearly be seen in the print) exhibits a spiky chained appearance which reflects the frictions and unhappiness of his childhood. Between the ages of 10 and 25 a large, wide island in the Venus line encapsulates the insecurity of his teenage years. The island resolves at the age of 25 corresponding to when he became a monk. After this point the line significantly improves, indicating the strong influence of the ashrama in providing security and structure in his life. There is also a parallel development of the Mars line at this point when the island in the Venus line resolves. This reflects the energy which he put into the hard work and discipline at the ashrama.

The whole of the Venus mount is heavily striated, indicating the extent of stress and tension within him. With this degree of striation it would have been very difficult for him to relax and be at ease with himself.

There is an inner section of what, in the absence of a simian line, would be a very long Mercury line. This subjective portion of the 'Mercury line' extending right down onto the Plutonic area of the palm is often seen in the hands of those who take drugs and have a 'mind expanding trip'. Whilst the line indicates a powerful development of their imagination, the degree of subjective awareness induced by the drug makes a person very introverted and unable to apply themselves to the world.

A very long Saturn line meanders along the palm (again the beginning section cannot clearly be seen in the print) and almost joins the Neptunian line. Since the symbolism of Neptune involves the influence of drugs, the relationship between the Neptune and Saturn lines reflects his aimless drifting through life in search of his next fix.

The prominence of the Neptune line indicates that the drugs did induce some profound insights, though the general criss-cross of lines marring its flow suggests that these would not have been without terrifying hallucinations.

The phalanges are intensely striated, reflecting the worries affecting his life. There are some prominent bar lines on the top phalanges of thumb, index and medicus fingers, indicating blockages in asserting his will-power, in drawing from his intuition and in the ability to structure his life respectively.

The second handprint (Figure 19.4) shows the change that all the discipline brought about in his life. Overall the hand is held in a much more relaxed position. The lines are more clearly defined and indicate that his emotional energy is flowing much more peacefully. Many of the ancillary lines have disappeared from the palm, indicating a release of his inner tension.

In the simian line, sections that were previously a Fire width have become consistently an Air width. This describes an increase in his mental clarity even if he still has difficulty understanding his feelings. This would certainly be linked to a reduction in his inner tension.

Though the island reflecting his insecure years is still present in the Venus line, the lines composing the island also changing from a Fire to an Air width show a dramatic decrease in his insecurity. Doubtless he well recalls his insecure years, but this decrease in intensity of energy indicates he is no longer concerned by them. The improvements in clarity to the rest of the Venus line show that his sense of security in life has become enhanced by his time at the ashrama.

The Venus mount has become clearer too. There is still a fan of stress lines coursing down to the Venus line between the ages of 25 and 44, but the overall clarity of the mount indicates that he has become much more relaxed and at ease with himself.

The very long subjective section of the 'Mercury line' has faded away to a length that stops underneath the annularis finger. This shows that he has overcome his introspection and is much more able to direct his ideas out into the world.

The long, meandering Saturn line has also faded away, leaving a clear basal portion. This shows the gradual development of his independence, formerly frustrated by his childhood insecurity.

The distinct Neptune line is no longer marred by criss-cross lines, which suggests that the clarity of his inner vision has improved, enabling him to derive greater inner nourishment from his meditations.

The phalanges are far less intensely striated, indicating that he is far less worried. It is notable that the bar lines on the thumb, index and medicus fingers have dissolved, indicating a freer expression of the energies associated with these phalanges.

A STUDY OF ASTROLOGICAL CORRELATIONS IN A HAND

Figure 19.5 shows the right (active) hand of a 28-year-old female and Figure 19.6 shows her natal chart timed at 01.12 a.m. GMT, on 20 Dec. 1962; Long. 08W37. Lat. 42N52.

The Ascendant is shown to be 5° Libra 51' with the Moon about to rise at 9° Libra 39'. The

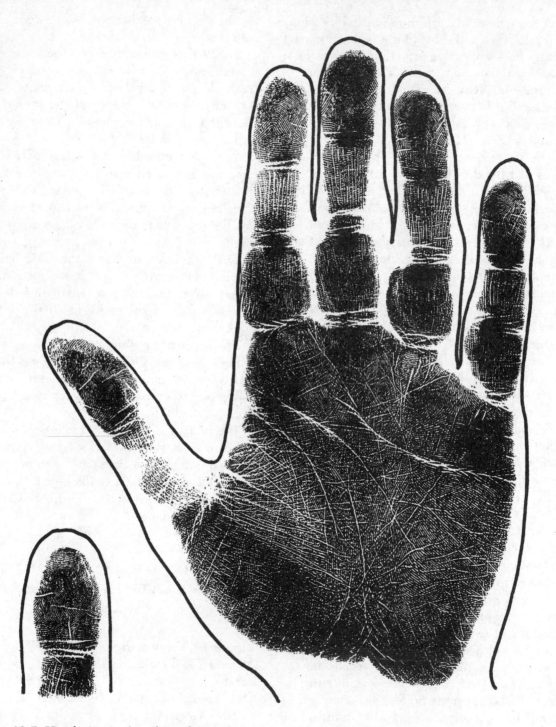

Figure 19.5 Handprint 4 – Astrological Correlations

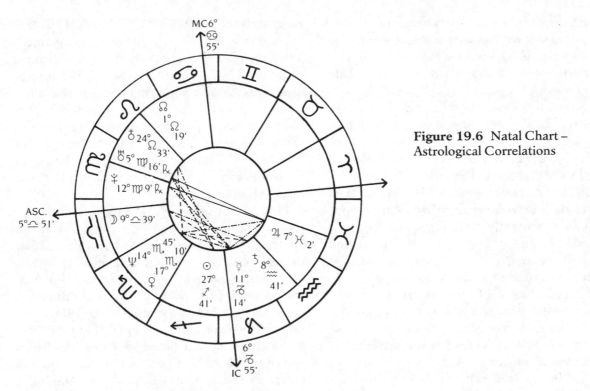

MC6°
69
55'

69

II

♌

♎
1° ♌
19'

♂ 24° ♌
33'

♅ 5° ♍ 16' ℞

☿ 12° ♍ 9' ℞

ASC.
5° ♎ 51'

♏

☽ 9° ♎ 39'

♐

♓

♒

♑

♄

Ψ 14° ♏ 45'
10'
17'
♀

☉
27'
♐
41'

☿
11°
♑
14'

♃ 7° ♓ 2'

♄ 8°
♒
41'

6°
♑
IC 55'

Figure 19.6 Natal Chart –
Astrological Correlations

Moon's close placing to the Ascendant as the rising Planet makes it symbolically very powerful in the chart. Since the 1st house of a birth chart describes the shape of the physical body, this is reflected by her hand having a Moon shape. The Moon has an affinity with the Water Element, and a number of other Watery features can be seen in the hand. The fine, smudgy skin texture identifies it as a Water skin, the Water quadrant, containing the Lunar mount, is well developed, and Water is the prevailing Elemental width of the palmar lines.

Venus rules the sign of Libra and is the 'Lady of the Ascendant'. Venus is located in the 2nd house at 17° Scorpio, 10', conjunct Neptune at 14° Scorpio 45'. The symbolic strength of Venus as the chart ruler is reflected in the hand by the prominence of the Venus mount. When the Moon is the sole Planetary influence reflected in a hand, the shape of the palm is distinctly curved. However, in this example the parallel development of the Venus mount gives the palm a squarer shape.

Despite being the ruling Planet, Venus is very poorly placed in the chart, being in detriment in the sign of Scorpio, and weak in the 2nd house (traditionally ruled by Jupiter). Furthermore the energies of Venus are weakened by the conjunction to Neptune and a wide square aspect to Mars, the lesser malefic, at 24° Leo 33'. Venus also has a sextile aspect to Pluto at 12° Virgo 09'. The lack of dignity to Venus is reflected in the condition of her Venus line in the hand.

The Venus line has a thin Water width and is chained until the age of 20, breaks at 40 and resumes again at 47. The break is, however, compensated for by the presence of a thin Water quality Saturn line which effectively 'seals' the break by reduplication. Just before the age of 40 there is a very thin branch line that reaches down towards the Pluto line. The Venus mount is covered by hyperstriation and grill patterns radiating down from the Mars active mount.

The conjunction of Venus with Neptune in the astrological chart suggests a dissipation of her vital energies while making her body very sensitive to drugs and alcohol. This is reflected in the thin Water width Venus line. The conflicting square aspect of Venus to Mars in the chart reflects the stress lines from the Mars mount which antagonizes the flow of the Venus line. In particular at the point where the Venus line breaks at the age of 40 the line is also hit by a distinct stress line from the Mars mount.

Whilst all these features powerfully suggest that her health is fragile and that physically she is very vulnerable to stress and extreme exhaustion, the placing of Venus in the astrological chart draws attention to other issues in her life. The 2nd house is linked with money and finances. The poor condition of Venus suggests that she has difficulties in earning money and consequently attaining security in her life. The fact that Mars rules the 7th house of partners and relationships in addition to the 2nd house, and is also the dispositor of Venus (Venus being in the sign of Scorpio ruled by Mars), suggests that her difficulties with money and security are aggravated by partners in her life.

At the age of 35 on the Venus line there is an influence line suggesting a relationship starting then. About five years later the previously mentioned break occurs along with the stress line from the Mars mount. It suggests this is a relationship where her partner takes advantage of her. The positive aspect of this situation will focus her energies onto such issues as love and self-worth, which will ultimately lead to her finding inner security.

Jupiter has a strong influence in this hand. It rules the 3rd house of her chart, which is

specifically connected with the hands. Jupiter is located at 7° 02' of Pisces, its own sign, giving it a strong placing in the chart. In the hand a prominent Jupiter mount is shown. The Jupiter line is also long and fairly clear, apart from a section between the ages of 10 and 30. This indicates that she enjoys being outgoing and expressive with her feelings. The placing of Jupiter in the natal chart in the 5th house of pleasures and entertainment indicates that she likes to be sociable.

Her 5th house is ruled by Saturn. In the hand the Saturn line is very poorly developed. It has an unclear start, a very thin Water width, and at the age of 30 the main line is taken over by two other lesser Saturn lines from the inner subjective side of the palm. One of the important qualities of a strong, unified Saturn line running up the centre of the hand is that it enables a sharp distinction between a person's inner and outer life to be made. The poor Saturn line indicates that she has difficulty in making a clear-cut distinction between herself and others in relationships. Unless she has enough space in a relationship to be herself, her innate sensitivity and vulnerability will be overcome by those with whom she becomes emotionally involved.

In the chart Jupiter is in opposition to Uranus which is located in the 11th house at 5° Virgo 16'. Correspondingly in the hand the Jupiter line is chained where it crosses the Uranus line. This suggests that her emotional conflict at the time came from following her ideals rather than listening to her intuition.

Mercury, at 11° Capricorn 14', also makes a wide sextile aspect to Jupiter. This is reflected by some ancillary lines crossing between the Jupiter and Mercury lines in the hand.

The 6th house reflects the illness of a person. Therefore with Jupiter placed in a Water sign and naturally ruling the sanguine humour, as well as the lungs and liver, she would be prone to cold, moist phlegmatic illnesses, chest infections, possibly asthma, water retention and oedema, weak digestion and anaemia.

Corresponding to the Saturn line, the placing of Saturn in the natal chart at 8° Aquarius 41' is interesting. Apart from a trine aspect from the Moon, Saturn makes no further contact with any other Planet in the chart and is almost peregrine. The 4th house of a chart shows the father while the 10th house shows the mother. Since Saturn rules the 4th house in this chart it reflects the influence of her father. The Moon is the ruler of her 10th house reflecting the influence of her mother. The trine aspect between the Moon and Saturn suggests a harmonious relationship between her parents. However, the fact that Saturn is almost peregrine it suggests that her experience of her father was distant, aloof, and cold. The symbolism suggests that the emotional vulnerability she experiences in relationships is linked to a poor paternal influence.

Of the Moon–Saturn aspect, where the main Saturn line ends, the two lesser Saturn lines draw up energy from the Lunar part of the hand. This feature suggests that provided she can find a harmonious environment within which to work, she has the potential to manifest the images within her imagination in the material world – an asset to any artist.

The placing of Mercury near the IC of the chart, at 11°14' of Capricorn, suggests the late development of her mental abilities. In the hand the Mercury line, though initially independent and clear, becomes chained and criss-crossed between the ages of 10 and 30. After this time her Mercury line significantly improves in clarity, showing that this is when her abilities come into their own.

In the natal chart the Moon has a square aspect with Mercury, suggesting that she has difficulty using her imagination. The Mercury line clearly forks into the Lunar mount, though precisely at the point where the fork splits, the Mercury line is cut by a section of the Uranus line. Mercury is trine a retrograde Uranus at 5° Virgo 16'. The 'severed' Mercury line indicates a reluctance to develop her imaginative qualities. Her imaginative abilities are also suggested by Mercury being in trine aspect to Neptune.

In the chart Mercury is also in trine aspect to a retrograde Pluto at 12° Virgo 9'. In the hand there is a very faint extension of the lower branch to the fork at the end of the Mercury line which leads down to the depths of the Water quadrant, where the Pluto line is normally found. The existence of this line suggests an interest in healing. This extension of the Mercury line indicates that as she gets older she will seek to discover more about herself and her inner resources. This is most likely to be after the age of 40, judging by the point when the branch line from the Venus line leads down to where the Pluto line is found.

The Sun in the chart is found at 27° Sagittarius 41' in an applying trine to the retrograde Uranus at 5° Virgo 16'. In the hand, energies within the Sun line are interspersed with the Uranus line, suggesting that much of her energy is directed into wishing for recognition rather than directly using her intuition to understand and resolve her various inner conflicts.

The most powerful aspect in the chart is the Sun trine Mars at 24° Leo 33' in Fire signs. This suggests she can be tremendously self-willed, with an enormous strength to draw from to create inner change. However, unless inwardly certain in her resolutions she is likely to aggravate her own situation. In the hand neither the Mars nor the Sun lines are clearly formed, indicating that this energy has yet to be positively directed.

CHAPTER 20

An Illustration of Cheiromantical Knowledge

THIS final chapter looks at the frontispiece to William Lilly's *Christian Astrology* (1647) Figure 20.1. This study shows how cheiromancy has been used to conceal deeper significance in an engraving. The symbolism of this frontispiece conceals many of the themes presented in the course of this book and their explanation forms a fitting conclusion to this work.

William Lilly (1602–81) was Britain's foremost astrologer of the seventeenth century, whose major work was *Christian Astrology*, in which he brought the writings of many astrologers from previous centuries together into one textbook. Lilly was a friend of the astrologer–cheiromancer Richard Saunders and he contributed a preface to Saunders' *Physiognomie and Cheiromancy* (1653).

A significant portion of Lilly's work was written during the Civil War (1642–9). It was a time when censorship prevailed, while the religious uncertainty of this era meant Hermetic knowledge could not have been openly discussed. The concealing of knowledge in visual form was a technique commonly used in alchemical illustration to communicate knowledge to those who could 'read' it while defying censorship. The frontispiece shown in Figure 20.1 has several symbolic themes intentionally incorporated into it, showing that Lilly's book is of a Hermetic nature and that it should be studied from this perspective.

Cheiromancy provides the key to unlock the engraving; the index finger of Lilly's left hand points to the 3rd house cusp of a blank astrological chart. The 3rd house corresponds to 'studies and writing'. The chart, together with an adjacent open text of Planetary and Zodiacal glyphs – clearly an astrological work – indicates that Lilly is 'pointing out' to the reader how to study his book. Jupiter is symbolically connected with the index finger; in Lilly's *Christian Astrology* under professions for Jupiter is found, '*young Schollers and students in an University or Colledge*'.[29]

The 3rd house has Gemini as a co-significator, the sign of the Zodiac that specifically rules the arms and hands. Lilly's right hand rest on a celestial orb showing some of the signs of the Zodiac with the stars in the heavens. If one looks carefully, one can see that Gemini is specifically shown to rise above the 'horizon' defined by the edge of the table and since the Planet Mercury rules Gemini, it is thus symbolically 'Lord of the Ascendant' or in this case, ruler of the engraving. When it is appreciated that Hermes is the Greek equivalent of Mercury, then it is apparent that Lilly is shown communicating a Hermetic work. This perspective is

Figure 20.1 Frontispiece to William Lilly's *Christian Astrology* (London, 1647); engraving taken from 1985 edition, published by Regulus Publishing Co. Ltd.

GULIELMUS LILLIUS Astrologus *Natus Comitat: Leicest:*
1° *May* 1602.

Guliel: Marshall sculpsit.

confirmed by the Hermetic maxim 'as above, so below'; for at his right hand Gemini is shown rising in the heavens 'above', while his left hand points to the 3rd house cusp, of which Gemini is a co-significator, in the chart 'below'.

In the background to the engraving is a simple rustic scene. It has been suggested that this scene was a view from Lilly's estate Hurst Wood at Hersham, looking across the River Thames to the Church at Walton-upon-Thames. However, Lilly only bought this estate in 1652 some five years after the publication of *Christian Astrology* which suggests that it cannot have been a view from his window. Certainly Lilly was connected with the Church at Walton-upon-Thames, for in 1663 he became its church warden and later he was buried in the Church on the left side of its chancel. It is likely therefore to be the Church at Walton-upon-Thames that is depicted here. Whatever is depicted in this scene, the inclusion of the Zodiacal segment at the top indicates that the whole scene should be regarded symbolically rather than literally.

As explained in the section on cosmology in Chapter 2, the Hermetic philosophers used the Five Elements to understand the universe. The Four Elements, Earth, Water, Air and Fire are all depicted in the rustic background of the engraving. Earth is the pasture with the grazing sheep, Water is the river with the fisherman, Air is shown by the spires and rooftops reaching up into the sky, and Fire is represented by a series of concentric circles that depicts light radiating from the Sun, which alludes to the source of Creation. Ether, the vital force which animates the Four Elements, is found within you, the observer of the picture – note how Lilly's eyes stare directly at you from whatever angle you look at them. When it is recalled that Ether is synonymous with Mercury, then it can be seen that Lilly is the symbolic embodiment of Mercury. He lists in *Christian Astrology*, under professions for Mercury, '. . . *literated Men, philosophers, Mathematicians, Astrologians, Diviners, . . . Messengers* . . .'[30] Lilly in gazing directly at you is communicating this link between Ether and Mercury, so showing that the key to understanding Hermetic knowledge is found within.

By abstracting the Four Elements, the Hermetic philosophers visualized the Creation of the Three Worlds; Fire is the Divine Light, the source of Creation. Air forms the mental or Intellectual World. Water forms the emotional or Celestial World. Earth forms the physical or Elemental World.

In the engraving the orb represents the Intellectual World in the heavens and the blank chart on the table represents the Elemental World on earth, while Lilly, the astrologer, embodies the Celestial World. In Hermetic philosophy the astrologer is seen to mediate between heaven and earth.

As already seen, Hermeticists have perceived their knowledge as consistent with and even fulfilling true Christian teachings. Lilly's *Christian Astrology* is a further example, particularly showing how symbolic ideas have been used to articulate certain metaphysical aspects of Christianity.

The conjunction of Jupiter and Saturn on the Pisces–Aries cusp can be seen pictured in the sky. The astrologer–astronomer Johann Kepler (1571–1630) suggested that the birth of Christ was heralded by the conjunction of these Planets in the year 7 BC, at this point of the Zodiac. Contemporary fellow astrologers would have immediately perceived the significance of this suggestion.

This connection with the birth of Jesus is apparent when the Realm of Light is equated with the 'Christ' principle. Saturn, 'the Lord of darkness', has its fall in Aries which symbolizes the descent of the Christ principle into matter. Jesus was described as the Lamb of God who, after being sacrificed, rose again from the dead and ascended into heaven. Jupiter being dignified in Pisces symbolizes His ascent into heaven, giving the faith for others to follow Him. '*Come ye after me, and I will make you to become fishers of men.*'[31]

The counterpart to this configuration in the heavens is found in the rural scene below. With regard to the shepherd tending his flock, Saturn rules shepherds and Aries connects with sheep, while the fisherman on the banks of the river would be described by the Jupiter in Pisces (see section on the index finger, Chapter 13). The precise placing of the fisherman immediately below the church symbolically identifies this figure as Jesus.

If our human condition is metaphorically described as 'lost sheep', then the shepherd (Saturn) leading seven sheep to the waters of the lake, describes how pain and suffering gradually lead us to thirst for inner salvation. Jupiter in Pisces symbolically describes the opening of the heart. As to the seven sheep, seven is the number of Venus the goddess of love, indicating that through love and forgiveness the heart opens to receive the teachings of Jesus. A particularly provocative detail is the shepherd's staff, which makes contact with the line of the fisherman

and, in so doing, leads the eye upwards through the spire to the heavens above; suggesting that Jesus, through the power of the Christ, is able to transform people's suffering and hardships, thereby guiding them on their spiritual journey.

The position of Lilly's left hand subtly emphasizes the index and middle fingers, linked to Jupiter and Saturn respectively which, echoing the above Christian theme, suggests that faith and discipline enhances the study of astrology. The 3rd house cusp, pointed out by Lilly's index finger, leads your attention to the words '*Non cogunt*' at the centre of the chart. This means 'Does not compel', and alludes to the statement on astrology by the Christian theologian Thomas Aquinas (*c.* 1225–74). Aquinas said 'the stars incline, but do not compel', thus further endorsing the Christian theological acceptance of astrology, while answering those who criticize astrology and other divinatory arts for taking away free will.

References

1. F. A. Yates, *Giordano Bruno and the Hermetic Tradition*, and *The Occult Philosophy in the Elizabethan Age*. Both highly commended source works on the history of the Hermetic tradition. The latter is the more accessible.

2. Paracelsus, *Selected Writings*, (1/12, 343), p. 198.

3. ibid. (1/12, 334), p. 199.

4. ibid. (1/8, 292–3), p. 204.

5. P. Curry, *Prophecy and Power*, pp.19–20. An excellent account of the political background to astrology from 1642–1800. Since the practice of cheiromancy overlapped with astrology much of the material also reflects the decline of cheiromancy since the seventeenth century.

6. *Job* 37:7.

7. *Luke* 17:21.

8. *Matthew* 5:8.

9. *Genesis* 27:28.

10. J. Dee, *Monas Hieroglyphica*, tr. C. H. Josten.

11. H. C. Àgrippa, *De Occulta Philosophica* III, Ch. 37.

12. N. Culpeper, *Complete Herbal and English Physician Enlarged*, 1843, p. 212.

13. N. Culpeper, *Treatise of Aurum Potable*, 1656, section – 'of the Element Earth'.

14. R. Boyle, *The Skeptical Chemist*, p. 43.

15. ibid. p. 283.

16. P. Curry, *Prophecy and Power*, pp. 62–3.

17. R. Boyle, *The Skeptical Chemist*, p. 350.

18. H. C. Agrippa, *De Occulta Philosophica* I, Ch. 52 p. 105.

19. B. Schaumann and M. Alter, *Dermatoglyphics in Medical Disorders*, Springer-Verlag (New York) 1976.

20. ibid.

21. P. G. Newrick, E. Affie and R. J. M. Corrall, *Relationship between longevity and lifeline: a manual study of 100 patients*, Journal of the Royal Society of Medicine, 1990.

22. These Elemental correspondences are shown in Robert Fludd's illustration within *Utriusque cosmi maioris scilicet et minoris, metaphysica, physica atque technica historia*, Vol. II, i, p. 217.

23. E. C. McCaffery, *An Astrological Key to Biblical Symbolism*, p. 133.

24. F. Gettings, *The Secret Zodiac*, pp. 97–117. The book is a study of the astrological symbolism within the Florentine basilica of San Miniato al Monte. The above section authoritatively deals with the changes in astrological conceptions between the thirteenth century and the present day. Many of the ideas raised are highly relevant to this presentation of the Intellectual World.

25. W. Shakespeare, *The Merchant of Venice*, V i.

26. F. Gettings, *The Secret Zodiac*, pp. 83–9. This book also studies the use of Zodiacal symbolism within Christian teachings.

27. J. Rothmann, *Cheiromantia*, Ex. (XV)

28. W. Lilly, *Christian Astrology*, is the most authorative reference to the astrology of the seventeenth century. Lilly was a personal friend of Richard Saunders. Contemporary presentations of this knowledge are found in D. Appleby's *Horary Astrology*, and O. Barclay's *Horary Astrology Rediscovered*. The latter work is the more traditional. All works deal with the topic of Planetary dignities.

29. W. Lilly, *Christian Astrology*, p. 63.

30. ibid., p. 78.

31. *Mark* 1:17.

Glossary

Aqua Vitae: The Four Elements have a quintessential relationship to the fifth Element Ether, whereby the four evolve out of the fifth. Ether was known to the alchemists as the *Aqua Vitae*, meaning 'the Water of Life'.

Ascendant: Called the horoscope in traditional astrology. This is the eastern horizon and the 1st house cusp of the astrological chart, which commences there.

Aspect: The angular relationship between Planets located in the signs of the Zodiac. The principal aspects and their angles used in traditional astrology are; conjunction = 0°, opposition = 180°, square = 90°, trine = 120° and sextile = 60°. [L. *aspectus* (*adspicere* = to look at)]

Benefic: A term used to describe Jupiter and Venus as Planets of good influence in an astrological chart.

Chart ruler: A term for a Planet which rules the Zodiac sign present at the Ascendant or horoscope of a chart, also traditionally known as 'Lord of the Geniture'.

Cheiromancy: The word comes from the Greek *chir*, meaning 'hand', and *manteia*, meaning 'divination', literally meaning 'divination through the hand'.

Descendant: The western horizon, and the 7th house cusp of an astrological chart.

Detriment: A Planet poorly placed in a particular sign is described as being in detriment.

Dexter: A Planet that has an aspect made to it by a faster-moving Planet further forward in the sequence of the Zodiacal signs. [L. *dexter* = to the right]

Directions (standard Ptolemaic primary): Directions are an astrological technique whereby all the Planets in a chart are moved at the same speed, in the same direction, either forwards or backwards. This particular kind of direction (standard Ptolemaic primary) is attributed to Claudius Ptolemy (*c.* AD 90-168).

Dispositor: A Planet which has essential dignity within a particular section of the Zodiac is capable of disposing any other Planet present within the section.

Essential dignity: A Planet strongly placed in a particular sign, usually a sign that it rules or in which it is in exaltation, is described as having essential dignity. A Planet may also have accidental dignity from its house position in the chart or through contacting the benefic Planets, Jupiter and Venus.

Exaltation: A particular placing of a Planet in a sign, different from one that it rules, in which it functions well. For example Mars is exalted in Capricorn.

Fall: Where a Planet is placed in the opposite sign of the Zodiac to its exaltation (q.v.), in which it functions poorly. For example Mars has its fall in Cancer.

Glyphs: These are the graphic symbols used to represent the Elements, Planets and signs of the Zodiac. [Gk *gluphé* = carving]

Grand trine: A particular astrological configuration whereby three Planets form a triangular pattern in the chart. Each Planet has a trine (120°) aspect with the other two Planets composing the triangle. A grand trines is usually formed between Planets occupying Zodiacal signs of the same Element or triplicity.

Hieroglyph: Literally 'The sacred symbol'. [Gk *hieros* = sacred + *gluphé* = carving]

House: An astrological term for the division of the sky into twelve sections, as represented in an astrological chart.

House cusp: The division in an astrological chart between one house and another.

House ruler: The Planet that rules the Zodiacal sign in which a house cusp falls, is called the house ruler. For example if the 3rd house of a chart is at

15° Aries, then Mars is ruler of the 3rd house. In this case Mars may be referred to as Lord of the 3rd house.

Horoscope: See Ascendant.

IC: Short for *imum caelorum*, meaning 'the depths of the heavens'. It is placed at the 4th house cusp at the bottom of an astrological chart.

Luminaries: The collective astrological term for both the Sun and Moon. [L. *lumen, luminis* = a light, an opening]

Macrocosm: The universe. [Gk *macros* = large + *kosmos* = world]

Malefic: An astrological term used to describe Saturn and Mars as Planets of misfortune in an astrological chart.

MC: Short for *midi caelorum*, meaning 'the middle of the heavens'. It is placed at the 10th house cusp at the top of an astrological chart.

Microcosm: The view of Man as a reflection of the universe. [Gk *mikros* = small + *kosmos* = world]

Mutual Reception: A relationship between two Planets occupying positions of each other's dignity or exaltation, whereby they can symbolically swap places.

Orb: A halo of influence surrounding each Planet in which it is effective. This influence extends a number of degrees either side of the position of the Planet. Each half of the orb is called the Planet's moiety. In modern astrology its is the aspects that have the orbs.

Peregrine: A Planet that has no essential dignity. [L. *peregrinator* = a wanderer]

Prima Materia: An alchemical term for the fifth Element of ether meaning 'the first matter' since it is the matrix from which the Elemental World was born.

Retrograde: The perceived backward movement of a Planet through the Zodiacal signs. Symbolically the retrograde motion detracts from the essential dignity of the Planet. The retrograde motion of a Planet is denoted by the symbol (℞).

Sinister: Aspects between Planets made forward in sequence of the Zodiacal signs. [L. *sinister* = to the left]

Key to Symbols

Elemental Symbols

Fire (△)
Air (△)
Water (▽)
Earth (▽)
Ether (✡)

Planetary Symbols

Sun (☉)   Jupiter (♃)
Moon (☽)   Saturn (♄)
Mercury (☿)   Uranus (♅)
Venus (♀)   Neptune (♆)
Mars (♂)   Pluto (♇)

Zodiac Symbols

Aries (♈)   Libra (♎)
Taurus (♉)   Scorpio (♏)
Gemini (♊)   Sagittarius (♐)
Cancer (♋)   Capricorn (♑)
Leo (♌)   Aquarius (♒)
Virgo (♍)   Pisces (♓)

Bibliography

Agrippa, H. C., *De Occulta Philosophica*, 1651.

Appleby, D., *Horary Astrology*, Aquarian Press, 1985.

Barclay, O., *Horary Astrology Rediscovered*, Whitford Press, 1990.

Boyle, R., *The Skeptical Chemist*, 1661.

Culpeper, N., *Complete Herbal and English Physician Enlarged*, 1843 edn.

Culpeper, N., *Treatise of Aurum Potable*, 1656.

Curry, P., *Prophecy and Power*, Polity Press, 1989.

Dee, J., *Monas Hieroglyphica*, tr. C. H. Josten. AMBIX, XII, 1964.

Fludd, R., *Utriusque cosmi maioris scilicet et minoris, metaphysica, physica atque technica historia*, Vol II, 1619.

Gettings, F., *The Secret Zodiac*, Arkana, 1989.

Lilly, W., *Christian Astrology*, 1647, reprinted Regulus, 1985.

McCaffery, E. C. *An Astrological Key to Biblical Symbolism*, Thorsons.

Paracelsus, *Selected Writings*, tr. N. Guterman, Routledge & Kegan Paul, 1951.

Rothmann, J. *Cheiromantia*, tr. G. Wharton, 1652.

Shakespeare, W., *The Merchant of Venice*, 1600.

Yates, F. A. *Giordano Bruno and the Hermetic Tradition*, Routledge and Kegan Paul, 1964.

Yates, F.A. *The Occult Philosophy in the Elizabethan Age*, Ark Paperbacks, 1983.

Tuition and Readings

Handreading

Dylan Warren-Davis gives handreading tuition, both privately and in seminar form, and also handreading consultations.

For further details of handreading tuition or consultations please write, enclosing a stamped and self-addressed C5 (230mm × 160mm) envelope or International Reply Coupon to:

Dylan Warren-Davis
PO Box 24
Chichester
West Sussex, PO20 6SQ
England

Please note that tuition and readings are **not** available by correspondence.

Astrology

For those who are interested in studying traditional astrology, Olivia Barclay runs a Qualifying Horary Diploma Course by correspondence. For details please write, enclosing a stamped and self-addressed envelope or International Reply Coupon to:

Olivia Barclay
Qualifying Horary Diploma Course
Mongeham Lodge Cottage
Great Mongeham
Deal, Kent CT14 0HD
England

Index